FAST-TRACK TO PROPERTY MILLIONS

Laurie Duncan, Alex Robertson and Conar Tracey

FAST-TRACK TO PROPERTY MILLIONS

Laurie Duncan, Alex Robertson
and Conar Tracey

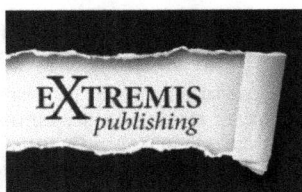

EXTREMIS publishing

Fast-Track to Property Millions by Laurie Duncan, Alex Robertson and Conar Tracey.

First edition published in Great Britain in 2023 by Extremis Publishing Ltd.,
Suite 218, Castle House, 1 Baker Street, Stirling, FK8 1AL, United Kingdom.
www.extremispublishing.com

Extremis Publishing is a Private Limited Company registered in Scotland (SC509983) whose Registered Office is Suite 218, Castle House, 1 Baker Street, Stirling, FK8 1AL, United Kingdom.

A CIP catalogue record for this book is available from the British Library.

ISBN: 978-1-7398543-7-9

Typeset in Goudy Bookletter 1911, designed by The League of Moveable Type.
Printed and bound in Great Britain by IngramSpark, Chapter House, Pitfield, Kiln Farm, Milton Keynes, MK11 3LW, United Kingdom.

Left to right: Alex Robertson, Laurie Duncan and Conar Tracey

Contents

Introduction

ET'S start with a thank you for buying this book – not just from us,
but we hope it will be a thank you from your future self too. The
future self that you may become if you allow this book to open your
eyes to the wonderful world of making money in property, and how
property can transform not only your future prosperity but that of your
family for generations to come.

Over a period of just over two years we have built our property
business, Real Estate Wealth Development (REWD Group), into a multi-
million-pound business, with more than 200 buy-to-let properties, a
successful development business with projects totalling a GDV of well over
£15 million, a growing building company, and finally a property training
business which focuses on specialist buy-to-let at scale strategies. AND we
are just getting started!

Property has transformed our lives, having both left stressful
corporate careers in 2021, to pursue a new life fully focused on property and
the growth of our business; a life which is ultimately on our own terms.
This book is a culmination of our experiences, mistakes and learnings within
our property journey, and it benefits greatly from the fact that we have
built a large property business in the modern age, where the political
landscape has been one that is strongly opposed to non-professional
property investment. We have faced all the challenges that property
investment in the modern age can throw up and overcome them, so the
good news for you is that you are in safe hands. We have made our fair
share of mistakes along the way, having built a modest buy-to-let portfolio
prior to working together in completely the wrong way, and subsequently
having to work through selling off these properties. The real game-changer
for us came only after we obsessively stalked those who were successful,
paid for the education we needed, and ultimately hit the books to learn
from the best and find solutions to the obvious problems that faced us.

Our aim is to fast-track your property journey by learning from our
mistakes, mis-steps and experiences, to allow you to skip past the serious
errors we made at the start and gain a fast-track ticket to success in
property. Note, however, that getting a download of our knowledge and

experience will not be enough to achieve this success; knowledge without action is like a tree without fruit. Only action-takers will benefit from the fruits of this journey. It is with this truth that we really identify what separates our success in achieving massive scale to those who don't get off the ground. We think differently and take massive action.

We speak to a lot of people who want to get started in property, and our advice is always the same: YOU MUST GET EDUCATED before embarking on this journey. The legislative and tax framework around property is such that anyone who is foolish enough to start investing in property without understanding the key teachings from this book is likely run into trouble along the way. In this respect we take on some topics such as property tax, which other property books may shy away from, because we feel it is essential to have a basic understanding of this subject or risk losing all of your profits to the tax man before you have even made any.

Whilst this book will cover a variety of property strategies, what will no doubt become clear as you progress through its chapters is that we are highly biased towards buy-to-let as the core property investment strategy. That's not to say that we don't adopt a variety of strategies; however, buy-to-let continues to be the foundation on which REWD Group has been built.

The information in this book is fully up-to-date at the time of writing, but you will be aware that things can change and over time. Some of the specific figures and facts, particularly in respects of things like tax and legislation, can change. The information, figures and strategies we are providing in this book are based on our opinion, and as such should not be relied upon for making financial investment decisions. As always, you should seek your own professional advice when making any such financial investment decisions from a suitably qualified professional. This is just a guide and is not financial advice, and the authors are not qualified to give financial advice. As such, they accept no liability for any financial decisions you make.

Okay, now that's out of the way, let's get into the good stuff.

First, a bit about the authors and their company, Real Estate Wealth Development. After all, your first, most valid question is: "who are we to be teaching you"? So let's hear from our first co-founder, Mr Laurie ("LD") Duncan, and find out what led him into property…

Laurie Duncan

I left school when I was 17 years old and didn't have a clue what I wanted to do. My older brother Jamie got me a place at the Glasgow College of Building and Printing to do the same course that he was doing at the time, which was multimedia design and technology. The course involved web design, graphics, programming, media creation and editing and so on.

I wasn't even really interested in all this stuff, but as my Mum said, it was better I was doing something than absolutely nothing! A couple of years later, HND in hand, it was time to go to university – and university was different experience for me. Really. You didn't have the hand-holding like you did at college, but instead you were expected just to go to lectures and turn up, take notes, listen to what these guys have to say, sit some exams.

And that was the education. I didn't really like that. I was used to the hand-holding and I couldn't really be arsed to work, and I was just really looking for something to be handed to me on a plate back then. So I went to Glasgow Caledonian Uni for about six weeks, then decided I was going to drop out because wasn't enjoying the course and really, I just wanted to be making some money.

At the time I was really into DJ-ing and electronic music production. Actually, if anyone wants to check out my dance tracks, you can go Spotify, type in Laurie Duncan and you will see a list of tracks that I've created. Even although I think they're all rubbish, it was a good experience and it is something I want to get back into in later life.

Now, I'm focused solely on REWD Group and massive wealth creation for myself and my family.

So anyway, I dropped out of uni – I was about 19 at the time – got a job at place called TSC (which stands for Telecoms Service Centre) and worked there for 6 months or so. After that, I worked for another call centre place subcontracted by Morgan Stanley. Maybe the call centre circuit is just something you need to do when you're in your late teens! When I was 20, and after I'd been at Morgan Stanley for a while, my dad then offered me a job in his company at the time, which was basically just making the teas and coffees and sending faxes (for anyone that existed before email)!

It was a general office admin job, with everything that went along with that. I started off really as a sales administrator. The company was a steel stockholder of pipes and fittings for the oil and gas industry. My dad was just trying to take me in under his wing to give me some kind of job, because I never really had any direction.

I worked there for about six months, but I didn't really like it. I was more interested in just going out and partying with my mates and stuff like that. I didn't really want to work or have a serious job, so I decided to go to Ibiza for the summer of 2005. I was there from May to October and worked for Carl Cox doing events promotions, which involved walking along the beaches, handing out fliers, attending the club nights and trying to maximize the crowds. The venue for Coxy that season was Space in Playa Den Bossa, and I absolutely loved that time of my life.

I don't even know if Space is still around anymore. Actually, I think they shut it a while back. But anyway, that was 2005...

After I came back from Ibiza, I think I was a little bit more kind of grounded. I felt like I had grown up after that, and was ready to settle down. I now wanted to get a good job and start having some money in my life and maybe look for a house! I think I was maybe 21 at this time and I had to grow up at some stage – right?!

So I came back from the White Isle and my dad offered me a job again back at his place, but in a different role; more like a kind of proper sales role. And I would be targeting customers, I would have a budget, I would be tasked with generating sales for the business, maximizing profit and selling these steel pipes and fittings into the oil and gas markets, refineries, power plants, steel fabricators, all this type of stuff.

I ended up getting quite good at it and I was quite passionate about it for a while. Long story short, I worked there for about 10-15 years in the end, and the business did really well from my efforts. It was a great learning experience but ultimately, I was looking for a bit more from life and I did always want to do my own thing really.

I'd been doing the same thing for a long time then, up to around 2017-2018, and I was looking to do more, have a bit more responsibility, and generally move up the career and life ladder. My older brother was the MD of that business too and he was always going to be ahead of me because of his age and experience and all of that.

So I could only ever go so far in that company. I decided I was going to make a move, I was going to set up my own business. At that time, I was going to start up a trading business in pipes and fittings – basically just buying from suppliers and sell it on to customers and take a margin for that service.

But then when I went to leave the UK company, which was now owned by an Italian Group, the President of the Group offered me a job to work with the Italians rather than at the UK office. The role was business development into Scandinavia and Eastern Europe. At the time it was really attractive – it was a cool thing to be traveling internationally for work and also ticking the 'more responsibility' box.

I felt very valued by that job offer and was really excited to get started. I got my teeth into that for about three years, but it became very obvious very quickly that I really didn't like being away from home – I didn't like living at hotels and hanging about in airports as my job!

I didn't like going out boozing every night and entertaining new, different prospective customers, then drive hundreds of miles the day after to then take more people out again. In all honesty, I was just completely knackered. This was one of the biggest drivers for me to get away from that kind of life, because Emma and I wanted to get married soon and I just did not see a life ahead of me that involved being away from home all the time. I had to do something about that.

We wanted to start a family soon after marriage (2018), and I really didn't want to be the guy that wasn't at home every night. I'd been doing the Scandinavia thing for about 2-3 years, but had now firmly decided that I wasn't going to do that any longer. I wanted to create something more for myself, for my family, for my and our futures, and to live a life on my own terms – a life that would be full of freedom, flexibility and an abundance of wealth.

I saw property as the opportunity to create that life – it was my vehicle of choice and I believed it would be possible to achieve everything I wanted, and more. Alex and I had started to talk about different ideas – we both already had a couple of properties each and were discussing options with what do to about them. We tell this full story in our 'Start-up Story' video – if you've not already seen that, check it out on Facebook – there's loads of really cool videos on there.

The government had recently launched what is better known as the 'Clause 24' legislation. They changed the tax situation so you didn't get full deductibility of your mortgage interest if you held assets in your own name. It changed the industry massively and we, like many others, were looking at selling our properties and finding another way to make some money.

But during those conversations between Alex and I, it was quite evident that we were both aligned on this property thing, and we both kept trying to find a way and to make things work. Even when the brokers, the banks, and everybody else kept telling us that what we were trying to do could not be done. We were quite determined to find a way.

We wanted to try and push forward through all these challenges and create something. We had to go and get some paid specialist education. We started reading and listening to lots of different books around property investment and the different strategies we could employ. And ultimately, back in 2018, we started making moves while we were both still in full time corporate employment.

I was buying my own properties and Alex was buying his – we weren't working together initially. Probably for about 12 months we were doing things separately, although we *were* speaking to each other on a daily basis, sharing lots of ideas around all the challenges we were facing. In Scotland, in 2018, there was VERY limited lending. In England, because it was a bigger market, there were a lot of mortgage solutions down there, but since Scotland was such a small market and all property transactions and lending was under Scottish Law, there was really very little appetite to support what we were trying to do. This has changed massively over the years, and now we have an array of lenders that we work with.

You will see from our start-up story on Facebook that we actually got our first investment for our first ever joint property deal at Alex's wedding. It was with a friend of ours and we were just casually chatting over some ice-cold Coronas, as the story goes! We explained were buying this two-bed flat in Alloa for £25 grand (off market) and we had agreed to buy it, but we didn't have the money and we weren't sure how we're going to fund it, yet.

You can't really get a mortgage at that kind of price level – definitely not for limited companies in Scotland and not back in 2019, so this investor was lined up and that was what kind of kicked us off shortly after that. Two months or so went by and we ended up getting a second opportunity, and the same kind of thing happened. We lined up another investor, tied them to that deal, and we were off to a flying start!

The second deal was a 125 square metre traditional style three-bed flat and was another cracking deal. At the time our business was called We Buy Property Scotland and we snowballed from there into REWD Group and our now-varied, but all highly synergistic, property related activities. We acquired the second property for only £60K and refinanced it around £110K – a taste of what is possible when you know what you're doing in buy-to-let.

We Buy Property Scotland only lasted about a year before we rebranded and called it REWD Group. We started getting into developments – it was commercial conversions we went after initially. And since then we started our own building company that does the construction work on behalf of the developments business, as well as the residential refurbs *and* the maintenance for the buy side of our business.

We then started REWD Training as we realised we now had some really specialist property knowledge that could help other people get started and accelerate their property journey. Now we are a very different animal – it's turned into something that I don't think either of us could have anticipated back then. We have staff, we have offices, we're constantly expanding and we've got multiple multi-million pound developments on the go. By the end of 2022 we should have around 350 properties under our ownership, and we've got cash flow swings like you wouldn't believe – a very, very different animal indeed!

But by taking action, by making moves, by stepping into the FEAR, by believing that whatever it was that we wanted to achieve was possible, and doing what many people wouldn't do… This has pushed us forward to a level that, I think, most would struggle to relate to. And I guess through this book, what we're trying to do is tell a bit more about our story, explain some of the strategies that we've used, and give examples of some of the deals that we've done.

If there's anyone that wants to be a bit more serious about it, get in touch with us and we can look to work a bit more closely with you on your own business and the specialist knowledge side for buy type property investment.

I really hope you enjoy the book. I am Laurie Duncan.

Here are some words for co-founder number two, Alex (Eccles) Robertson, about his journey into property...

Alex Robertson

Usually, the first thing someone wants to know about the history of someone who has achieved success in business, is whether they had a helping hand. Do you come from a wealthy family? Are your parents in property? Is this a family business that has been passed down through the generations? These questions are all designed to help the 'asker' justify why they cannot emulate the success. I am sorry to say you're not getting off the hook that easily! There was no head start in life, there was no silver spoon, golden carrot or any other mystical object that gave either Laurie or me a head start.

Growing up, my parents worked hard and we were fortunate enough to live in a good area, whilst being acutely aware that were at the bottom end of the wealth spectrum in that area. Really, as a kid I had all that I needed, if not everything I wanted. I have never been a particularly creative person; my brain is driven by logic and structure, so a life as an entrepreneur is not something I had ever envisaged for myself.

My path through the early years of my life was very normal, completing school with very average grades; more an indication of my effort levels and interest rather than my capabilities. The next step was university, and what did I chose to study there? Well, logic took over when the career advisor had told me the three top-paid jobs were doctors, lawyers and accountants. My average grades excluded the first two options, which only left accountancy... and so there it was. Decision made. Why was I so focused on the most well-paid job? Well, whilst I had a fortunate upbringing in a good area with two conservative parents who were very protective of me, I had a massive appetite to have the finer things in life. I wanted to climb the social ladder; I wanted be noticed, and I wanted to escape the feeling of being at the bottom of the wealth spectrum.

At university I employed the same tactics at school, putting in nowhere near enough effort to reach my potential grades. I knew I needed at least a 2:1 in my degree to get a half decent job, so unsurprisingly that is exactly where I landed. After university I was lucky to land a great job working in finance for a Canadian oil and gas company. This spawned a fifteen year career that saw me travel the world spending four years in Russia, two years in Norway, four years in Azerbaijan, one year in Spain, one year in Tunisia, six months in South Africa, and finally a six-month stint in Texas.

My job within the company quickly became that of being the guy they sent in when they were setting up a new facility in a new country. I would be responsible for negotiating land deals, setting up companies, hiring staff, implementing the systems and processes, and negotiating supplier agreement. This was a fantastic training ground to learn how to get a new business off the ground. My last major project for the company was in Azerbaijan, where my boss and I visited for two weeks to discuss a potential project in 2014, and I eventually ended up staying more than four years. The project was for BP and involved pipe coatings for one of the largest subsea pipeline projects ever, transporting gas from the Caspian Sea to Europe. A small team of us negotiated what became a $500 million project. We agreed a deal to upgrade and run a state-owned coating facility, and we hired a full new team of around 350 staff – all in a matter of months. This project became one of the largest and most profitable projects the company had ever completed. We had a profit target somewhere in the region of $50 million, and we achieved about $20 million more than forecast. I personally and successfully negotiated a $1 million Forex variation order with BP that our company didn't want to pursue, as they believed our chances of success were remote. This was probably the most intense four years of my life. My boss and I, along with a small team, had built a monster operation with little help from the organisation. I gave up Christmases and weekends. I missed family events, weddings and countless birthdays. I had several failed relationships along the way. I put on weight and didn't look after myself, and ultimately all I focused on was work. At the end of it all, after all the tens of millions of dollars I had made for the company, I got a 'special bonus'. Was this finally going to make me rich? NO! I got a $12,000 bonus.

That was the catalyst; the point where I said that I would no longer allow myself to be leveraged by a company. I had all the skills to do this for myself and now (in my early 30s) it was time. It was time to build my own business; time to leverage other peoples' skills to make myself wealthy. But in what industry? Well, I went back to that basic thinking I had as a kid, which had led me down the path of accountancy. I asked a simple question: how do all the rich people make their money? The *Sunday Times* rich list answered that question for me – PROPERTY. Of all the wealthiest people in the country, an overwhelming majority of them made their money in property; even the ones that made it in other industries eventually invested their gains in property. We will get into more detail on just why property is such a great place to make money in Chapter 2: The Basics, but for the moment let's just say that for most people the biggest purchase they will ever make is the property they live in. It's not therefore surprising that there is serious money to be made there.

The Story of REWD Group

Now that we have heard what led both Alex and Laurie into property, let's get an understanding of how Real Estate Wealth Development came about and how it became a multi-million pound property business in just a few short years.

Whilst we were friends from school and both started our journey in property at the same time, we had no intention to work together – both of us having had bad experiences in the past when getting into business with friends. The start of both our property journeys were not pretty. Both of us were managing our properties by ourselves. We had no strategy, no systems and no real understanding of what we were doing. We couldn't differentiate between a good deal and a terrible one because we didn't have the proper knowledge to understand what a good deal really was. Now, when we look at those numbers, we cringe really hard because they just don't stack up. We went ahead for another year with our patented strategy of not really having a strategy, buying up some properties we thought were good and enjoying a decent return.

Fast forward to 2018, and it was the night before Alex's wedding. While he was busy arranging the wedding decor, he got a notification from Facebook about an opportunity to buy a flat. Since Alex was busy with the wedding, he didn't have the time to analyse the deal or negotiate with the owner, and so he asked Laurie to help him out. The plan was that if the deal worked out, both of us would go 50-50 on it. Laurie did a fantastic job in getting the deal, and it became our first joint venture. The only slight snag in our plan is that we had no idea how we were going to finance the

£25,000 purchase price. During the evening of Alex's wedding, whilst we told the story of this successful deal, one of our friends from the wedding heard this and wanted to be involved. He had recently sold his house and was looking for a short-term place to put his money in exchange for a return. And how much money did he have to invest? £25,000! The power of the universe or what? And with that, we had our first private investor.

After the success of this first deal, we found ourselves doing a second one when a property deal in Ayr came across Laurie's desk and he was unable to attend the viewing. This time Alex did the deal and secured the private investor to buy, and thus deal number two was done. Over the course of that first year we did about ten deals together, by which time it became very clear that our efforts together were worth much more than what we had achieved separately, and so REWD Group was born!

By year two, REWD Group had grown to own over 200 buy-to-let properties across Scotland. How had we started with that one £25,000 deal and, just two years later, we had over 200 properties? Undoubtedly a large driver of this staggering growth was the combination of Laurie's vision, drive and ambition, coupled with Alex's logical, analytical and financial astute mind. But most importantly, it came from the fact we think differently. We employed many of the strategies that we will educate you in throughout this book, but critically we wanted to understand how these strategies could be scaled and done on a bigger scale. This gave birth to our portfolio acquisition strategy, and the buy-to-let at massive scale model that we will cover in Chapter 9.

No story about REWD Group and its success would be complete without talking about our third contributor to this book, Conar Tracey – the Head of Group Development. Conar joined REWD Group in May of 2021, but his involvement in the success of our business started much earlier. Almost 25% of the deals the company bought in the early days were sourced by Conar. At only 26, Conar had been in property from an age of 19 and – through his hard work, dedication and keen eye for a deal – he had become one of Scotland's top property sourcers. Whilst the balance of Laurie's drive and big ambition and Alex's analytical and financial savvy was creating great results, it was clear that to reach the next level we were missing that industry experience and connection. Enter Conar Tracey.

Here is Conar to tell us about his experience in the industry and the part he plays within the group...

Conar Tracey

It's true; I really do manage to find property deals that would have your mouth watering at the prospect of getting your hands on them. Even if you don't know a thing about property, it's not hard to understand that buying a flat for £10,000, renting it out for £400 per month and having it revalued at £40,000 just five months later, is a good f***ing deal. I'll get into the specifics of return on investment and yield in later chapters but, for now, if you see a deal like that come up, you do everything it takes to get the deal done!

I'm Conar Tracey, and at the time of writing this book I'm 27 years old with nearly ten years' experience as a professional within the property industry, having been directly involved in over 1,000 property transactions across the UK. From the age of 19 I began my career in property as a Trainee Estate Agent with a small real estate firm based at George Square in Glasgow. It was a bit mental how the job came about, to be honest. I had basically been messing about with my future and, although I was a genuinely good kid, I was just pretty lost with who I was and what I wanted to do with my life. It got me into to some bother; much to the delight of my parents!

At school I was very switched on and things came naturally to me, but I seriously struggled with the rigidness of authority and this prerequisite that you must go to university to be successful in life. I honestly couldn't stand it, and I had this burning desire to do things my way – even though I had no clue what my way even was yet. Nonetheless, I told my mum that I wanted to chuck school and walk away with only one higher, despite the opportunity and capability to go after a career in law or medicine based on my performance at school pre-exams. My mum's response was that of any single parent: 'Well, if you're not going to be at school, you'd better get your arse out there and start working!'

So as the feisty 5ft 3in Drumchapel-born mother of mine demanded, I set about getting a job. Now, it's true that intelligence can only get you so far in life, and I'm definitely a big believer in that. So although I was fairly bright, my biggest attribute to this day is my ability to adapt to any situation and build solid relationships with people within a very short timeframe. Sales came so naturally to me that I honestly didn't even feel like I was working. I've sold gas and electricity in call centres, I've sold cars, luxury furniture, high-end retail, gym memberships – you name it, I've sold it. I was the best performer everywhere I went, and I gained so much value from each experience; understanding how people from all walks of life interact and engage with you. I practiced various techniques and responses to gauge what worked best when and why, and honestly I just loved the challenge of building a relationship with a stranger, identifying their problem, and presenting them with a solution. I have also always been crazily money-motivated, so if the rule of life is 'the more I sell, the more I earn', you can bet your f***ing arse I'm going after every deal that's there to be done.

So anyway, after moving through the ranks of various sales roles in different industries from the age of 16 to 19, I stumbled across an advert for a trainee estate agent role and I was instantly drawn to it. The path I had started to take had went from selling bigger and more expensive products each time, so it made sense that property would be the next thing for me – as well as the fact I always knew there was a lot of money to be made in property, so of course I got the inevitable erection over the idea. I had just been offered a full-time sales role with Arnold Clark in Springburn and it came with an £18,000 salary, company car and a tidy commission structure. But it was at this point I decided to make a move that would be a career decision and not just the next sales role.

The job dropped me right into the deep end, getting hands-on with both sales and lettings for residential and commercial property. It truly was a traineeship that served me with a solid foundation of all aspects of how a property business operated and the processes involved. I'll always be grateful to the owner of that company for the opportunity, but it was clear to me that there were bigger opportunities and I had the bug for property now. There was no going back.

I ended up hounding another company in Glasgow that I felt would catapult my knowledge and experience of property. They had a quick selling estate agency, an auction company and an investment fund, so it really ticked all the boxes for career progression. I sent my CV to them and kept phoning every two days to make sure the Associate Director had received it. A side-note, actually; I was naive back then and I always used to put my date of birth on my CV which, unbeknown to me, usually had a detrimental effect because I was a 19-year-old kid who had a CV of a 40 year old – and a new job every six months. So you can imagine how that looked. But I mean, I was learning, and at least they couldn't say I didn't have any experience!

I actually gave my CV to a property recruitment guy, who told me I was best to get back in touch in a few years because I was too young to really have a chance of getting the kind of position I thought I deserved. I was very tempted to send a swift 'f*** you!' text message to him when the Associate Director of this company eventually phoned me back and offered me an interview. This was my moment and my opportunity to make a serious move in the right direction, so I did what any overzealous teenager would do: I went in and told them I would work for less than anyone else who applied! I'd like to think that's not the only reason they hired me at the time but, either way, I had officially became the youngest Property Valuer in Scotland at 19 years old.

From that day on, I worked with what I still believe to be one of the best valuation teams in the country. There were two guys I worked with who showed me the ropes and, although they had very different styles, they were both listing machines and they knew how to identify a deal and get paid handsomely for it. The Associate Director was also a machine. She knew the property game like the back of her hand and, honestly, I couldn't wait to get into the office every day to be surrounded by these people and just absorb all of the knowledge and experience they had to offer.

My first deal was a two bedroom house down in Creetown, past Stranraer. I remember it so clearly; the seller was a female in the RAF and she used to live in the property, but was always travelling with work and just left the property empty for about two years. It needed fully renovated and she had been trying to sell it on the open market with a local estate agent, but was getting nowhere. So there I was on the other end of the phone: a virgin in the property valuation game, but ready to offer this woman a solution that she couldn't refuse. I opted for auction as the best exit, as she wanted it done quickly and securely but with the opportunity to get the best price. I set a guide price of £35,000 and it sold for reserve at £37,500 at the first auction. I charged her £1,500 + VAT, and we got

£2,000 from the buyer at the auction as well. My commission was 10%, and I was f***ing elated at that £350 going into my next month's pay; more so because I agreed to work for £1,000 per month to get my foot in the door whilst the two guys doing the same job were being paid double that! But the main thing was, I was certain this was the life for me and I would do everything it took to become the best in the game.

I worked in that role for three years, and had established a reputation as one of the best in the company with a reputation of securing the highest fees. I focused on quality and not quantity, and it worked in my favour. I went on to run the whole of Scotland for an English-based quick selling estate agency, fully transforming their business in Scotland before eventually going on to run an Auction and Estate Agency with a former colleague who had set up on his own.

My ability to adapt to situations and build relationships with people is undoubtedly the reason for my success. The more complex the situation, the better for me. However, as the old saying goes, 'you can't sell to an empty chair.' It became very apparent to me that I was not in control of the leads and that at any time, someone else could turn the tap off and I would have no one to phone, no appointments to attend and ultimately, no money to make. It was clear that this was going to be the biggest risk to my business, and I had to eliminate it ASAP. I've spent the last few years learning and understanding marketing to a very intricate level, and building sales systems to ensure that the tap can never be turned off and that I always have people in the chair to sell to. This is something I have brought to REWD Group across all of the businesses, and is the main reason I have the title of Head of Group Development which essentially means I make sure we are constantly growing in every way possible.

I see myself as more of an intrapreneur. I don't need to take all the credit of an idea or build something from scratch; in fact, there are so many benefits of not doing this, but I do have to fully believe in what I'm doing and the company I'm representing. I have to be absolutely, fully invested in what I'm creating in order to reach my true potential, and I am proud to say that I have that. Alex and Laurie are the co-founders of REWD Group, but I am every bit a part of REWD Group as they are, and we share a relentless vision for where the Group is going.

Property and business can truly change lives, and I am testament to that more than I'm willing to reveal in this book. But I promise you this: you are going to want to keep reading, and you are going to want to learn how this stuff can change your life. Now, as we write this book and REWD Group is in its third year, the company is on track to have well over 300 buy-to-let properties in the year. We have a building company, a training business and a development business that does both large-scale commercial to residential projects as well as new-build development. It's been an amazing journey, and the most exciting part is that we are just getting started!

Testimonials

Before we end this chapter, we want to tell you that the key takeaway from our start-up story isn't that you should postpone your investing journey until you learn every little aspect of real estate. Not at all. What we want you to understand is that no matter how imperfect our start was, we took the plunge. We took action, even though we only knew about the basics of investing, and we could still reap decent rewards.

If you keep postponing until you learn everything, you'll never achieve your dreams in this lifetime. To paraphrase legendary entrepreneur Sir Richard Branson, if you get an amazing opportunity but you are not sure you can do it. say yes – then learn how to do it later (unless you're going to fly a plane, in which case, don't). So, take the first step. Stop postponing. Stop procrastinating. Unlike our start. You'll have us guiding you every step along the way, telling you what to do and what to avoid.

This stuff really can be life changing if you are willing to take the ACTION, but don't just take our word for it; let's hear from some of our training clients and their experiences…

- 'I would recommend REWD Group to anyone looking to get involved in the buy-to-let market. These are the guys to speak to – [they'll] point you in the right direction and give you all the proper information that you need for moving forward.' – Gary
- 'If you actually want to build a sustainable business and build a sustainable portfolio, then I definitely recommend REWD Group.' – Callum

- 'Absolutely, we'd recommend REWD Group. The way we see it is you can spend years and many thousands of pounds making mistakes, or you can get educated and learn from people who have done it, learn from people who have made those mistakes and ultimately, you'll be a lot further forward.' – Eshan
- 'Incredibly impressive – specifically relating to the finance and systems of financing, and how ultimately it all fits together for them to achieve some pretty incredible growth in a very short space of time.' – Eshan

REWD PRO, January 2022
- 'If you were trying to learn all this yourself, it would take forever.' – Alexander
- 'What they're achieved in the last 2-3 years... quite simply phenomenal.' – Brian O'Neill
- 'We highly recommend REWD Group to people whether they've got properties already or they're starting up from nothing.' – Laura & Michael

The REWD Group in Numbers: 2019 to 2022

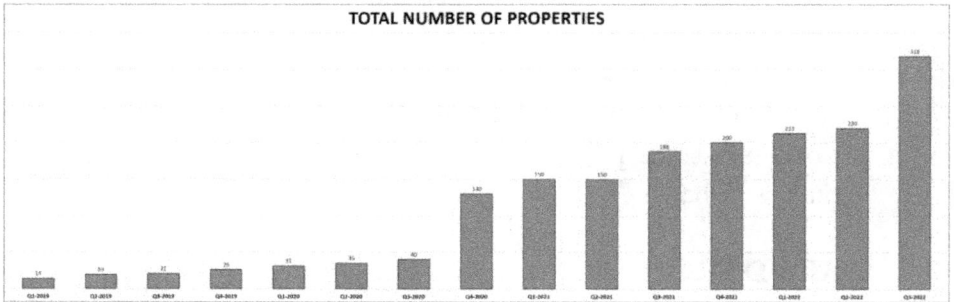

TOTAL NUMBER OF PROPERTIES

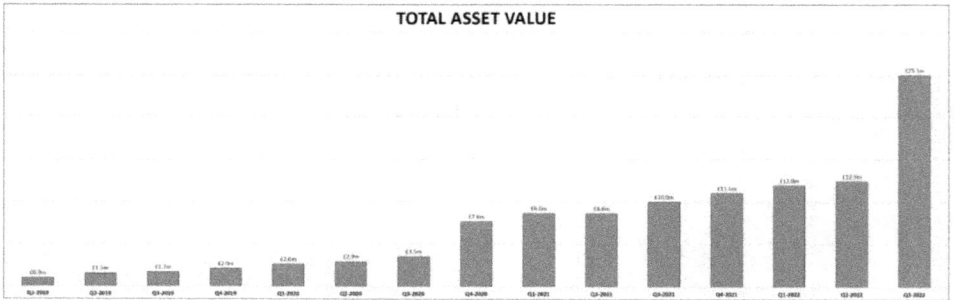

TOTAL ASSET VALUE

RENTAL INCOME PER MONTH

FAST-TRACK TO PROPERTY MILLIONS

Chapter One

Mindset

Laurie Duncan

L ADIES and gentlemen, boys and girls, professional property investors... welcome to *Fast-Track to Property Millions*! This book is
an introduction to property investing, designed to demonstrate all
of the different ways that you can make money with property. This is the
first section. The reason we always start with mindset is because the
number one thing that is going to come between you and your success, or
lack of it, is the same one thing that's going to come between you and
achieving your dreams.

Thinking, one way or the other, is definitely what's going to cause
you to take different actions. And this is why it is so fundamental for
people to get their mindset right. Now, I was one of the worst believers
when it comes to state of mind. The thing is, I would have slated anyone
just a few years ago that was
talking to me about mindset;
you know the sort of thing:
when people used to talk about
'belief' and 'focus' and blah,
blah, blah. And it is quite funny now to look back, because I
have had a massive mindset
shift about a lot of different
things I'm going to be talking
about in this chapter. I do actively know that (and I firmly
believe that) if it wasn't for

applying all these different things and being consistent – that is, being persistent with it – that success wouldn't be forthcoming. Even when you know how to think constructively, it still often seems like it's a little too far out there – or you start to think it's never going to happen or whatever, so you have to continually push forward and apply these factors to your state of mind. I believe this is what has made the difference for us, and what separates us compared to a lot of other companies that got started around the same time, about two to three years ago.

Really I just want you to just be open-minded to these ideas; just read what I have to say and let yourself absorb it. Even if you think some of it is in the realms of hippie nonsense, just give it a chance. Maybe try some of the stuff yourself and see how it helps you move forward, because I know myself from practicing these things that it can be a real game-changer. I firmly believe if it if it wasn't for the things you're about to read, we wouldn't be doing what we are.

What is mindset?

Welcome to the idea of Mindset. Let's get started. A lot of people are looking for some kind of perfect scenario in life. Right? Well, the reality is that the perfect scenario just doesn't exist. If you are sitting there waiting and waiting and waiting for this perfect scenario that will never come along, you're never going to make a move. You know, the deals that we started off on, they were by no means perfect. There were some good ones and there are some bad ones. But one thing we were determined to do was just make our moves and keep moving forward. Because perfect doesn't really exist. And I think you just need to be aware of that, because your mind is always going to hold you back from making a move: it can make up all sorts of bullshit excuses to try and stop you moving forward.

The most important thing is just to get started; make a move, get educated, get your first deal, get your second deal... just keep going. Because every time that you make a move, every time you do a deal, every time you take that step forward – you're always going to learn a little bit more. And it's only really when you look back that you can see how far you've come.

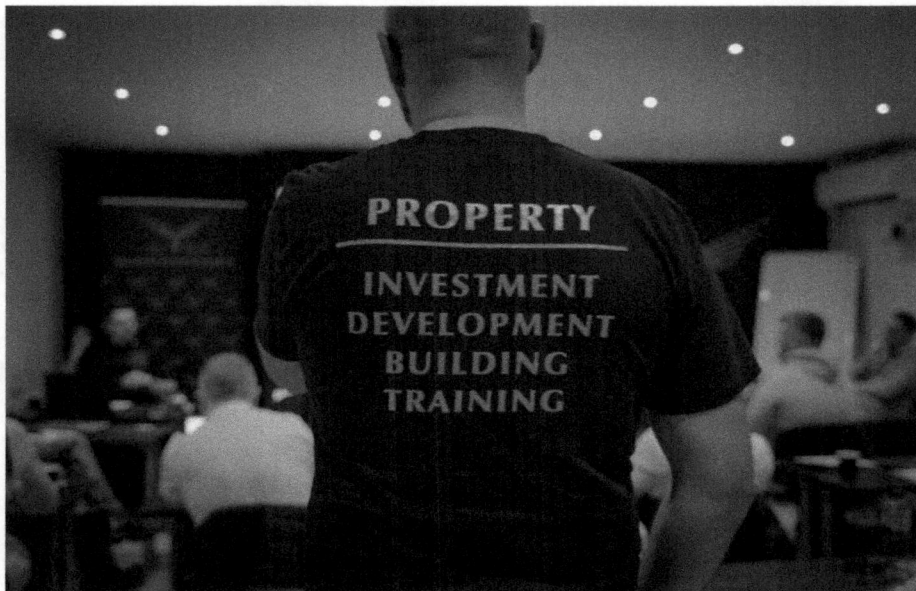

It's a strange thing, but your mind is definitely going to try and hold you back when it comes to looking for this perfect scenario. So the point here is just to recognise that 'perfect' isn't going to come your way, and just get started: make a move, do something, start first and get past any stumbling blocks later. You need to realise that, genuinely, you and only you can determine the course of your life. Too many people try to blame and complain when it comes to justifying what happened when things go wrong. There's always a reason that, somehow, it's always somebody else's fault. It's never on you, even when you know it's only up to you. Who else is going to create this life that you're dream of? No-body! Because no perfect scenario is going to come your way. No-one is going to come along and just provide this for you. Not one source out there is going to provide you with all of these deals; you need to put the effort in, and you need to realise that you need to work for your dreams.

Going on a course is not, in and of itself, going to make you rich. Right? By applying this knowledge, applying this education, taking actions could help you to reach your goals, but you have to recognise that you are the only one in this equation who can make your dreams come true. Whether they happen or not is absolutely up to you. Don't blame other people. Don't complain about all these other external factors in your mind as means of justifying to yourself all these reasons why you know you don't have what you want yet.

So it's important to know that the responsibility for your success lies solely with you, and you need to recognise that fact. The sooner you do this, you will start taking different actions because you're no longer reliant on the actions of anyone else. It's all on you. Anyone can always produce excuses for any decision, right? I've got my own excuses for things not happening in my life and in business, and everybody out there is the same. Don't think that you are any different from anyone else. This is just your mind justifying to you why things haven't quite worked out yet. But coming up with excuses is ultimately a pointless endeavour. You've either achieved what you set out to do or you haven't. And if you haven't, there's no real point in generating excuses about why you've not done it.

There are perfectly legitimate reasons why things might not work out right way. Life can be challenging; when your life is hectic, it can have an impact on how you do things at work. Imagine if you have a new baby to care for. Your sleep may be affected, health and fitness can definitely feel off-kilter, you can start to feel tired at the office. You know, the difficulties involved in looking after a new-born can very easily become an excuse for not doing things – and a very plausible excuse, at that. This is just one example that comes to mind. But you know that the excuse is just that: an excuse. 'We've got young kids, therefore we couldn't possibly do X, Y and Z'. And it's a legitimate reason, right? Because it's tough. In fact, it can be very, very tough. But at the end of the day, it's still an excuse. We've either done the things we set out to do or we haven't, and if we've not done them because of such-and-such a reason... well, maybe that helps us to put the situation into perspective. But at the end of the day, you still need to recognise that you've either taken action to move forward, or you have an excuse for why you haven't. But the excuse isn't going to help you advance your career.

Discomfort is something I have come to love. Why is that? Well, it's quite a strange thing to feel uncomfortable because, generally speaking, it's not a nice state to be in. Yet I've come to love it and to respect it, because I recognise that when I am uncomfortable in a situation I am actually growing in that scenario. For instance, we sometimes talk about the first time we completed a commercial acquisition. That was 'the Poundies Building', as it's known; a two-and-a-half thousand square metre commercial building. We bought it for £200,000, and that purchase was made with a bridge plus a private investor. It was a very creative way to fund 150% of the purchase price, so we ended up with cash in the bank. It was cool in the end, but at the time it was scary and really we didn't know exactly what we were doing. We were very fortunate in the end with that project, but the whole acquisition process – and even after the acquisition – felt like an uncomfortable experience at the time. It was the first time we undertook a project where we were planning to convert a property via commercial-residential conversion. After we concluded, it was something like the 10th of January 2020. Very early in the year. That was just when the work started. Your mind goes into overdrive. You start to worry that your money might have gone down the drain. I couldn't sleep for a few nights, because I kept having bad dreams about the roof getting ripped off. It was just crazy. I worried continually, because it was a new and uncomfortable experience. But now we've got about six commercial projects on the go. Every one of them gets slightly easier because of the moves we made in the past. We wouldn't be doing all these projects at the one time if we hadn't have made that initial move. It may have felt uncomfortable back then, but we pushed through that fear barrier anyway.

That's just one example. But you're going to be uncomfortable when you start something new, right? It's just a natural and understandable state of being. So if you've not yet bought your first property or perhaps you're looking at the prospect of scaling up – maybe you're looking to buy your first portfolio, something like that – it's going to be uncomfortable, because you're going to be doing things that you've not done before and that's just part and parcel of having a fear of the unknown. Yet I've really come to recognise and even appreciate this feeling of being uncomfortable. I respect it now, because when I feel it I know that I'm growing. And you should respect it, too. Once you realise the positive benefits of discomfort, it makes growth a lot easier. It can make dealing with other decisions easier when they come along, depending on how big you want your opportunities to grow or the different range of things you want to get involved in.

We couldn't have done everything on day one. It takes some evolution, ultimately, to build a business. So, you see, the feeling uncomfortable thing is really a good thing. It's a mindset shift, but try to take that on board and accept it. Make a genuine attempt to implement it, because that will serve you very well. How you deal with fear is the number one thing that's going to hold you back or push you forward. Stepping into the fear and confronting it is necessary to allow you to grow.

Dealing with fear

The bottom line is that it's fear that's going to make you uncomfortable. The fear of worst-case scenarios appearing all too real. Your mind will go into overdrive with fear, and unless you deal with this it'll hold you back from doing all sorts of different things. But eventually you need to step into the discomfort and confront the fear directly. You need to take that decisive move forward, because otherwise you're just going to be moving round and round in circles. The same old circles, the same the same things you've always done... the same way you've always been. You're never going to get out of that circle, that loop, unless you step into the fear and push yourself forward. And we still experience fear. Don't think that we are any different because of our experience. Every time we make a move, it's still scary if it's new. But again, we recognise this feeling of discomfort. We talk it through; we talk about all the risks, all the challenges – it's true of everyone, all over the world – and ultimately we step into that fear.

Fear moves us forward and we grow, but recognise when you have that feeling of fear and harness it. It doesn't have to be in business; it can be in life in general. If a wild tiger decides to run towards you and bite your head off, you know, that's what *proper* fear feels like. Run away, get back into your safari van or whatever happens to be heading in the other direction. Basically, that's natural fear, and we all experience it. You need to recognise that fact, because both good and bad can come from it depending on how we deal with it in any given situation. But you know, when it comes to business and decision-making in life, recognise this feeling of fear and step through it when you can. Push right through it.

I still maintain to this day the biggest difference between us and others is that we choose to step into the fear, and that makes us think differently. Because we think differently, we take different actions. And because of those actions, we end up with different results. So, standing between you and your goals is action, behaviours, habits, daily practices, mindset, focus and belief. Realising this is the difference that transformed our minds and made us start to think in a new and constructive way. That's what we did, that's now what we're doing, and that's what we're going to teach you how to do.

Thought processes, learning and mental self-discipline

If it wasn't for us having had a strong goal to begin with, our thought process would be different. In fact, it would be entirely different. If you've never written down your way of doing things, or perhaps sat down and thought about why you think the way you do, I'd strongly encourage you to do it. Because you're going to encounter challenges, and you need to chart a path to get yourself through them. Your thoughts will take you over if you do not control them, so you need to be disciplined about any intentions of boosting the economy, creating positivity, generating opportunity and massive success foryou're your stakeholders. We include you, reading this now, as a stakeholder of REWD Group.

I want you to ask yourself: are you living in Cuckoo Land? You might never have heard of Cuckoo Land before. Maybe you have. Maybe this is your first time. Who knows? But Cuckoo Land is this weird place where some people's minds exist and, basically, it's just a place of confusion. It's a place of chaos. It's a place where a fake reality is conjured up that people think they are living in. And what I mean by that is, if you're getting started in business and your expectation is that you're going to make a billion pounds of profit... well, that would be awesome, right? And, hey, if you can do that, respect is due. But I don't know how many folk have made a billion right away. And in the first year of trading, your goal should be big – but not too big. I'll return to that topic a little bit later on, but while you know you're not going to make a billion, you should still not be afraid to set the bar high.

When we got started, I think it was our objective in the first year to have ten properties, and then it was 30, then it was 50, then it was 100, then it was 200 and then... a thousand. So yes, set yourself ambitious goals, but they should be relative; while they should be challenging, a billion pounds as the target in your first year is a Cuckoo Land objective.

The more we were locked down during the coronavirus pandemic, there's not been too many live business events up and down the country, but we are going to be getting right back into the habit of attending them and we would encourage you to come along. Why? Because there are always new things to learn, and it's always a great experience to get involved in. You will experience a genuine interest in those people attending, and there's loads of value to hear from the people that talk at these events too. These are people who run their own businesses and in different guises, so such events are really worthwhile going along to from a networking perspective as well. But I look at a lot of these events taking place across the country, and there's a lot of folk out there who just see sunshine and rainbows. They think that everything's fine, everything's rosy, everything's great. You know the kind of thing: 'I love life and life is awesome, and blah, blah, blah.' And it's almost as though they are eleven years old and living in Cuckoo Land, or maybe they're just very happy with their lives – and that's perfectly okay. However, they tend to say things like 'I'm just going to be me' or 'I just want to be me.' Look, I'm quite a positive guy and I do talk about 'awesomeness' all the time, but it's not like every single day is awesome. You know, challenges can crop up, there are problems, and there are all kinds of issues that can flag up when you least expect them. New problems will emerge that you need to overcome to push yourself forward, and you know you have to do your best to try to figure it all out.

Life is not all sunshine and rainbows. I do like that kind of positive energy, positive talk, positive mindset ethos that goes on – and not just at these events I'm talking about. But, you know, it's maybe best explored through the personal development industry. There are a lot of folks who think that life is all sunshine and rainbows, and it just isn't. So don't be lured into that Cuckoo Land thinking that lures you into believing that everything's all rosy. You'll need to be ready for these problems and challenges that are going to come up and be ready to grow. So it's good to attend events and training courses, as well as taking part in other educational programmes – whether it's business, property, mindset, e-commerce, social media, management, marketing... any combination of all those different courses that exist out there. And there's a lot of them these days. You can go along again and again, obtaining paid education for any kind of specialism you want. So while I don't know what your specific goals and objectives might be, I'd urge you not to limit yourself to studying only the strategies involved in the property market. We ourselves are already looking at doing more education and high-level learning. The process never ends.

There are plenty of people out there that will go to all these different courses, one after the other, and they never make a move. They never take action. But they will talk the talk because they've been on this course and been on that course, and as a result they've done this and they've done that. Don't fall into the trap of becoming a 'course jockey'. I mean, go along to the courses by all means; learn as much stuff as you want, as long as you're going to implement it. You need to take the action after you've got the knowledge. Otherwise, what was the point of it? Why have you even paid for a course in the first place? For the same reason you are reading this right now. Naturally you want to get the maximum value out of education, but the only way you can get that value is by taking action. 'Course jockeys' don't make that leap from theory to practice. You can meet up with them like a few years down the line and say, 'Hey, how are you? I haven't seen you in four years. How have you been getting on since you started?' And the reply will come: 'I'm just waiting to make a move.' So don't let your mind hold you back from making a move; don't be a 'course jockey'. Go on the right courses, implement the knowledge, grow. Go on a different course, implement the knowledge, grow. A tree will not exist unless a seed has been planted. A crop will not exist unless a seed is being planted.

And you will get there. It is not possible for you to get results unless you've first taken action. Now, if you keep taking the same old actions you're still going to get the same old results. That is a fact. Einstein's definition of insanity was to do the same thing over and over and over again and expect a different outcome. Stop and think about that for a minute. You need to take different actions in order for you to get different results. So don't think if you are fixated on this Cuckoo Land vision that things are just magically going to change for you. If you keep doing what you've always done, you won't get the results you're aiming for. You will have to plant the seed. You need to take the action before you can get the outcome. This is the comfort zone I've talked about, and it's fundamental that you break out of that way of thinking. If you think you're going to get different results from staying in your little comfort zone and not making any moves, you are making a big mistake and you need to break outside of that mindset.

You need to be okay with that idea. You may encounter problems, and you may have issues along the way. You will find help if that's what you want. There are plenty of mentorship options out there to try and keep you on the straight and narrow, but recognise that you need to break outside your comfort zone. You need to escape from it, so say to yourself that you need to take different actions. Come to think about what you're spending your time on. Be very aware that you might be sitting and watching *Love Island* and just watching the next series on Netflix. Maybe it's the TV news or some other drain on your time or energy. Or are you watching educational stuff on YouTube instead? You can listen to audiobooks, or you can tune in to podcasts. The range of podcasts out there is unbelievable now. There are audio presentation companies like Audible, as well as some amazing podcast platforms. These audio presentations can be listened to when you are walking the dog, making your breakfast, cutting the grass... any number of activities. Why not check out the *Real Wealth Podcast?*

Any points in your life that would normally be considered 'dead time', you can fill with learning new knowledge. And at night, you know, you're watching things that inspire you and motivate you. I mean, I still flick the news on them every now and again. I also watch like shows like *A Place in the Sun*, because I might be interested in properties over in Alicante. I enjoy watching programmes like that; it's not necessarily educational, but it motivates me, it inspires me, and it makes me want to do more.

There's a lot of worthwhile material on YouTube, which is just loaded with the different presentations from people and different special-isms. I play *Lemmings* as well; that's my game of choice on my phone and like usually just before I go to bed, I have a game of *Lemmings* to unwind. The thing is, I don't sit and play *Lemmings* all day every day. (Maybe if I'm on holiday, I'll give it a blast!) But the important thing is to recognise what you're spending your time on. Because you can fill that time with knowledge, with education, with inspiration, or even with fellowship.

The benefits of effort

You may be reading this book for yourself primarily, but who else is go-ing to benefit from your successes? Your wife, your husband, your partner, your extended family? You know, we talk about generational wealth, and who benefits from generational wealth? Our kids. That's what we are thinking about. And you will generally find that if you are doing something for someone else, you tend to put in a bit more effort than if you were just doing it for yourself. It may seem like a strange thing, but it's a natural thing. Unless you're very selfish – and of course, some people are, and they would they would do more for themselves than they would do for others – you tend to find that most people will put in a bit more effort to go after whatever it is that they can achieve so that other people can also benefit from that.

Think about this scenario. Suppose that your wife motivated you to succeed when you first started. Keeping this relative to property, say your initial goal is only five properties. Well, that might be your goal right now – for maybe five or eight properties. But you're determined you're going to get five. You get five on the open market and, having done that, you know it wasn't a big enough challenge to motivate you. You know your goals have to be ambitious. Like I mentioned earlier, it was our company's first goal to have ten properties, then it was 30, then it was 50, then 100, then it was 300, then 1000... whatever these numbers were. But at every stage they had to be a little bit bigger, because we had to be motivated for them. They had to be big, because they had to change the way we were acting. And certainly the reason we bought our first portfolio deal is because we were thinking about a goal at that time which was, I think, about 300 properties – and in the end we acquired 82, all as part of that goal. So if it wasn't for us thinking about these goals, we wouldn't have taken these actions and we wouldn't have been motivated. If we had said the goal was ten properties, we might only be on eight right now.

You have to recognise how powerful your thoughts are, because that will determine the outcomes you are capable of. A lot of people will talk about doing whatever is necessary, committing to whatever it takes. And the reality is that most people don't. They don't commit the time, they don't make the effort, they don't sacrifice; short-term sacrifice should never be long-term, because actions have consequences. Doing whatever is necessary means doing whatever is necessary. We see so many people coming through the training programmes and they say they're hungry for success. They get fired up by the course, and they've got all this new knowledge that has pumped them up, driven them, motivated them. And then they're talking about going to do this and going to do that. But in the end they do nothing. They go back to where they've always been, going around in those circles. They're not making any moves, not making these sacrifices, not getting up a bit earlier, not working a little bit late, not committing time from the week to focus on their property venture, or whatever the other goal might be in their life.

You need to recognise that if you want to succeed, you have to do whatever is necessary, and that will be outside your comfort zone. Very likely, sacrifices will be talked about. You're reading this right now because you're looking for a new reality and you're hoping that this content, this education, is going to give you the key to that new reality. But can you imagine if you really thought about it, if you considered what life is going to be like if you implement all this stuff and – when you are successful – can you imagine it? What does it mean? Is it a bigger house, a nicer house? Maybe a fancy car... or a supercar, such as a Ferrari F8 Spyder? (That's my one.) Perhaps a Range Rover or a Rolls-Royce? It's just a question of time. I can imagine that new reality. Just as importantly, I can imagine that it doesn't have to be these material things.

You know, maybe success looks like more time, more flexibility, more freedom.

You might want to still keep your job. You might like your job. You might want to just kind of work less and do more in property, but still do them both. Nobody's saying that you have to own multiple companies, and everything that goes along with that. You know, that sort of thing isn't for everyone. Maybe your goal is just ten properties for now, or 20 or 50... or even buying your first portfolio. Perhaps you're focused on getting that first deal over the line. But what does this new reality look like for you? Can you imagine it? How do you envisage it? (Later I'll look a little bit closer at visualisation, a very, very powerful technique that I use daily. It plants a seed in your subconscious mind.) So think about this new reality and make sure you have this vision in your head, as it's a really powerful means of motivation. If this ends up going back to confronting fear and inaction and all those sort of things, imagine that by taking all these actions, the end result was guaranteed.

Would you do all these things that push you out your comfort zone if you knew the result was guaranteed? Of course you would. Would you make a financial sacrifice? Would you make a time sacrifice? Would you do whatever is necessary? Absolutely you would. The problem is that your brain, your mind, doesn't know. But then it comes back to belief, right? How strong is your belief in the end result? If you knew the end result was guaranteed, you would take whatever action was necessary in order to achieve that goal. Think, because you can think of everyone and anyone, and nobody else needs to know. It's all in your mind. I love that. It's just for you. It's your special little place where no-one can interfere.

The importance of thinking and self-belief

What are you thinking about right now? You might be sitting there thinking that an old character on a TV soap opera hasn't aged well. Or you might be thinking, who fancies bowling? I wonder what I'm having for my dinner tonight? What is going on? And that's all happening in a world of your own, because it's one thing to consider the inner world and another thing entirely to think about the outer world. But if that's a new concept for you, think about that. Thoughts about what is going on reflect that world of yours, because your thoughts can lead to a feeling, that feeling will lead to an action, and the action will lead to a result. There's no 'hippy mindset' bullshit about that. That is a fact. The principle is called TFAR: Thoughts lead to feelings which lead to actions which lead to results. Now, you're reading this because you want to get results, right? We want you to get results. We want you to get better results. We've achieved big results because we think differently to most.

As you know, in order to get the result you must first have the thought, so what are you spending your time on? Are you spending your time thinking about the right end results? Because if you start with that thought, see how it makes you feel. The way it makes you feel will force you to take actions, and these actions will be in different shapes and forms. But these actions all lead somewhere, and depending on what actions you take is what's going to lead you to result A, B, C or D. There'll be different results based on the specific actions, so be very aware of what you're thinking about and don't allow your mind to control you. It's *you* who should control your mind. Your mind just a muscle in your body, and training it is just like training your biceps, training your quads, training your chest muscles. You can train in these things, and your mind is just a different kind of muscle – one that plenty of people operate subconsciously, unconsciously, and they don't take the time to think about controlling their output. They just walk around day by day: they wake up in the morning, they get in the shower, they have their breakfast, they drive to work, they do their day job, they come home, they stick the telly on and watch it, they go to bed and they repeat these unconscious operations. And that will go on and on and on the whole way through many people's lives, just because they don't stop and take a minute to think.

Just think. Focus your thoughts, because if you don't do that, you will operate unconsciously. The unconscious is a really difficult thing for people to get their head around – particularly if they are operating unconsciously. But if you are operating consciously, you're thinking about things; you're assessing, you're not necessarily acting on the emotions you're sussing out. Then you can take the actions that will move you towards your goal, whatever that result might be. But if you are operating unconsciously, be aware of that. Stop sending different messages to your subconscious mind, and that will change your output. You literally have the power to choose whatever you think; whatever it is that you want to think, you *can* think. Anything can be absolutely anything. This is your inner world, and nobody else's. Nobody can take that away from you. So think wisely about the things that are going to move you forward.

Think about your end result. Think about all the actions. Think about your growth. Think about all your successes. Visualise this new reality. But choose what you think about, because it's within you. I guarantee you, thinking differently is what's going to lead you to the outcomes: the results that you desire. And hey, if you think small, you're going to get small results. You see, if you just want small results – and I don't believe that for a second – that's all you'll get. If you don't heed the lesson that I mentioned about mindset, talking about property, talking about all the different ways you can make money, then you won't get where you need to go.

You'll have seen that our business growth has scaled up massively, right? Massive scale. I don't know anyone else that's achieved anything like we have, to be fair. But it happened because we did not think small. We thought *big*. We thought that right back from the start. We had a group vision from the beginning. The group has evolved since day one, but we thought big – and because we've been thinking big, we've got big results. So how can you possibly think that you want small results? I don't believe you want small results. I believe you want big results. And I know you can get big results, but I need you to think big. Think big and watch what happens.

Visualisation

I mentioned earlier about our visualisation. Vision generally is a very, very powerful concept. You must have one, and that vision can look very different to each and every one of you. But the vision is just a point in the future for things to be a certain way. Visualisation is playing the scene over and over in your mind; it can be still images of this future moment in time. Mine is a moving picture. It's a scene and I'm not going to go into detail, as it's personal to me and I get very emotional anytime I describe it. But it's a very, very powerful thing to have going on in your subconscious. And if you've not got a vision, spend time creating one – and you can be as creative as you want. You can make up in your head, you can write it down… but however you do it, I encourage you to do it. Write it down, because writing things down – simple as it may seem – is a very powerful and effective process.

Personally speaking, I've got different visualisations for different scenes: different moments in time, in life and business and fitness. All of that. But I do visualise daily. And the thing is that you will often find that successful people generally talk about the same stuff. I mentioned that at the beginning of the chapter. You know, originally I would have been the first one to just take a hard pass on this kind of thing. So anybody that was talking to me about visualisation and mindset and meditation and affirmation, and whatever else – I would have been sceptical. But the more I started going to these events, all the successful guys were talking about this stuff, and all these successful guys were visualising, they were meditating… in other words, they were all doing things that I didn't do. And I thought, well, if that's what these successful guys are doing… perhaps if I just do that, can I be just as successful? Surely it's going to give me at least a bit of a chance. So now I do visualise daily, and it's so powerful. If you've never tried it before, just give it a try.

See how you get on, but recognise how it makes you feel. For me, I find that it fills me with fire. It fills me with passion. And it's really helped us to grow to the scale that we wanted. It continues to help us to go out there and breathe life into visions. Even if they seem 'out there' right now, they're not Cuckoo Land. That is to say, they're not Cuckoo Land 'out there', but they are 'out there' in the sense that many people might laugh at them. In fact, on my wedding day, part of my wedding speech was (and you may even have seen this video, because we had an edit of it done for social media) that I mentioned I had a vision for the future, and I said – a little bit in jest – we'd have our ten kids running around. My wife was laughing at the time.

The other part of that section of the speech went on to talk about five German Shepherds and 200 houses. Now, I said in jest about having ten kids because I love kids. Whether we'll have ten in the end, I don't know. And five German Shepherds. I admit that they're big dogs, but I do love having dogs around as well. So I would love to have a pack of five German Shepherds – even if it sounds a little bit 'out there'. Then again, so is having ten kids and 200 houses. But everybody was laughing, and it was a wedding speech after all. So it was meant to be fun.

However, only two and a half years after that, we had achieved that goal of 200 properties. But as that vision was out there, nobody could grasp that it could become a reality. Everybody laughed at the time. And even when I talked about it – aside from the wedding speech – everybody laughed at me. And that's cool. I laughed myself a little bit, but I knew in my mind I was going after my goal hard and I believed that it would be possible to achieve it. I didn't always believe it, but I set the bar high for my objective. The visualisation may have seemed a little out there, but it wasn't Cuckoo Land. I didn't even put a timeline on it, but I knew we were going to do it, and quickly.

So if your vision seems a little bit unrealistic, that's okay: you want to set goals big enough that people might laugh at you like that. That's what happened to us, and yet we achieved them. That's just one exam-ple, of course, but I always think it's quite cool to think back about that time. That was the 4ᵗʰ of August 2018 – the day we got married – and yet, only three years later, we had already achieved our goal. I'm still working on the kids and the German Shepherds, by the way, but I'll get there one day.

However, be wary of who you decide to share your visions with. Because like-minded people like us, and the REWD Group generally, will understand your ambition because we think big. Only talk about your vision with people that think big, because they're the ones who are going to get it. They're going to support you, they're going to help you, they're going to have different ideas. And certainly people that have achieved big goals already are the ones who will be able to relate to these visions. Suc-cessful people are like-minded people when it comes to visions and goals. Big goals are interesting. They're attractive. So be excited to share your visions with like-minded people; discuss them with your mentors and your peers. Talk about them and share them. You'll find that you can be inspired and motivated by other people's goals, visions and dreams. Dis-cuss them with the people in your circle. But I can't emphasise enough:

don't share your visions with people who might be obstacles to your success. They may well laugh at you, and equally they might drag you down. But, personally, I don't mind seeing this because I like them to laugh at me. That inspires me to do more, and ultimately I'll be the one having the last laugh.

I don't worry too much about other people's views of my radical goals if they don't 'get it'. You know, some of them just think I'm nuts. Maybe I am, just a little bit, if you knew what's going on in my inner world. But it motivates me. It inspires me to take more action, make more moves and grow more. I think you can tell a passionate person when you hear one. So, talk about your own goals, your dreams, your ambition, your vision. Talk about that with people that are on a similar wavelength to you, and just be wary of who you share it with. One person might build you up, and another may well pull you down. But don't let negativity affect you. Instead, harness it; let them motivate and inspire you. Recognise how you feel, because you're going to experience emotion one way or the other, depending on who you share these things with.

So that's vision. It can be powerful stuff. But there's also the issue of belief – in particular, do you believe in your vision or not? Well, I certainly believed in the goal of 200 houses. Dreaming of owning so many properties was very ambitious, but I believed that vision. Do you believe in your own? Do you believe that you can achieve whatever it is that you're going after? Because if you don't believe in your own vision – if you do not believe in yourself – then why is anyone else going to believe in you?

If you're going to look to try and secure your first investor or negotiate your first purchase, or if you're going to deal in an attractive sale, and you're trying to secure that property... if you don't believe you can secure that property and acquire it, if you don't go and meet your private investor who might be able to support you in the acquisition... you'll never know if you would have succeeded or not. If you don't believe that you can go and achieve it – secure it, get financed, get the deal over the line, maybe a seven day completion – whatever it might be... if you don't believe you're capable of doing all of that, why would anybody else?

Overcoming self-limitation

It's really important to recognise that limiting beliefs are like carrying a big bag of negativity with you. Don't let those limiting beliefs overwhelm you. No doubt they will try to pull you back to your little comfort zone with nothing more than negativity. But you can overcome limiting beliefs. Trust me, you can. You just need to think about it. You need to operate consciously, not unconsciously. Confront those limiting beliefs. Think about it and put a stop to them. We teach a lot of material about dealing with negativity, and they are very powerful techniques. Don't let these things hold you back, because they will – and recognise that fact.

Don't forget that every professional was once a beginner. We didn't wake up one morning and just have all these assets and experience. We didn't wake up one morning and have a group. We didn't wake up one morning and have all the different companies that we operate now. We had to start off at beginner level and work from there. We had to buy one. Then we had to buy a couple. Then we had to buy five. Then we had to do a first portfolio deal. Then we had to operate the group structure. It's the same for businesses in every profession. Richard Branson, Jeff Bezos... they're all in that same category. They had to start somewhere. But the point is that we all have to start somewhere. We were all beginners at some stage.

Now, we are involved in property investment development, building, training, there will be some other businesses to add to that list soon too. But we had to start somewhere. We were once beginners, just as you might be right now. So think about what you can do. And I'll tell you what: if you think about why you *can't* do whatever it is that you want to do, then take a notepad and write down all of the reasons why you cannot do them. You will soon find that you have tons and tons of reasons why you can't do these things. But then you think about reasons why you can, and your list will be much smaller. Why? Because it's a natural thing that goes on in your mind. Everybody thinks about the worst case scenario. The worst case seems very real, though some folks instinctively think of a best case. Perhaps you may end up somewhere in the middle. But don't accept these justifications from your mind about why you cannot do whatever it is that you want to do. Because you can.

• • •

You can succeed if your faith is stronger than your fear; only then you will push through the pain barrier, this uncomfortable zone that holds you back. If you push through that, you'll move forward toward your success. Or does your fear seem stronger than your faith? Because I guarantee your faith can be stronger than your fear. If you do not act upon this belief that to calm that fear, it's going to distract you from moving forward. So if you believe that your faith is stronger than your fear, you're going to move forward easier. If your fear seems stronger than your faith, you really need to work on this, because otherwise it's really going to hold you back. So keep asking yourself with an ever-stronger focus. Focus, focus, focus, focus, focus.

You will need to focus. It's essential that you do so. You must not let yourself get caught up in all these slick offers that fly around the Internet. You know the kind of thing: cryptocurrency offers where you can make a million quid with one click of a mouse button from your home in Barbados. Blah, blah, blah. Instead, focus... and stay focused. Find the right strategic involvement and remain focused. Don't allow yourself to become distracted. Get tuned in. Then *really* get tuned in. So don't let these other external factors influence where you're going. You're here now; you've paid for this book and the knowledge within it. You're interested in learning about property investment development. But if you allow yourself to get distracted by other things – if you find yourself distracted by cryptocurrencies and Forex, and then you add in yet more diversions – you're never going to get anywhere.

Stay focused on property as your specialism. Hunt it down, focus your goals, keep learning. What are you going after? What is your aim? And if you've not determined your goals, don't you need to write them down? You need to write them down to realise them. You can then look back over a few years and consider how your goals have changed over time... but whatever it is that you're going after, at some point you need to go after it. You need to go out there and hunt it. Nobody else is going to hunt it down for you.

We've looked a bit at distraction already. It can very easily pull you away from going after what you want in life. Focus means sacrifice. But it should only be short-term. Don't allow yourself to sacrifice everything in life. You don't need to work 100 hours a week for five years solid. No nice garden, no nice house, you don't eat in restaurants and you don't see your family and friends... all that sort of thing. That's no way to live life! So don't sacrifice life for five years. But all the same, you might need to get up in the morning a little bit earlier than you're used to. You might need to work a little bit later at night. You might need to work some weekends to move your business forward too. Why would you not want to do that?

So being focused does mean sacrifice, but it should not consume your life. It should only ever be a short-term thing to move closer to your goals. A lot of people talk about the work-life balance. And for me, the work-life balance thing can be summed up as follows: we take actions and they have consequences. And I live more and more by that because it can lead to a very relatively free, flexible life. I can take time off when I want, work when I want, travel when I want. But I'm only able to do that because of the actions and sacrifices I've made in the past. I don't mind working from abroad or on holiday or whatever. I mean, we've all got mobile phones these days, right? What I'm saying is, you can do whatever you need to do. So even when you're traveling, it only takes two seconds to send out texts and email from your mobile phone and keep things moving forward. That's my view. It's not to say that it should be this way for years on end, but by taking all of those little actions, cumulatively they allow me to live a very free and flexible lifestyle.

So it's not really about the work-life balance for me. It's about the actions I choose to take creating the consequences. Action, action, action. Do what 99% of people don't do. Most people don't do what is necessary; in other words, to take the action required to move you forward. What's your goal? You must, must, must know this lesson. This is a big, bold, capital letters message: it's critical action. Vital to your success or failure. If you do not take action, you're not going to move forward. Please, please, please take the action you need to take. If you find that you've got issues and you need support, consider mentorship. But you need to take the actions. If you don't, you'll go nowhere.

Start now. Do something. Make a move. Because you either bought that property or you got that portfolio over the line or you didn't. And we've plenty of examples of these types of things. But the whole 'chimp mindset' thing... the reality is, that could break a deal. Stay on the straight and narrow when your inner chimp tries to take over. We either secure the investor and we purchase that property or we don't. We either complete that development project or we don't. We either secured that portfolio or we didn't. It's so important to realise that it's action you need to take. And depending on the action that you take, it's going to either conclude, move you forward, grow... or not. And that's true of literally every single deal that you engage with. As the deals get bigger, the tensions greater, the amount of personalities you're dealing with increase, there will be more and more different things to fight through. And those are the kind of problems that can come up just by going through the completion process. But the fundamental thing is either that you did or didn't – and if you did, you move forward. If you didn't, you did not move forward.

If you don't try, the failure rate is 100%. So, did you make that investment in a property that you tried to secure? Maybe you felt that you could have done things better? But if you didn't try, you have no chance of succeeding. If you tried to get it done, but didn't quite get there, there are ways to make sure you succeed the next time. You paid for the education, spent more time with people that can help you move forward towards your goals, and you're ready to accomplish your goal. You either make the move or you don't. There is no in-between. It's so important to know that action is going to be the key to making your objectives a reality. Action is going to be the key. Even if it doesn't work out as you planned, even if it isn't the best case scenario, you will still have learned by going through that experience. Take the action, make the move, get the knowledge, apply the knowledge. How can you possibly expect to get an outcome if you don't know the strategy and you don't know what you're doing? This baffles me.

Combating negativity

Negatives are one of my favourite things to control, because negativity is going to be detrimental to your progress and ultimately your success. If you allow them to, negatives will hold you back, big style. They have done for me in the past, and I'm sure you won't be any different. Learning how to control negativity and your emotions is crucial. Finding ways to deal with those feelings can really serve you well. And again, this isn't really stuff that people study; it isn't stuff that people often think about. Sometimes, for a number of reasons, people just become negative. They get negative, and that's the end of it. But thinking about it, we get back to the issue of operating consciously: recognising this negative scenario and then controlling that emotion can be very powerful for you. If you don't control it, it will take control of your mind instead and your thoughts will wander. If it gets extreme, your mind will start coming up with all sorts of random crap; crap that doesn't even exist. Just negative stuff. And once your mind gets into this way of thinking, it will be endlessly held up unless you deal with it directly. Unless you control the negativity, your mind really can't cope. But it can once you get a good degree of control over it.

A lot of people that suffer with anxiety are affected by this type of thing because they can't control what's going on in their lives. Obviously I'm talking about applying this type of stuff in business, and certainly to your property investment journey, and dealing with negatives is a big factor in all of that because there are going to be plenty of them. So it's essential to learn how to control that. They can really distract you from reaching your goal. I know that I go on and on about achieving the end result of whatever these goals are that we set ourselves. That's because, for me, it's all about the end result. Everything between the thought and the goal being decided upon... anything that lies between me and the end result. Everything in there is just noise. It's just noise. It doesn't matter. All that matters is that you achieve that goal, and negativity will definitely distract you from your goals and objectives. I'm sure you can relate to this. I'm sure everybody who is reading this can directly relate to this negativity thing, but the key thing is to know that you can control it.

So don't think that you can't deal with it. You can. It's just about levelling up your knowledge to help you deal with that scenario. There are life hacks I apply to my own life on a daily basis. All these different things have value. Some of them might seem very obvious, some of them maybe not so much. But for me, using all of these things daily and in different shapes and forms have been beneficial. Applying these things to-gether is massively powerful, and I really believe they have helped us massively to move forward.

Deep breathing – by which I mean, breathing right through the thought – can help you in business and in life. Every single day I do deep breathing exercises. They really work. It slows your heart rate. It puts your mind in a state of calm. And I don't believe I could take cold show-ers in the morning if it wasn't for breathing through that initial shock going from the hot water to the freezing cold! I mean, I am a big lad. At time of writing I currently weigh about 114 kilos. I need to get to 100 or less; that's one of my goals. But I mean, you would look at me and you wouldn't think, 'man, this guy stretches – I can't see him in the saddle pose!' Yet maybe when you come in to see us in a live event, ask me if I'll do a live demonstration of a saddle. I mean, I probably won't. I'd proba-bly kill myself trying. But I love this stretching thing anyway. However, I wouldn't be able to do those stretches or hold those poses for long peri-ods of time. It can be uncomfortable, really uncomfortable. Bordering on pain. Some of these poses that I do are part of what's called ROMWOD, which stands for 'range of motion workout of the day'. It's pretty cool. But I don't believe I could do these stretches if it wasn't for breathing. Breathe in through it: the deep breath, focusing on the breath count, and using my heart as a natural timer. When I do these stretches, I meditate. Sometimes I let my mind wander to let it clear. Other times I focus my mind on certain things: goals, objectives, visualisation. I've talked about it before. You know the kind of thing: playing scenes over in your mind, visualising future scenes situations that you want to achieve, affirming to yourself. I find value in this type of stuff.

I am a property millionaire. I can do anything, whatever it might be for you. But I like to do the meditation, visualisation and affirmation as I stretch and as I breathe, so I'm combining all these things together. When it comes to exercise, Alex Robertson talks about reducing your cortisol levels, and it's true. Before any type of exercise, you might feel a bit pissed off. You might be frustrated. 'I don't even want to do it', you might think. And you know the main reason that's holding you back? Your mind is making you lazy. Your mind is saying: 'Stay comfortable.

You don't need to put your body through this exercise nonsense.' But you push your body and you do the workout anyway. How do you feel? You feel awesome! Then you take a cold shower, breathing through, slowing your heart rate. Then after the exercise, sleep well. We all need our sleep!

The only reason I make that point is because when I first got started, I was working crazy hours. I wasn't really sleeping as much, and it was obviously impacting on my performance. I would get up at 4am and I wouldn't go to bed until 11pm. I was doing all sorts of different things over the day, and at night I was networking. At the same time, I wasn't eating right. I wasn't sleeping properly, and it was impacting on my performance. I was shattered all the time. And now, I actually make a point of getting as much sleep as I can at night. I really value sleep now and I didn't before. We need to understand the health benefits, too. I've got a Fitbit which tracks my sleep. All of these things really go together. And I've called them life hacks – though, as I say, some of them are natural. Some of them you've maybe never thought about before. Go and try them out.

All of these things combined puts you in a different zone compared to not doing them. So again, as I wrote at the start of the chapter, let yourself be open-minded. Just give this stuff a chance. Try it. I would love to hear how you get on with doing these things as well, because really I think this is all very effective and advantageous stuff. You know, I'm not saying this stuff to fill up space in this book. I really believe that doing these things can help you. So check them out. Being organised, being systematic and having good communication is essential in any business. It's essential in life, in my view.

But organisation is key. You need to communicate, you need to organise, you need to keep things moving in the background. And even if you don't have a clue what's going on, communicate with confidence and clarity, especially when you're negotiating. At all times, communicate with confidence and clarity, because that's *always* necessary. If you are communicating ineffectively and waffling all sorts of different crap, you're not looking confident. If you're looking at the floor the whole time, that's going to impact on your results.

• • •

Likewise, files and folders need to be structured. They're going to be essential for finance and all the other stuff you're going to be doing. Assuming you're looking to buy a lot, a great deal of admin goes along with that, and you need to be prepared for this to take up a lot of your time – feeding a whole load of information back to the bank and the brokers and all that type of thing. So you should be structured, and you should you should plan things in advance. At all times, be organised. And look, the buy-to-let thing in particular is a very passive income stream, and you have your power team – which is all of your key stakeholders, your lawyers, your broker, your agent... all of that stuff. They should be taking care of things in the background, if you have organised that as you should have. You should have that level of systemisation in place, and you should communicate clearly and confidently with these guys to keep things moving along.

Your role as a professional property investor is to find deals and find finance. That's your role. Everything else should be systematised and be taken care of in the background. Focus your time on these vital things. Allow your team to deal with everything else. This is where you find most value, because you only have a limited amount of time each day. Everybody all has the same amount of time each day. So how come some people get more stuff done than others? Is it because some systemise the process every time they start a new business? We ask ourselves, how can we systemise this? How can we make it better? How can we make it more efficient? How can we remove the time that we have to be involved? And just as importantly, how can we remove our time from that? And it's all about effective systematisation. Everybody's got a different view if too many people are involved in the organisation process; there's no leadership or direction towards goals, but if everyone has a place within different scenarios then things can move much more effectively. We have become good at this, depending on the scenario. Sometimes one of us will take the lead and the other will step back, while in another situation the other one takes the lead. But depending on the scenario, one of us will take the lead and one of us will step back. We're quite happy to adapt to these roles, and it makes us work very, very well together.

Establishing your goals

I talked earlier about setting your specific goals. This will be very important for you. Your objectives need to be big, but not Cuckoo Land big. They need to be 200 properties, not a million properties and more. But make sure that you write them down. Write down your goals, as just by writing them on paper you send a message to your subconscious mind. Just try it, and be open-minded. Write the goals, then take time to think about what you want and why you want it. Who else can benefit from your efforts? Write all of this stuff down.

Most of you have probably heard about the smart goals, right? They should be specific, measurable, achievable, realistic and timed. But really, reality is just a perception. So do all the rest of the stuff, but just be aware of when it comes to your realistic objective, don't let it be a Cuckoo Land objective. Let it be a big objective... just not in the realms of Cuckoo Land. Vision boards are cool. I put together vision boards for 2018, 2019 and 2020. However, I didn't do one for 2021 because that was when we were moving into our new office and event space. But we did create a board for 2022. It was organised, systematised and put on dis-

play. Why? Because it's quite cool to look back at these goals and reassess them periodically. Think about whatever your goals are on a regular basis, because they are going to change.

They're going to change as you grow, so make them big. Focus, believe, think about the outcomes, reassess. I like to do it on an annual basis, maybe every six months or so. It all depends on what you want to do, but definitely write them down. Think about what you should put on your vision board. If you were to see mine from 2018, you would be able to read about some of my crazy goals. At that moment in time it was 100 properties. It was scary. It was new. I didn't have a clue what was involved in it. The point is, I've not achieved every single one of these goals from 2018. I don't look like a Navy SEAL yet, and I've not got to my 95 kilos target weight yet. But these are things that go on in my mind, and they've always been in my mind since 2018. Some of them I have achieved, some of them I have not achieved. That includes the fancy car. I don't have a Range Rover yet. The big house I did buy, though.

Anyway, at that time the goal was still 100 properties, and I think we had maybe 40 or 50 at that time. I don't remember. I sometimes talk about holidays, so they are on the vision board. But as my lifestyle goes, I don't really want to go on holidays anymore as such. I'd rather have a secondary home; I'd like one up in the Highlands somewhere, and I'd like one in the Alicante region. I'd like to live my life between these locations, as I don't have to be in the office every day. Between 2019 and 2020, at that point the property goal was changed from 100 to 300, so as you can see over these years the goals were changed, and the 'mastermind' goal that I had on my vision board eventually ended up becoming the training company that we operate today.

The training company started with mastermind, and it has since morphed into a full training business. Our business is bringing you this education. There are now joint ventures involved. We've come on leaps and bounds since we started. We buy portfolios regularly; something I could never have imagined at the start of 2020. We didn't have a portfolio deal until around October 2020. There was our commercial residential projects; I mentioned that we've got six projects underway at time of writing. One was our ten bedroom HMO restaurant conversion. The purchase price equals 100 times the rent; that means you're going to get 12% yield. I look back at these old vision boards from past years, and I see how they change over time. The 2022 vision board, of course, has entirely different goals on it. So you can see why it's very powerful to write all of this stuff down. It's funny to look back on this kind of thing and see what we've achieved. You should do the same.

Perceptions of reality

I want to talk a little bit about reality and what it means to you. Because reality is a perception, and you could be limiting yourself by living in your current reality. And I see how your current reality could change, because my own current reality is very, very different to what my reality looked like a few years ago. It's going to be the same deal for you when you start making moves, when you start pushing yourself forward. But don't limit yourself by observations of this current reality, because reality is going to change. It's a perception. What does it look like? And what about one year, two years, three years from now? Or even five years, ten years?

What does your new reality look like? Will you take the necessary actions I mentioned earlier? You're either going to move forward or you're not, and that's down to the actions that you take. So imagine you take the necessary actions. What kind of reality is it that you want to be in? Do you want to be living in Monaco? Do you want to be living in a billionaire's reality? Maybe you think that's too crazy. Perhaps you want to be living in a multi-millionaire reality. Think about your reality; what it looks like. Think of someone that you know – maybe somebody you see and like. It could be on social media or the TV, maybe someone famous or influential. Do you want to be living in their reality? Think carefully about that. Think about whose reality you want to be living in, because you can create whatever it is that you want.

You need to realise that your current reality has come about because of the decisions you have made so far, because of the choices you have made to date – that is what has created *your current* reality. To create your new reality, you're going to need to take other decisions. Different decisions. You're going to need to think about that, and see how it makes you feel. You're going to need to take actions that are going to

produce that result of your new reality and shape what it will look like in one, two, three, five, ten years' time – whenever it may be. But realise that your current reality looks the way it does because of the decisions you've made so far. This is all about getting you to where you want to go, because you need to recognise how you're going to get there.

You need to gain the knowledge. How can you possibly expect to move yourself forward towards that goal if you don't have the knowledge? Well, this educational content is knowledge, but you also need support. And while you might not feel as though you want support, it will massively help you in the long run. It will help you stay on track. It will help you stay motivated, and help push you to take the right actions. It may be uncomfortable, but you need to have the knowledge and you need to have some kind of support – whether that's through mentorship or otherwise. You need a good team around you. You need a good lawyer, you need a good letting agent, you need a good refurb team, you need a good accountant. In short, you need people that know what they're doing. You need a good, solid team around you, because if you don't, that's going to slow you down from getting to where you want to go.

As I mentioned earlier, everything between now and the end result is noise. Recognise that it's noise and block it out. Stay focused. If you

● ● ●

knew that you were guaranteed this end result, you would know how important it is to keep focused. If you knew you were guaranteed the outcome, you would do all the stuff that is in this section. What is your mind saying to you right now? That you're in the unknown? Maybe you don't know, but the knowledge, the support, the team and all these techniques that we've taught you about can make all the difference. This chapter, and everything else that's involved in getting started, is detailed in this book, and it can help move you to where you need to go.

We love working with people. We love helping people achieve whatever it is they want to achieve in the property world. We've obviously done great ourselves, and all this educational content is based on our own experiences. So, we are very excited for anyone planning to undertake a similar journey.

The REWD Group directors and staff members pictured on location in the Falkirk area. (Images Copyright © Sara Amelia Photography, all rights reserved).

Chapter Two

The Basics

Alex Robertson

WELCOME to the next chapter in *Fast-Track to Property Millions*. This chapter will be all about the basics. And in this section, we're going to be going through some of the more fundamental elements of property investment. We're going to touch on things like: the question of why to invest in property; the keys to successful property investment; the buying process; and also some of the basic terminology you need to know.

The fact that you're here suggests that you already have an idea of why property investment is such a wonderful opportunity to create wealth. However, we're going to go into more detail: the 'must dos' of property investment and certain key things to avoid. We're also going to cover some of the key terminologies within property, just so you're not bamboozled by some of the property jargon that you're likely to encounter. And we're going to talk about the property buying process so you can understand from start to finish the process that's involved in purchasing property. Then we're going to end up talking about what strategy might be right for you now. Obviously in this section, we're not going to be going through all the various strategies that are available within the property market; this is merely to get you thinking about what you are looking to achieve from your property investment strategy.

Why invest in property?

Before we get to that information, it's important to have a think about what you're looking to get out of property investing. What is the objective? What is the goal? These are the questions that can help you decide what strategy you might want to focus on, coming at the other end of this introduction to property investing. So, let's get into some of the key reasons why property is such an amazing investment vehicle.

Solid asset class (supply vs demand)

Why property? Well, firstly, it is known as one of the most solid asset classes – as the old saying goes, 'safe as houses'. The reality is that people will always need a place to live. If you think about Maslows' hierarchy of needs, the most fundamental human needs that we have beyond our physiological needs, which are the needs for food and water: we have the safety needs, which is ultimately a roof over our head. It is one of the most fundamental things we need as human beings. You know, we all need a place to live. Moreover, the UK housing market has extremely strong fundamentals. When we look at the UK market versus the likes of Spain, for example, the UK market has a massive undersupply of housing, unlike Spain that has excessive housing provisions.

There are some surveys that estimate that there is a shortage of 4 million homes to meet the current demand for housing within the UK, which is continually growing. Moreover, we've got around about a million homes empty throughout the UK. So, as well as the requirement for more new homes we have an under-utilisation of stock. We've got under-supply versus demand, we've got a growing population, we've got an ageing population... so there is continually increasing demand. Ultimately, we're only building somewhere in the region of 250,000 to 300,000 houses per year. So, it's just not enough to catch up on that demand.

The fundamentals for property are very strong in the UK as an asset class. When you look at somewhere like Spain, where they have massive oversupply, they really require a lot of people coming from abroad and to have their holiday homes there to meet the demand that they have, because they have such a large tourism base. If that tourism goes away, the local demand is not enough to meet the amount of development that's happened in Spain. So, for instance, they were extremely badly affected by the crisis in 2008 when property prices crashed because the fundamentals of their market were weak. There was this massive oversupply in construction for the tourism market that wasn't necessarily required. Ultimately, they suffered, and the recovery for them from the 2008 crash was a much longer and more significant process than it was for us here in the UK, where the fundamentals were ultimately quite strong. We talked about the undersupply estimate: 4 million shortage estimate, 1 million empty homes, and only building about 250,000 to 300,000 properties a year. All these factors lead to quite a strong fundamental indication that the UK property is a solid asset class.

Debt leverage

So why property from a debt leverage perspective? Property offers one of the most unique situations insofar as you can leverage quite a substantial amount of bank debt against the property. Because banks see property as such a safe asset class, they are comfortable with higher levels of lending. They will lend a sizeable amount of money towards the purchase of a property, and the beautiful thing about this is that the debt is relatively cheap. This is because it's safe, because it's a solid asset class, because it has a very comfortable market for resale. The bank is willing to provide these relatively low costs, because they see it as a relatively low risk. So in a buy-to-let mortgage, for example, you will be paying anywhere between 2% and 7% interest per year for some of the more specialist stuff within that threshold. Especially at the 2% level, you're talking about very, very cheap; that's the leverage that you have available to you.

If you look at other investment categories – different investment types such as, for instance, stocks and shares or if you're investing in cryptocurrencies or fine wine or classic cars – you will not find the same level of debt leverage that's available against a property investment. There are not many banks that are going to provide you money, certainly on any scale to invest in stocks. Property is quite unique in terms of the level of leverage that's available. And the beauty of all of that is you get the full return, the value of the asset, even although the relative level of cash that you've put into that investment is likely to be quite low. For instance, with the average property, you could probably get somewhere in the region of 70% or 80% of the cash to buy that property from the bank. You're only putting in a 20% to 25% deposit: a relatively low amount of cash. But when the value of that property increases, you get the entire benefit of the value of that increase; you get the rental income in its entirety, less the cost of the mortgage interest which again is relatively low. The value the property investment can bring in terms of that leverage is huge, with the potential to accelerate the amount of return that you can get from your cash.

When we get to the chapter that talks about understanding the numbers, understanding your return and how to calculate that, you will see that the percentage returns that we can achieve through property – particularly with that leverage – is incredible. It can dwarf a lot of other types of investment opportunities. it really is quite exciting, the level of financial return that we can gain.

Capital growth

Next, let's talk about capital growth: another one of the massive reasons why people invest in property. If you look back over the last 40 years, for example, property prices have almost doubled every ten years. Now, that's inclusive of market corrections; it's inclusive of a cycle which says that roughly every 12 years, the market crashes. Over the last 40 years, in Scotland, property has almost doubled every ten years on average. Now, to put this into perspective, in 1980 the average home in Scotland would have cost around £15,000. This is an incredible figure; I think it seems so cheap, because today as we stand in 2021, the average property price in Scotland is £166,000. It probably doesn't take too much to work out that as an annual increase over that time period, it works out at 6% per annum – or what we call a compound annual growth rate of 6%.

Now effectively, if the figure of the annual increase was 7% or just over 7%, that would equate to prices doubling every ten years. It's just slightly under that line, but that's still a huge return: 6% just from the capital growth. Year on year, your investment has increased 6%. That's even before we have considered the rental income.

Then there's the fact that you don't even pay for the entire property. You only pay for a portion of it. There's a huge ability to leverage debt and get a massive gain from capital growth on the full value of the property. And the beautiful thing about it as an investment is that growth is only taxed when you sell. So even though you're making this annual return, you don't have to pay any tax on it unless you sell. Now, ultimately, if it's your principal residence and we're talking about your own house, then you wouldn't have to pay any tax when you sell anyway. Your principal private residence is exempt. However, if it's an investment property, you do have to pay tax when you sell – but only when you sell, not on a year-on-year basis. And because you get an increase year on year, and ultimately, you're only taxed when you sell, that leads us to the conclusion that capital growth is a massive reason why people are investing in property.

Passive income
The next subject is passive income. A lot of the time when people are talking about passive income, we're talking about buy-to-let within the property investment world. While other types of property investment can be passive, ultimately buy-to-let is the investment that's most passive of all. If you think about other strategies like flips, for example, you constantly must keep finding new projects, finding new deals to be able to gain profit. Whereas with buy-to-let, you can buy some properties and then have an agent manage them. And effectively, there's very little involvement from you on a day-to-day basis with the agent being responsible for the property. They collect rent, are the first point of contact for the tenant, and they deal with any maintenance issues. The agent takes all the calls from the tenants, and they pay you at the end of the month.

The tenure of the tenants can be quite long term, so there is no regular job to fill properties and even when tenants do leave, the agent would be responsible for finding a new tenant. If you intend to be a professional investor it is critical to systemise your buy to let business and have it managed, as the day-to-day management of your own portfolio can be very difficult, with tenants calling at random times, co-ordinating repairs and marketing vacant properties. It's no wonder you get so many 'tired landlords' when they are managing their own properties; no one wants to be fielding calls for an angry tenant on Christmas day when they are about to tuck in to their third Chocolate Orange. Leave it to the professionals.

REWD Group has gotten to a point now where we are paid for each one of our portfolios once every month. Cash comes in at the start of the month. Beyond that, we don't have much involvement, other than the monthly KPI performance reviews we do to ensure there are no issues. Of all the businesses that REWD Group has, our buy-to let portfolios are by far and away the most passive. This passive income truly is the key to financial freedom, as so many people create a new stream of income that requires their close involvement and time and, in that case, all you have created is another job. We sometimes talk about the 'financial freedom figure'. This is how much money you would need to generate via a passive income source to replace your current income. If you want to be able to have a hands-off investment where you take money every month, and it replaces your income, so you don't necessarily have to work, then buy-to-let is by far and away the best strategy. Why? Because very few other investment opportunities can create such a passive level of income where you create a deal, you buy the properties, you find your agent, you set it all up and the money just comes in every month.

We normally look to be aiming for about £250 per property, per calendar month of net cash flow. That is your rental income, less direct cost of land. You know if your financial freedom figure is £2,500 then you're going to be trying to aim for maybe 10 to 12 properties to meet that financial freedom number – and then, suddenly, you've got the money coming in every month to cover your bills and you find that you don't necessarily have to work. You know you can do what you want to do. You can enjoy life and have what we would call financial freedom, or financial flexibility. Property is one of the most unique investment vehicles to create passive income, which will allow you to spend your time on other things. And ultimately, we've used a buy-to-let portfolio to allow us to create monthly cash coming in that we can fund to grow other businesses.

We have a development business, a training business, a building company. A lot of the funding for those businesses, certainly during the initial period when we were growing them, came from our buy-to-let properties and the strength of the rental income that we had there.

Inflation and future growth

Property benefits from inflation, so let's look at an example to try and make this clear. Using the example of the average home back in 1980, imagine you bought that home for £15,000 and you bought it with a £5,000 mortgage. Whilst that seems very little money now, back in the 1980s and considering the average salary back then, that could have been a significant cost that could have affected your ability to go on holiday, or your ability to spend time with your family because you had to work overtime, for instance. You could have had a significant impact in your life having to pay that mortgage, especially with capital on interest; you're not only paying the interest on that loan, but you're also repaying the £5,000 capital over a longer period. That that could have had a significant effect on your standard of living at the time.

Imagine a situation where effectively you didn't do that. You let the £5,000 loan remain and you just paid the interest on it. That would have significantly brought down your monthly payments. You could have potentially ended up with more money to enjoy life and now, in 2020, your house is now worth £166,000, if you remember back in the last example. That £5,000 loan in today's monetary terms is not all that significant. It may only be a couple of months' salary for you and that's it – the mortgage is paid off. The decreased value of money has worked in your favour; inflation over the course of those 40 years has deteriorated the value of that loan.

Inflation in real terms is probably around 5% per annum. As the value of your property continues to go up year on year by 6% (as in the capital growth section), it outperforms inflation in terms of growth, while the amount of debt you have against that property stays the same.

Just to further emphasis this point let's look at our buy-to-let portfolio at REWD Group, which currently sits around £11 million in value with around £8 million of bank debt. Assuming Laurie and I did nothing with that portfolio for the rest of our lives (other than collect rent and maintain them) and we live to the ripe of age of 87, the value of our properties would have doubled more than 4 times and the asset value would be in excess of £200million, whilst the level of debt would still be £8 million. That is some serious gains in our lifetime.

Money generation from property

The next big reason why to invest in property is that there are many, many ways to make money in property. If you look at the later chapter on strategies, you're going to see all the different ways that you can make money with property. There are so many ways: whether you've got money, whether you've not got money, whether you're a novice, or whether you're a more sophisticated investor. There are various strategies that you can employ within property. You don't even have to own the property to make money on it. You know, that's the beauty of all the strategies that are available to you as a property investor. There are strategies for everything, and we will detail them all within that later chapter. As I said, it doesn't have to involve owning the property.

You can do things like, for instance, assisted sales – where you effectively agree a price with the vendor (the person who owns the property) that you're going to guarantee them for their house. You'll then spend money to improve that property to sell it at a higher price, which will give you a margin; you'll make money on the sale, they'll get the agreed price that they signed up to at the front end, and everyone's happy. So there are strategies like that, which don't actually involve owning property. I've talked about assisted sales, and we have other strategies within property like buy-to-let, flips, property sourcing, rent-to-rent, commercial to residential conversions – there are many, many more. And we cover all of that within the strategy chapter.

The amazing thing about property is that you do not need your own money to invest. That's the beautiful thing about it. You don't have to have money to be involved in property. And I hear a lot of people saying, so many times, 'I want to get involved in property, but ultimately I'm trying to save up a bit of money first', or 'property is only for rich people', or maybe 'I can't get involved in property investing until I have X amount of money in the bank.' The reality is that those are all excuses. When you know the strategies and when you are educated in property investing, you will understand that you don't necessarily need money to be a successful property investor. A lot of what we have done in building the group to the size that it is just now, and building our more than 200 buy-to-let properties in the last few years, has been done without using our own money.

We didn't start as millionaires. We had to find the skills necessary to bring money into our business. This is a really important point for anybody that's thinking about getting started, but think they need this imaginary big pot of cash to get started: it's just not the case. If you don't have any cash, there are strategies like property sourcing that you can pursue, where you find deals for other investors and take a fee, or joint ventures where you bring the deal and you manage the project whilst someone else brings the finance, or a rent-to-rent deal where they may not need a huge amount of front end cash, and certainly an amount of cash that you might be able to finance in other ways – maybe a short-term credit card or whatever. If the money returns quickly, where perhaps you're only paying for a small refurb or you're only paying for a couple of months' rent vacancies on a on a rental deal before you implement a sublet, for example. These are strategies that maybe require a smaller amount of cash versus purchasing a property.

Private investor finance is another huge one; it's a big thing that we've implemented over the years. This involves finding good deals but then having private investors, who get a return on their money secured against that property, to allow you then to buy it. So, you know, you're not even using your own finance, but you're still providing a service to investors who are looking to get a return of the cash. And there are many, many other financial strategies besides, some of which we will cover within the finance chapter of *Fast-Track to Property Millions.*

Success leaves clues

I like to keep things very simple. When I first started looking for a profession when I was at school, I looked at where the money was and who was making the most money. At the time, back in the day, it was before the tech age. It was accountants, doctors and lawyers who had good salaries. So I thought, 'Okay, I'm good with numbers, I'll be an accountant, because there's good money in that.' That's what I did, and when I was trying to choose an industry to set up my own business, I took the same approach. Where are people making the most money? Where's the best place to be? It was obvious, property. Aside from the fact it's generally the biggest purchase someone ever makes, you just need to look at *The Sunday Times* Rich List. You'll see what each of the richest people in the world do to make their money. The largest majority by a mile is in property. Most of the richest people in the country are making money on property. 'Success leaves clues': look at what the most successful rich people are doing and copy them – adding your own spin on things, of course. It's not rocket science.

The key to success in property investment

Next, we're going to talk about matters of property investment. What are the key things that we need to do to be successful property investors? We must buy right. That's the old saying: you make money when you buy; 100%. You need to add value through refurbishment. We'll talk more about that in a minute. You need to make profit. Of course. This is a business, so it's fundamental that we make money, and you need to understand the numbers. How can you understand if you're going to make money? If you don't understand the numbers, you know, it seems fundamental. And then you need to understand the buying process. That is one of the key elements to purchasing or doing any property deal: that you know what the process is, the steps involved, and how long it's likely to take. So, let's get into some of these elements in a bit more detail.

Buy right

So first, ask yourself: can you make the money when you buy? I hear people talk about this time and time again, and it's never been truer: it's so easy to get caught in a property deal where you like the location, you know the area, you like the look of the property and envisage yourself living there. You think it is a great investment. And you'd like to point to that property and tell all your friends that you own this property: *that is not property investing*. That's when your heart has started to lead your head; you're not looking at it like an investment. You're being led down the wrong path. Ultimately, so many people make that mistake. It's key to focus on the numbers and make sure that you find a target price.

● ● ●

You want to buy any property at the right price to make sure that this is going to be a good deal for you. If you fall at the first hurdle – if you've negotiated the price, and it's way too high – you're never going to be able to recover that situation, especially in markets like Scotland. Scotland has relatively low property prices, so buying at the right price level is important because it's not so easy to add value through refurbishment. The reality is if you're looking at a £50,000 property, it's unlikely that a brand new £10,000 kitchen is going to be able to give value to that type of property because it has a maximum achievable price – that no matter how nice the property is, it's not going to achieve a price beyond that. So, you need to be clear on those things, and ultimately – because prices are relatively low to start with in Scotland – adding value through refurb when the costs of doing work are going up and up, and the cost of building materials are similarly going up and up. It becomes much more difficult to create value through refurbishment when ultimately a lot of the value that you create as a property investment comes from buying at the right price. BMV becomes a critical measure – BMV standing for 'below market value'.

How much in terms of percentage have you paid, versus the market price of that property? If you've got a £100,000 property, and you bought it for £75,000, you've got 25% BMV. We're always aiming for somewhere in the region of 20-30% BMV. But ultimately that's only one measure. We need to understand the whole deal in its totality, and that's something we will look at within the understanding the numbers chapter. Here you can see a little bit more detail on how to calculate the investor's view of how a deal works.

Direct to vendor

So how can we get these great BMV deals? Well, the most likely scenario for a good BMV deal is negotiating direct to vendor. You can't get BMV without having some sort of leverage in the situation. You know, if something's on the market and there's two of people that are going to view that, you're not going to get the best price because it's going to go for the high end of highest price – and ultimately, you're not going to be able to secure any leverage. So that's the frustration for a lot of people just now, as the market is strong and it's difficult to get these good deals unless you're dealing direct to vendor; say if you're dealing with someone who's selling it rather than dealing with agents or intermediate third parties or auction houses. You're dealing with the vendor directly, because you can negotiate directly with them.

Dealing direct to vendor is only the first element of securing a BMV deal. You're also looking for that seller to be a motivated seller; people who are in a rush to sell the property for whatever reason. Motivations can be broad and vary from someone who's received it as an inheritance to someone who just wants rid of the property because it has a negative emotional connection, or perhaps someone who's bought a new property and the sale of their property has fallen through; the chain is broken, and they need a quick sale, or they will lose out on the new home. And you can help them with that. Perhaps it's someone who maybe has an impending action; someone whose property is about to be repossessed and has an urgent need to get a sale to pay off the bank. There are many varying motivations which can affect the price that you can negotiate with the vendor. And if you're able to do a quick cash deal – if you're able to secure a property and offer to pay cash in two weeks with no mortgage, and no complications that extend the period – that can be attractive to a lot of people. So that's where the best deals come from.

Negotiation

You must understand the key negotiation tactics to get the best prices. Obviously, the ability to negotiate is a key part of the business as a property investor. So, let's talk negotiation. If you are in a position where you can get in front of a vendor and be negotiating with them directly, what are some of the key skills and steps that you need to know as property investor to make sure that you get the right offer?

The first strategy is: never be the first person to mention a price. I'll never be the first to put out an offer, and there's a very good reason for that. I will give you a good example of one of the first negotiations we ever dealt with, and it was where we managed to secure an ex-local authority property for £22,000. Ultimately, throughout our negotiation, we didn't mention a number. We just tried through discussions with the vendor to extract their number – that is, the number that they're looking for. What is the number that solves their problem, and allows them to move on? The reality is that they came away with this figure of £22,000. The vendor eventually said, 'If you could just maybe get to £22,000 then that would let us move on. We can live with that'. This was staggering, as if we had been asked to put a number on what the property was worth, our number would have been between £40,000 and £50,000, so we could have automatically removed £18,000-£28,000 of the profit from that deal – or more – just by putting a number on it first. But because we let them take the lead and let them explain to us what their 'freedom number' was, we got one of our best deals.

In this specific case it was an older couple that wanted to downsize, and by then they already had their new property, so they were keen just to move on. And this is a thing that we see quite a lot with these local authority houses – most people have bought them from the council for a relatively small fee of around about £8,000, as that was the going rate back in the day. They don't have a particularly large value in their minds against those types of property, and so £22,000 probably represented a good return on their money over the period that they've had that property. So that was the right number for them, and it was a huge deal for us because at the end – after maybe only about £3,000 or £4,000 worth of investment – we were able to refinance this property with a market value of £75,000.

The next key negotiation skill is the use of third person authority, and this is something that a lot of people do when they are negotiating. If you go to buy a car, they'll use this third person authority of: 'You want to deal? Well, I need to go and ask my manager. You know, he's the one that makes the decisions.' This is great to diffuse a lot of the negotiation tension, because it's not the person that's standing in front of you that's ultimately making the decision. There's this third person strategy within negotiation that can really help you. You become the helper in this situation, as the person that is trying to get them the deal. But I need to get through this other person first. In property investing we talk about private investors – the investors that sit behind the business – and those are the guys that call the shots and need to say where the money goes.

Whether or not they exist or it is in fact you that's the investor, use of a third-party authority in the transaction can really help diffuse any tension.

The next negotiating tactic is to use extremes, which literally just means outlining the best and worst-case scenarios for the vendor to encourage them to deal – and of course, the best-case scenario would be your solution. Let's look again at the example of the old couple that sold to us their flat for £22,000. The worst-case scenario in their head was where they'd have to put their property on the market, and it could be sat there for months. That could well have been the case, because the property wasn't in the best condition. Maybe in this instance they would have two properties. They've already got the new property ready to go. They move into that, and they have this property sitting empty, and they must continue paying bills on it. There's also a risk that it might be broken into. It might take a long time to sell. And you must deal with estate agents constantly going back and forth to this older couple. People are viewing the properties; no-one puts in an offer. You know, you can build up this this worst-case scenario to paint a very bad picture. And the alternative is that we give you an easy out: two weeks, cash in the bank, no issues, no stress, at the number that you're looking for. Using those extremes of the best and worst case can be very powerful.

Finally in negotiation we have the use of scarcity. This essentially means scarcity of time or some other measure to encourage the seller to agree to your terms. For example, there are always other deals. There are always other places to put our money as investors. Any deal that you're proposing is never permanently available. We have other investment opportunities, or private investors are keen to move forward with this deal, but they have other deals to consider. So, you know, if we're not willing to move fast, then then we may lose the opportunity. So again, scarcity is common. It was a negotiation tactic to ensure that you're able to get the best deal and move it forward at the right price. And so, these are just a few outline negotiation tactics that are used during the sale, to make sure you get the best deal and that you get the best value price when you do so.

Adding value

The next thing is a must in property investing; adding value. As I mentioned at the start of this chapter, it's important to add value anytime that you spend money on a property. However, it's not always easy. The industry has this philosophy that for every pound you spend, you should add £3 of value – especially in markets like Scotland, where property prices are already low and the cost of work is continuing to rise all the time; it's not so easy to achieve that level. As we've said at the start, you really make your money when you buy. For us, doing the refurb is all about keeping the cost to the absolute minimum; it's about understanding who you are refurbing this property for. So, if you are doing a refurb for a flip where someone's going to buy it to live there, they would expect the standards to be high.

Such a purchaser will have views of this being their main asset; they want to see themselves living in the property. It must be finished to a higher standard versus a property that is to be rented, where you would still want to make the property attractive to a tenant, but you know they're less likely to be living there in the long term, so they don't have the same connection to it in terms of expectation. You're also going to want to make sure that you create a property that has as low maintenance as possible. For example, carpets should be hard-wearing, and you should always go with wet wall in the bathrooms instead of tiles, as it's cheaper to install and requires less maintenance. Tenants tend not to look after the property as if it were their own – at least, some of them don't. You must make the property more hard-wearing, and you're not going to want to spend as much money as you would if you were doing up a flip.

You need to know your strategy. You need to understand what you're providing, based on the strategy that you've undertaken. For instance, if you are creating an HMO (a house in multiple occupation), the refurb might be much more significant because we have legislation such as fire compliance plus the local authority's licensing requirements to adhere to within the remit of the work being undertaken. There's much more cost to be factored in than just the initial strategy. You're going to get caught up in small details, so don't get too personal. You don't want to get too much into the colour schemes and interior design of what you refurbish, especially with a buy-to-let refurb. We have a formula. We have a standard that we've set, and our guys know our expectations of what we want to achieve with it. We don't have to get into the fine detail every single time. We don't have to go into a property and say, 'No, I want this colour rather than that colour.' They know what the standards are that we want them to adhere to, so don't get too caught up in those things. You're not going to live there. It's not your home.

So many people will make that error and call up and ask what tiles they're going to use, what carpet they're going to use, what colour paint on the walls... all that sort of stuff. It's just not what we're about. That's why, as property investors, we need to professionalise. There should be a standard that we should meet that matches the cost criteria that we have, based on the overarching strategy. Like I said, keep it simple.

Analysing profit

The next thing we must look at is profit within this basics chapter. We need to make a profit; it goes without saying. But how can you make profit without being financially literate, without understanding the numbers, without understanding how to calculate what your costs are? You need to know what your profits are going to be, and then understand, ultimately, is it worthwhile? Am I going to get enough return for my money? How am I going to finance it – what could affect the profitability, and am I going to pay so much tax that I have nothing left by the end of this? These are the most fundamental questions you need to understand as a property investor, and ultimately our aim through *Fast-Track to Property Millions* and our introduction to property investing and all the various sections we have from property taxes to understanding the numbers to understanding strategies... they are all covered by this overview, which is going to help you to understand whether you're making profit.

You've got to understand the numbers, understand your strategy, complete your due diligence, understand the tax elements – all of that. All these things create a picture of any deal: you're trying to analyse if the costs associated with the income and ultimately the profit that you're going to walk away with must bring the return you'd expect to see.

The buying process

Understand the buying process. Earlier we talked about securing below market value and some of the things that might help us do that. Securing a property investment is all to do with being very professional in what we do, and making it very clear to anyone we're dealing with that we know what we're talking about. We understand the processes. And moreover, when we commit to delivering something, *we can do it*. Dealing with delays distresses sellers, who are key to securing a BMV deal; it will be essential that you can deliver on your promised completion date, otherwise the deal may fall through. Therefore we must understand the buying process.

Understanding the buying processes is fundamental for the purchase of a property, from as little as nine days – which is the quickest we've managed to close on a deal – to months and months. You know, one of our longest commercial deals took six months to get over the line, so the length can vary significantly based on the type of deal. Understand the process and control the steps, as this will help you accurately assess the timeframe required to get the deal done. For a distressed seller, getting a deal completed on time could mean the difference between recovering some equity and moving on, to losing it all in financial ruin, so this is a serious business.

So, it's important to understand the process, and it's important to understand what steps can be removed to speed up the process. Let's have a look at that over the course of the next few paragraphs, so we can cover the step-by-step process to acquire a property. Our process includes 18 steps. Not all of them may apply. For instance, if you're buying cash a lot of this stuff we're going to talk about – in terms of the steps of getting a mortgage, the valuations, all that stuff – is not going to apply because you're just going to be going straight into cash. You don't need it. So it's key to understand that. As we said, it's vitally important that as a professional, you know what's involved in the process and understand that it can take more than eight weeks based on the standard process. Okay, so let's look at the first step find the property that meets the criteria.

Throughout the course, the chapters of *Fast-Track to Property Millions*, I'm going to teach you all you need to know to set your own property criteria. What boxes are you looking to tick? You need to view the property. You need to assess the work that needs to be done on it. Consider your budget. Then it's a case of analysing the numbers, completing your due diligence – and all of that is covered within the due diligence chapter. We also deal with this process within the understanding the numbers chapter. You must put together those numbers, assess the deal in its totality, and understand whether this stacks up for you and what value you should be negotiating around.

These are just the first few steps of analysing the deal, understanding the numbers and making sure that the deal stacks up for you. Then we can start negotiating. If you are dealing directly with the vendor, use all those negotiation tactics we talked about earlier. Then, once the price has been agreed, it's a case of instructing your solicitor to make a formal offer based on the terms and conditions that you've already agreed. Start the mortgage application process at that point. If you're using a mortgage to purchase this, you'd be contacting the broker in advance. The expectation before the end of this process is that you would have already contacted the broker. You would have already been in discussion with them about what your investment criteria is, and broadly what you're looking for. Then, once you have a specific deal ready to go and you understand the numbers, the acquisition price and so forth, they can then go away and look at a much more specific proposal for that that property and give you a very clear recommendation as to what mortgage product you should be looking for to start that mortgage process. That is just the start; once you have the mortgage product identified, it's time to submit the mortgage application. Your broker will take you through this, but you will find that the information required is broadly similar for each application you make, so have things like verified ID, list of assets and liabilities, monthly income, payslip etc., all saved in a folder, so the information is to hand.

As soon as the mortgage product is agreed, then a valuation will be instructed. Sometimes the valuation is paid for by the mortgage company. Sometimes you must pay the fee yourself, and it can be anything from a few hundred pounds to the £500 or £600 range, depending on the property itself – even although in Scotland we have a Home Report which gives a valuation on the property, the chances are the mortgage company will still want to do their own valuation on it. It's not the case that the Home Report would necessarily replace this valuation; it may still need to be done. This can be the biggest driver behind delaying the property deal completion, as the surveyor will have to arrange access to the property and coordinating that may take time. This process can take 1-2 weeks and is a big reason behind why we always recommend that when time is a factor, do not buy with a mortgage, buy with cash – although it doesn't always have to be your own cash (more about that in later chapters).

Next, the solicitors will agree terms of sale. In Scotland this is called a missive contract. They're going to go back and forward and be very specific to agree the terms of your purchase of this property. That may include things such as what furniture fixtures are included within the sale. It may also include things like any limitations on warranties available for the white goods within the property. There is a list of standard things that need to be agreed within a property sale while it's going on, and they'll constantly be referred to you to get your input on any specific issues.

The solicitor at this point will also start to conduct property searches. These include searches with the local authorities. The local authority searches would cover anything from whether the property is listed to whether it's in a conservation area, up to whether it is historically subject to any subsidence issues or anything like that which may have been reported. It would also list any historical issues that the local authorities have had with the property. For instance, if there is an environmental health order on the property, or if there is mandated repair work to be undertaken. It will also cover planning for future things around the property that could affect you, such as if the council were thinking about running a motorway through your property; you would know about that through these searches.

Searches are a critical part of the due diligence process that solicitors would undertake on your behalf. Other searches include things like looking at the flood risk of property, or perhaps specialist searches like mining reports. If it's been a historical mining area, the lender might want to see a report to understand the likelihood of subsidence or any historical issues concerning past mining in the immediate region. These are the sort of things that are happening within the search process.

Then, finally, the mortgage offer will be issued based on the valuation. So once the valuation reports are back and you're comfortable with them, and the value ties to your expectations, there will be a formal offer of the mortgage explaining how much they're willing to lend and detailing the terms under which they're willing to lend to you at this point. You can also check the valuation report. The mortgage company don't always give it, so it's something you may need to push to ask to see it. But you know that you can check the valuation report to see if there are any specific issues on it.

Next step, completion dates are sent through the lawyers who will discuss between themselves a date to aim for a term of completion, and that will include when the mortgage company can finalise its checks and transfer the funds to be able to complete the sale. So, there will be an initial discussion about when they should be set to complete. The mortgage lender's solicitor will complete their due diligence. There may be other things that they need from you or from the vendor to be able to understand the completion date and find any issues with the property, perhaps looking to see if there have been changes made to the property that may affect future saleability or mortgagability; for example, if modifications have been made to change the property without the proper planning or building warrant approvals in place, the mortgage company is unlikely be will to proceed with the transaction.

Essentially, all these sorts of things are going to be carried out by the mortgage lender, and – when they are satisfied the property is suitable for lending – your solicitors will request your deposit funds to be transferred. As it's getting closer to completion, here's how much money you will typically need to put in. Assuming that your mortgage is 80% (of the price being paid), you will have a 20% deposit to pay plus all the fees. We will work through these various fees and costs in a later chapter on understanding the numbers. You're going to have to start transferring funds, and you're also going to have to prove where those funds came from under money laundering regulations. They will want to know that these funds haven't originated from an illegal source; they need to know where this money has come from. They will ask for things like bank statements and documentation to support the larger receipts within that bank statement. This is a legal obligation for solicitors, and they take this process very seriously, so it's best to have this done earlier in the process to ensure there are no delays.

Finally, you have insurance to consider. It may be a case that you have to do the insurance in advance, because the mortgage company usually won't advance funds to your solicitor until they've seen an insurance policy. You might have to do this a few days before completion, even if it doesn't take effect until the completion date. The mortgage company are going to want to see that, so you must make sure that the property is insured. So many people, when they're dealing with cash and they're not dealing with mortgages, forget to insure the property because no-one's asking for it. It's not like you've got a mortgage company asking to see your insurance certificate. This step is important; last year we had a fire in a block of flats where we owned 10 properties out of the 12, and the cost of reinstatement was over £300,000. If we hadn't had the correct insurance, this would have been a major loss for our business.

Now the mortgage company will finally transfer the funds to your solicitor after deducting their legal fees. As I said before, generally they will deduct fees accrued from searches or other additional legal services. In Scotland, your solicitors are going to make sure that you do not sign a missive until you are actually in a position to complete, because if you sign in advance of completion there are significant liabilities if, for whatever reason, you're not able to conclude on it.

Let's have a look at what might happen otherwise. Say there was a deal where effectively someone agreed to buy a property and signed the missive themselves. It cost £200,000 to buy this property, and the vendor can then go back and sell the property on the open market for say £100,000. Then the person who originally signed may be liable for the other £100,000 shortfall versus the original price that was agreed. Signing a missive can have huge implications. That's why I would strongly advise that you don't sign your missive until the very last minute, when the money's pretty much down and you know that you're good to finalise a deal. Because if all falls apart for whatever reason, you can find yourself seriously on the hook with the missive.

Once all that's done, and the missive has been signed, the cash transfer takes place and everybody's happy. The keys to the property will be released to you, either from the selling agent or from your own solicitor, or from the vendor's solicitor. Then you finally have access to the property, and you can start to develop the space. So broadly speaking, that's the whole process from start to finish. It does vary slightly depending on whether you're taking on a mortgage.

You'll notice that five or six of those steps were just solely dependent on a mortgage. It's quite clear to see that a mortgage being a part of this can really delay the process. As I mentioned earlier, if you're taking on a mortgage, the minimum delay to each transaction can become eight weeks. Using cash really speeds up the process, because you don't have to wait on that valuation or for the mortgage company. You won't have to wait on finding the right product, the right mortgage deal, and going through the application process. You won't have to wait on the process and all the valuation information to make the final offer, nor will you have to wait on them doing all the extra due diligence. If you have to involve a mortgage company it is likely to be the biggest risk in your deal falling down, even though you have gotten a mortgage acceptance at the start of the process; if they find anything in their due diligence that doesn't meet their detailed criteria, they will pull this offer and you will be forced to start all over again. The big change is that buying with cash dramatically speeds up the process and reduces the risk in purchasing the property, which is why so many people are keen to receive cash offers.

Terminology

Next, we are going to get into some of the property terminology. I don't want you to be bamboozled by some of the property jargon that you will come across, so the aim of this section is just to simplify it for you and make it very clear what each term means. This will avoid confusion on some of these abbreviations, and there are a lot of them within property investing.

Understand some of the key industry terms we use throughout the *Fast-Track to Property Millions* chapters. There is an explanatory table at the end of this chapter. We have already focused on some of the jargon that we are going to be talking about all the way through this book. In fact, some of the stuff that I've already mentioned in these early chapters is straightforward.

Let's start with the first abbreviation: BTL. 'Buy-to-let' – most people know that one. But just in case, it means buying a property to rent and holding the property for the long term for capital growth and rental income. To lease and make a profit through buy-to-let rental income over months and months, and capital growth over the long term. Ultimately that's all buy-to-let means.

CTR is another common abbreviation. All it means is 'commercial to residential'. It's the conversion of a commercial property – that could be anything from an office to a shop to a warehouse – into one or multiple residential units. It's another core strategy that REWD Group uses, through redevelopments; we create new residential property from historically commercial buildings. All it really is, is buying property to refurbish and sell it in the short term for profit. It's very much a short-term strategy. Normally six months as a minimum, because of the mortgage restrictions. But you know, you're buying very much with the intention of selling on for a profit in the short ter.

HMO: I've mentioned this term earlier in the book, and it refers to a 'house in multiple occupation'. All it means is a property rented, by the room, to several unconnected parties. You may have a three or four bedroom house and, rather than renting that entire house to one family, you rent each of the bedrooms on a room-by-room basis. That's all it means.

And as for BMV, we've talked about this already. 'Below market value' is the agreed discount in percentage terms versus the full market value. Say it is worth £100,000 and you need to buy it for £75,000. You have a 25% BMV deal, meaning you've got 25% discount on the value of the property. Each of the above is common terminology within the world of property.

HR is a Home Report. Really, it's just Scotland that has these reports, but a Home Report is basically a property condition and valuation report. It's going to have everything from a condition report on the key areas of the building – be it the superstructure, the roof, the internals, the electrics, heating, plumbing, all that sort of stuff – and is going to cover those key condition areas insofar as the surveyor can physically see things. There will be things that they won't be able to identify, purely because they don't have access to building walls or to go into the internals of the building. It'll also give a valuation for mortgage purposes. The assessors will also cover some of the details on how the property is constructed and all that sort of stuff. It will have an energy performance report on it as well, which talks about the energy efficiency of the property. There will also be a property questionnaire at the end where the current owner has responded to commonly asked questions about the property. It's a comprehensive report that you can get in advance of buying the property if you just request it from the agent. But it's only available in Scotland.

PCM: we use this terminology a lot throughout the book, and it stands for 'per calendar month'. That's all it means, and usually it's mentioned in reference to rent. When we talk about a rent of £500 PCM, we mean £500 per calendar month that's paid.

Then there's LHA – not a common terminology – which stands for 'local housing allowance', which is the total amount that a local authority is willing to pay for a particular type of property. That's the monthly amount. It's paid by the Council for rent for those who are on local housing benefit. Ultimately the amount will change, depending on whether it's a flat, whether it's a house with a particular number of bedrooms, etc. If you want to understand the lower end rent values for any property that you're looking at, LHA rates are always a good place to start, and each council will have these published on their website.

EPC: I've already mentioned this in the context of Home Reports. EPC is an Energy Performance Certificate. It's a report of the energy efficiency of property. This is becoming more and more important now as the legislation changes to ensure that properties are becoming increasingly more efficient as we transition over the next few years. The level of energy efficiency for any property that's going to be made available to the rental market is gradually increasing. Historically they had to be a level E, which is quite low, and it's gradually moving up through the levels currently going to level D grading. EPC is a common factor within a home report. All rented properties must have an EPC in place.

APR is 'annual percentage rate'. Normally in the context of a loan, we're talking about annual interest; we mean the rate of annual interest as well as standard fees payable. And so the APR will not only include the interest that you have to pay on the mortgage, but will also factor in the fees that you've had the pay and the front end for that mortgage.

LTV is a 'loan to value' ratio. This is the percentage the bank is willing to provide against the value of a property. For instance, a 70% LTV on a £100,000 house is going to be a loan from the bank of £70,000. It's as simple as that: just the percentage of loan that you get from the bank, respective to the value of that property.

ET stands for 'early termination' charges. We're talking about this in terms of loans and mortgages. Normally when you carry a mortgage, you agree an initial period for that mortgage. For instance, you may have a fixed rate interest mortgage guarantee for three years, which means generally you're going to have to pay termination fees if you try to terminate the mortgage within the initial three-year period. So that's all that means. It's important when you're stacking up your deals, especially if you're buying with a mortgage and refinancing onto another mortgage. When you refinance to a new mortgage within this initial loan period, usually 2-5 years, you will have to factor in early termination charges, which will be in the range of 1-5% of the outstanding loan value.

LBTT refers to 'Land Building Transaction Tax'. This is a tax payable on the purchase of a property based on its value. There are two different types of LBTT rate: the residential rates for residential property, and then non-residential rates for everything else (mainly commercial property). It's a tax on, for instance, some residential properties. If it's below £145,000, you don't pay anything and thereafter the different rates apply at an increasing level as the property values get higher. Normally it's calculated for you by your solicitor, but it's important you know how to calculate this so you understand your full costs associated with a deal; this will be covered in detail within the understanding the numbers chapter. The equivalent of LBTT (which is only in Scotland) in England is

SDLT (Stamp Duty Land Tax), and it's more commonly known as stamp duty. Most people who have purchased a property are at least familiar with the term.

ADS was introduced in 2017, and it's essentially another type of stamp duty called 'additional dwelling supplement'. It is a tax that applies for anyone who has an additional property, a property that is not your principal private residence (where you live). It's an extra transaction tax on that additional property. In Scotland that's an extra 4% stamp duty on the value of the property fee. In England it's 3%. It applies to the full value of the property and paid on all property purchases above £40,000.

PGs, or personal guarantees, are individual legal promises made when credit is issued to a business for which a person serves as a shareholder or director. When a limited company takes on a bank loan, then it is highly likely that the lender will ask you to sign a personal guarantee which means if they can't recover that loan from the business, they will be pursuing you personally for the money. Many people think when they're investing through a company they have this protection – you know, the fact that a company can go under, and the individual's assets are protected. That's not necessarily the case with property investing because quite often the banks are going to want personal guarantees. They can also come after your assets if the company can't pay.

Let's talk about some other terms. Net yield: this is something that we're going to cover extensively in the chapter about understanding the numbers. Ultimately, this means the net return on the property investment: in simple terms, the annual rent less associated costs divided by the value of the property gives you the net yield percentage.

ROCI is common terminology; we often talk about a 'return on cash invested'. ROCI is just the cash that you get back based on the cash that you've invested. The beautiful thing about this calculation, unlike the other yields calculations, is that it doesn't look at the value of property; it looks at how much money you put into that property, accounting for the fact you have got debt leverage in the deal. This makes ROCI a good formula to use as a comparator against other types of investments, like stocks or shares. We're going to cover that topic more fully later in the understanding the numbers section.

A 'goldmine area' is really common terminology in property invest-ing – however, we hate this terminology. It refers to an area of at least 10,000 houses, which you target as the area for your property invest-ment. When people refer to a goldmine area, that's effectively an area that you know well; quite often it can be where you live, where you know the market, and so you go there, and you know it's a safe place for you to invest. We don't really buy into the concept of a 'goldmine area' as we feel it is overly restrictive and in the modern age of technology, where so much due diligence can be completed online, geography should not be the limiting factor on your investment, but more your ability to manage the property via your 'power team'.

'Power team' refers to the key professional support to your proper-ty investment business who give advice, provide services or manage on your behalf. It's the accountants, letting agent and the skilled tradesmen – all those key people that support your business and help you achieve what you're trying to achieve.

'Private investors' just means individuals who are lending money to your business.

Think about strategy

Before we finish the section, a reminder that this section is simply about some of the basic elements of property investing. Before you move onto the following chapters, it's important to take a step back and think about what strategy might be right for you. Of course, you haven't been through all the strategies yet, so what I'm asking is that you think about what you might be trying to achieve through your property investing journey and that, in turn, will influence your decision about which strat-egy works for you. Have a think about whether you're looking for short-term returns or longer-term returns. Now, that could be the difference between trying to do a few short-term flips and building up some cash, or it could be gradually building a buy-to-let portfolio that's going to return strong cash flow in the long term, but not so much in the short term.

So have a think about any personal dynamics that might affect this decision. Whether you're looking for short-term or long-term returns, also consider the amount of time that you're able to commit to this new venture. Before going into this, really reflect on how you can make time available within your life to make sure that your property investing is successful. You can't implement this kind of activity without committing some of your time to get it off the ground. That's not to say you must give up your life for it. We managed to build REWD Group while we were still in full time employment and only left our day jobs at the end of our third year of trading. We achieved this using 'leverage': perhaps one of the most powerful words in property. Entrepreneurs use other people's time as well as leveraging systems and processes to maximise what they can achieve, with minimum personal time input. But you still must put in the time at the front end to make that happen.

You need to start looking critically about how you spend your time; look at what you're doing in your life, and work out what you can outsource at low cost or what you can eliminate completely. Eliminate things that are not adding value to your life, and allocate this time to accelerate your property journey. The amount of time that you can afford will also affect the strategy that you are able to employ; there are some strategies that you just may not have the time to implement. Flips may not be realistic for someone who can't get on-site regularly. You can review some projects, but some people just won't have the flexibility to be able to come and go and get involved with that type of project, whereas buy-to-let might be a more passive option where you would have an agent and managers, and ultimately, you'd have very little direct involvement.

When choosing a strategy also consider: What are your skill sets? What are your interests? What is your passion? You know, there's no point in going down the route of a strategy that you think may tick all the other boxes, but you're not that interested; then you just become fenced in with your other restrictions.

It's important to think about the strategies that we're going to introduce you to, to consider what really sticks out – to see what evokes passion within the property world, and to think about whether that's going to massively affect the energy that you're going to put into making your investment work. And ultimately, what we are all about is generational wealth. For us it was about building a business that would last for generations. We wanted to build something that was going to be around for a long time. Buy-to-let is a fundamental part of that. But then, we have all these other strategies and all these other businesses we're growing on top of that. So, think about what your goals and objectives are. The reason we are discussing strategy even before we have even taught you what they are, is simply that it is the most critical decision you will make at the start of your journey. The road of an entrepreneur in any business is tough, so you must be singularly focused on the result and have passion for the process.

We will end this chapter with the three tips we would give to entrepreneurs embarking on their first business journey:

1) FIND YOUR WHY: The journey is tough and if you don't have a big enough reason to push through the difficult times, you are likely to give up. Maybe it's your family, your kids, a deeper purpose to help or achieve a mission. Whatever it is, it must be a big reason that stirs something inside you.

2) FIND YOUR VEHICLE: Again, the road ahead to building a business or empire will be very tough, so you need to love what you do. Choose your business wisely. Many people would say our vehicle is property, but for me it's not. It's deal-making and problem solving; it just so happens to be within a property business. Whatever you are passionate about should drive this decision, which massively impacts the strategy you chose to implement within property.

3) LEARN ABOUT LEVERAGE: Leverage in business is massive, in both meanings of the word:

(a) 'Debt leverage' and 'leveraging something for a greater result'. Debt – it was the great business author Robert Kiyosaki who said, 'The two things that separate the rich and poor is debt and taxes'. The rich leverage 'good' debt to accelerate their wealth by buying assets, while the poor use 'bad' debt to buy things they can't afford. Taxes – the rich use companies to legally avoid taxes, whilst the poor pay tax before they even receive their salary.

b) 'Leveraging something to achieve more' – realising that you are limited on the money you can make from your own time. Leveraging other people's time, or systems, or outsourcing, or eliminating non-value-added activities, can all massively accelerate your wealth and success.

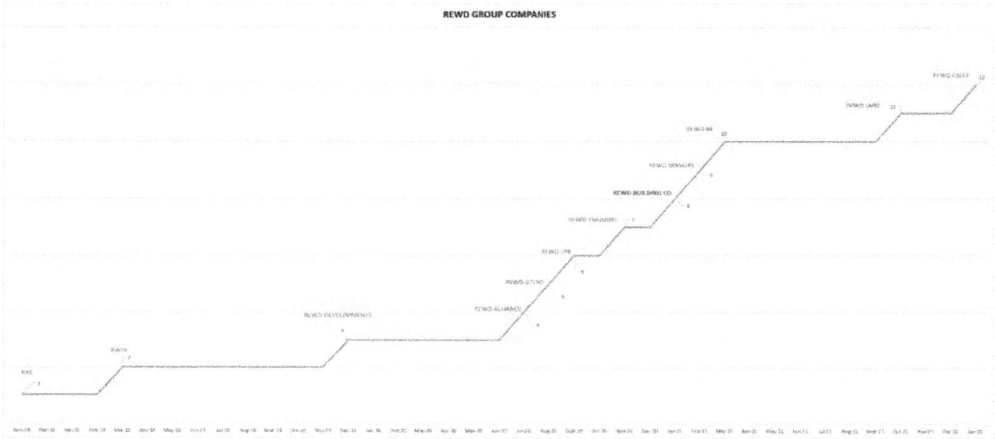

REWD GROUP COMPANIES

COMMONLY-USED TERMS AND ACRONYMS

ADS	ADDITIONAL DWELLING SUPPLEMENT
APR	ANNUAL PERCENTAGE RATE
ASB	ANTI-SOCIAL BEHAVIOUR
BFC	BOND & FLOATING CHARGE
BMV	BELOW MARKET VALUE
BTF	BUY TO FLIP/SELL
BTL	BUY TO LET
BTR	BUILD TO RENT
C2R	COMMERCIAL TO RESIDENTIAL
DD	DIRECT DEBIT
PSF	PER SQUARE FOOT
DIP	DECISION IN PRINCIPLE
EICR	ELECTRICAL INSTALLATION CONDITION REPORT
EPC	ENERGY PERFORMANCE CERTIFICATE
ETCs	EARLY TERMINATION PENALTY
FOI	FREEDOM OF INFORMATION
GDPR	GENERAL DATA PROTECTION REGULATIONS
GY	GROSS YIELD
HMO	HOUSE OF MULTIPLE OCCUPATION
HR	HOME REPORT
HSE	HEALTH & SAFETY EXECUTIVE
IFA	INDEPENDENT FINANCIAL ADVISER
ILA	INDEPENDENT LEGAL ADVICE
IO	INTEREST ONLY
LA	LOCAL AUTHORITY
LBTT	LAND AND BUILDINGS TRANSACTION TAX
LHA	LOCAL HOUSING ALLOWANCE
LTV	LOAN TO VALUE
NY	NET YIELD
PAYE	PAY AS YOU EARN

PCM	PER CALENDAR MONTH
PG	PERSONAL GUARANTEE
PIP	PERSONAL INDEPENDENCE PAYMENT
PRT	PRIVATE RESIDENTIAL TENANCY
ROCI	RETURN ON CAPITAL INVESTED
RTB	RENT TO BUY
SAL	SCOTTISH ASSOCIATION OF LANDLORDS
SAT	SHORT ASSURED TENANCY
SDLT	STAMP DUTY LAND TAX (N/A IN SCOTLAND)
SECURITY	THE ASSET THE FUNDS ARE LEGALLY ALLOCATED TO
SIPP	SELF INVESTED PENSION PLAN
SO	STANDING ORDER
SQM	SQUARE METRE
SS	SINGLE SURVEY
SSAS	SMALL SELF-ADMINISTERED SCHEME
SVR	STANDARD VARIABLE RATE
UC	UNIVERSAL CREDIT
VAT	VALUE ADDED TAX

Images from training events organised by the REWD Group to date.

Chapter Three

Strategies

Conar Tracey

I N this chapter, I'm going to give you a detailed understanding of the key strategies that provide the opportunity for you to make serious money through property investment. We're going to be looking at some of the pros and cons of the most effective investment strategies within the UK property industry.

I'm going to broaden your outlook throughout the course of this chapter, so that you can start to implement some of these strategies and get involved in property investment. Regardless of your current circumstances, how much time you have, what your current financial position is or the skills that you're currently equipped with, there will be a strategy that you can utilise to make significant income.

You may have already heard of some of these strategies that we're going to be looking at; even those who aren't involved in property will typically have heard some of the common terminology or have a reasonable understanding of how the most popular strategies work, but the main idea of this chapter is to really open your eyes to the multiple different methods that you can implement. It may even be a case that you have heard of these strategies under different names, but the fundamentals are the same and these are the main money-making concepts that we're going to look at in detail:

- Buy-to-Flip (sell)
- Buy-to-Let (rent)
- HMO (House of Multiple Occupancy)
- Deal Trading/Property Sourcing

- Assisted Sales
- Commercial Conversions

Different strategies for different situations

Property investment presents endless opportunities to make money, with many strategies offering the ability to get started with very little or even NO MONEY.

We'll start by breaking down the most effective investment strategies in the UK and the things we have to consider before choosing which strategy is best for your circumstances.

One of the first things that we need to take into consideration is the **location**: think carefully about your target area. Certain strategies will only be effective in a location that commands the product you wish to offer. Focus on the key factors each location provides and match it to the strategy you want to use, then see if it makes sense.

We have areas such as city centres, suburbs, local authority/social housing, coastal locations, etc. All these areas have very particular elements that determine the demographic of the people who live there, and we need to understand what their habits are and what kind of property and services they are looking for.

- **City Centre**: Heavily populated by students and professionals with typical demographic aged 20-29, who prefer to walk rather than drive to work/education. They are attracted to immediate access to a large variety of amenities.
- **Suburbs**: Typically populated by those aged 30+, married or in a civil partnership and living together. They usually have children and are heavily reliant on cars and good public transport links. Local schooling is a significant factor in these areas.
- **Social Housing**: Typically populated by working class and low-income families/individuals who require support from DSS/Universal Credit.
- **Rural**: Much larger properties with significant land. Typically farms and agricultural businesses, but also increased interest for holiday homes and people looking for privacy in the countryside.

- **Retirement Villages**: Private community exclusively for those aged 55+ in quiet, secure locations.
- **Beachside/Coastal**: Estimated 3 million people in the UK live in coastal locations. Popular holiday/retirement areas that attract spikes of tourists during holidays and summer months.

You may choose to focus on location first and try to make the appropriate strategy fit; however, a better solution as to not limit yourself geographically would be to establish the needs and wants of each potential deal and its location, then apply a strategy that you believe will be successful in that area. This approach will massively support your growth.

Key components of property strategies

What kind of property are you looking to invest in and what purpose does it serve to your target market?

Just like location, different property types will serve a different purpose to different people:

- **Flats/Apartments**
  Usually preferred by individuals or couples, and often found in densely populated areas. The position of the flat within the building is also important to consider: the elderly or those with physical disabilities will usually prefer a ground floor position. You may also get a garden area with a ground floor flat; however, the internal floor space is often smaller because the entrance to the building that serves as a communal hallway often restricts the area available for living accommodation. A top floor position can be perceived as the most desirable as it usually has the most privacy and the best views, but if there is no lift access you could be restricting your market.
- **Houses**
  More suitable for families and those who require more space. The key benefit of a house is the simple fact of having a private main door access to the front and back. Houses usually benefit from ex-

ternal space such as gardens or driveways, providing much more adaptable accommodation to meet a lot of requirements. There are various styles of houses: terraced, semi-detached, detached, bunga-low, cottage, etc. There is no real standard template for what should be provided under the category of 'house'. However, it is well known that a three-bedroom semi-detached is the most popu-lar property style throughout the UK. They are by far the quickest property to be sold or rented on the open market because of the huge demand.

- **Traditional Conversions**
  Transforming old churches, schools, banks – essentially buildings that have a lot of historical features and are usually found in con-servation areas classed as 'listed buildings', to reinvent a new purpose such as converting an old church into residential apart-ments. These projects can be costly and tend to have a lot of hoops to jump through to satisfy any conservation restrictions; however, they can be statement projects that attract a lot of attention (and value) in the right market.

Other factors to consider include size of property and whether you want to target the high end of the market or find a strategy that works in the lower end of the market.

- **Size of Property**
  Number of bedrooms and the overall size of the property will at-tract totally different people. Studio apartments or one-bedroom properties are only really suitable for single individuals or a couple. 2+ bedroom properties offer a product that would be suitable for more people who are in need of an extra bedroom. It is always as-sumed that the bigger the property, the more value it should command, but the reality is very different. You will find countless hotels or B&Bs available on the open market, saturated with op-portunities because the demand for large buildings like that isn't the same as smaller residential properties. Likewise, bungalows are typically positioned best for those who are looking for their final

property to settle in for retirement, and therefore bungalows with large gardens and loads of external space tend to have less interest than much smaller alternatives.

- **Low End vs High End**

  Depending on your target market, you may have to provide a higher end product in order to fulfil your chosen strategy. If you're targeting a family home in an affluent area, it's likely you will need to focus on a higher quality finish in order to attract attention and command the best value from your desired end user. If you focus on the lower end market, you have to appreciate that the attention to detail from the end user will be significantly less compared to those operating at the opposite end of the market.

Do your research and collect all the data to understand your location, the type of people that live there and what kind of product they are looking for. Study the available data within the location that you're looking at and consider whether they're more likely to buy or rent.

We need to collect all of the information based on the market demand that will help us select the best plan to try and guarantee as much as possible that we're going to make money. It's important to do all of that before we start to look at the strategies themselves.

Restrictions and considerations

I want to bring your attention to one of the most common issues you will be required to navigate your way around when investing in property in the UK- The dreaded 'six month rule'.

It's time consuming and draining. It's a rule that has been applied by mortgage lenders which essentially stops you from being able to sell or refinance a property until you have owned it for at least six months.

Now, in terms of sales format, you can very much still purchase a property, then the very next day sell it to someone else, as long as they are a CASH BUYER: there is no issue with that at all. The only time it becomes an issue is if the person looking to buy the property from you requires a mortgage; this is when the 'six month rule' kicks in. The mortgage lenders will not support the transaction until you have owned the property for at least six months. Essentially what this means is that you now have a six-month lag on operations of your property business if you require some form of mortgage to allow you to exit the deal.

This is particularly frustrating when it comes to buy-to-let as an investment strategy. Unless you own the property for at least six months, you won't be able to refinance. So, if you purchase a property with cash, spend thousands on refurbishing and then put a tenant into it, you won't be able to get any of your money back until at least six months down the line; in fact, in most cases you can't even start the mortgage application process until you've owned it for at least six months and one day! By the time the valuation has been carried out, the application has been processed, funds are released between the solicitors etc., realistically it's closer to eight or even nine months before you have your funds back in play.

It's worth mentioning that this is by no means a law; it's simply a new industry standard that most mainstream lenders will abide by. There are some specialist lenders who may support a deviation of this so-called rule, but it is likely they will not be flexible to the same level that you would ideally want them to be. Often you would be offered much less of a loan value from them if you wanted to do things quicker.

The 'six-month rule' is very much a key consideration with all investment strategies – certainly those that involve actually purchasing the properties – and it's vital you realise that you may be restricted on your exit because of this. You just need to factor it in before you proceed with anything.

There are more advanced strategies that you can use once you have built up your credibility as a professional property investor. Commercial lending will basically allow you to cut through this problem of needing to wait six months. These are the kind of advanced level strategies that we cover in detail on our *REWD PRO: Professional Buy-To-Let Investing* training.

Effective basic strategies

Now that you're up to speed with some of the key considerations, it's time to look at the most effective strategies to make money in property.

I always find it best to explain the mechanics of how things work through real-life examples and give you an in-depth understanding of the background behind each deal and how I identified the correct strategy to apply. This should give you clarity on what lies ahead in your own property journey, with references that are legally documented on the Land Registry so that you can fact-check and know for sure there is no bullshit in this book!

Buy-to-Flip

This is simply the process of purchasing a property with a view to selling it for more than it has cost you, in order to make a profit. To be successful at that, you want to be looking for a property that offers the opportunity to add value. In many cases where the property requires considerable upgrading, you can negotiate a much better price, therefore creating the equity position that will ultimately become your profit. A common term you will come across in property is 'BMV', which stands for 'below market value' and essentially just means that you're purchasing a property for less than what it is currently worth. Securing a property at a discount or 'BMV' will be critical in any investment strategy.

An example of a successful 'Buy-To-Flip' project that we bought is 11 Haddow Grove, Burntisland, KY3 0DA. This was a 3-bedroom mid-terraced house that we secured off-market at a considerable discount,

added value through refurbishment and then resold through an estate agent on the open market.

Purchase Price: £70,000
Sourcing Fee: £10,000
Additional Dwelling Supplement at 4%: £2,800
Legal Fees: £1,000
Refurbishment: £20,000

Total Invested (TI): £103,800

New Valuation (NV): £145,000
Utilities & Council Tax (RC): £1,306
Selling Costs (SC): £3,500

Total Profit: (NV) £145,000 – (TI) £103,800 – (RC) £1,306 – (SC) £3,500 = **£36,394**

This property was brought to us by a property sourcer (another fantastic strategy that I will discuss later in this chapter), as the seller had recently inherited the property and was simply looking for a fast and secure sale so they could move to England. The property was in poor condition throughout and required a full refurbishment including new kitchen, bathroom, electrics, decoration and flooring. Typically, our core model is buy-to-let; however, this was a three-bedroom house with an anticipated end value of £140,000 and a rental value of £750 per month. When considering the loan value and interest payable on a property of

this value, we decided that given the demand for properties of this size and style in the area, we would be best suited to resell the property and use the profits to reinvest into lower value properties where the yield and returns would be much more attractive. We had significant interest in the property as soon as it hit the open market for sale, and we actually accepted an offer of £150,000 after only two days. Unfortunately, with any strategy there are risks, and when your exit is dependent on the financial position of a new buyer there is always the potential for the transaction to fall through. We had been advised that the buyer would be using cash and therefore didn't require a mortgage: this was true... however, the client needed to sell their property to raise the cash, and the buyer for their property needed a mortgage. This is known as being in a 'chain', and unfortunately the link broke at the other end. We relisted the property on the market and within a couple of weeks we accepted an offer from a new buyer at the valuation level of £145,000, giving us a tidy pre-tax profit over £36,000.

The price at which you secure the property is ultimately where your profit is created. The adjoining neighbour had just sold for £120,000 in not-so-great condition when we were presented this opportunity for £70,000, so we knew we were securing well below market value. In order to maximise our return, we knew we would need to refurbish the property to sell to the end user, which we anticipated would be a young family who would purchase it to live in; therefore, they would have much higher expectations in terms of condition and want a property finished to a good standard ready to furnish and move straight in. Our alternative here would be to reduce our profit margin and sell straight on to a cash buyer/fellow investor who was looking for a flip project, as buying this at £100,000 and spending £20,000 would still have been attractive enough to an investor but we would have reduced our profit from £36,000 down to about £15,000 – albeit we would get this much faster, and not need to outlay any refurb costs.

A great example of a straight flip or a 'property trade' following this alternative exit is Braidwood Cottage, Penicuik, EH26 9LW.

This was a four-bedroom detached cottage in a semi-rural setting that was in dated condition and required significant upgrading to make it an attractive family home. It had a valuation of £475,000 when we managed to secure for £325,000. I know what you're thinking: 'How the f*** did you get a £150,000 discount? Who on earth would sell at such a drastic drop?!' And I get it; it's a seriously difficult thing to understand when you're not used to this game. But I assure you, property may be bricks and mortar… but just like everything in life, it is driven by human psychology and that will always create opportunity.

Our original intention was to reconfigure the layout and fully refurbish with an anticipated end value of £550,000. Throughout our due diligence process to get a building warrant for the structural changes we planned to make, we realised that the costs to carry out our plans were going to exceed £100,000 as opposed to our original expectation of £70,000. If we proceeded with the original plan, we stood to make approx. £100,000 profit, but we would have a lot of financial exposure into a single property and would be fully dependent on someone paying the £550,000 for it – and at the time of this project in 2022, we were heading into a very volatile market with inflation and interest rates going crazy. We reassessed our position and considered the product we had, and we decided it would be best not to carry out the refurbishment and instead resell as is. We got an updated valuation less than six months after we

had bought it, and it came back at... £475,000! We acknowledged that this would be too high a price expectation given the level of work required and who our end user would be, and therefore we opted to list on the open market for a fixed price of £450,000. Within days we had over ten viewers and accepted an offer to let the property go, making a very tidy sum.

Purchase Price: £325,000
Sourcing Fee: £0
Additional Dwelling Supplement at 4% + LBTT: £18,850
Legal Fees: £1,000
Refurbishment: £0, but we spent a about £1,500 on drawings and planning for the building warrant.

Total Invested (TI): £346,350

Sale Price (SP): £450,000
Utilities & Council Tax (RC): £2,780
Finance Costs (FC): £16,575
Selling Costs (SC): £4,500

Total Profit: (NV) £450,000 – (TI) £346,350 – (RC) £2,780 – (FC) £16,575 - (SC) £4,500 = **£79,795**

Okay, we reduced our profit margin by 20%, but we also made nearly £80,000 and didn't touch the property! We reduced our financial exposure and ultimately made excellent profit within a much quicker timeframe.

How was this possible? Because we bought at the right price.

With the buy-to-flip strategy it's critical that you consider all the costs. Purchase price, professional fees, tax, refurbishment, council tax, utilities, surveys, selling costs... it all mounts up, and if you don't have a clear overview on the costs of the project, you will most certainly be setting yourself up for failure.

It's also important to be realistic about your sale value expectations. Make sure you understand the product and the market, use up-to-date evidence to support your end values and make sure you have a back up plan just in case the refurb costs get out of control. If you buy correctly from the outset, you will always have a positive outcome!

The final point I will make on the buy-to-flip strategy is to consider your personal financial position. The reason I mention this is to under-stand the tax implications employing this strategy can have. If you operate in a personal name, then any profits you make from a buy-to-flip project will be taxed as income. Everyone is allowed to make gains of £12,300 (2022 figures) per year, but over and above this will be taxed at whatever rate of income tax the balance of the profit will put you into based on your income. This means that if you're already employed, doing a deal that earns you nearly £80k profit will instantly put you into the higher tax bracket and you could be giving over 40% of your profit away! Make sure you seek out professional advice to fully understand the most effective way for you to operate so that you can keep as much of your hard-earned profit as possible.

Buy-to-Let

This is our core investment strategy at REWD Group. There are count-less benefits to this strategy, but for us the main one is the ability to generate significant cashflow on a regular basis – the ability to create in-finite returning assets gets us really excited, and you should feel the same way!

Buy-to-let is simply the process of purchasing a property with a view to allowing someone else to occupy it and they are known as the 'tenant'. The tenant then pays you for the use of that property every month in the form of rent, and allows you to make money from the asset every single month as opposed to waiting until you sell the property.

The standard form of investing for buy-to-let (BTL) is simply by using a BTL mortgage product, where typically a bank will give you 75% of the purchase price. This allows you to enter the market with a signifi-cantly reduced level of cash.

For example, let's say you were buying a property at £80,000 as a buy-to-let. The bank will give you £60,000 towards this purchase, meaning that you simply need a deposit of £20,000 plus enough to cover any legal costs, taxes and refurbishment on the property. You can then rent his property for say £600 per month, use this income to cover the costs of the mortgage, insurance, letting agent and any maintenance etc. The balance leftover each month then becomes the income you have generated from the property that you can keep. Here's how this might look:

Purchase Price: £80,000
BTL Mortgage @ 75% of purchase price: £60,000
Deposit Required: £20,000
Legal Costs: £1,000
ADS @ 4%: £3,200
Refurbishment Costs: £2,000

Total Cash Required: £26,200

Rent: £600 per month
Letting Agent @ 10%: £60
Insurance: £20
Monthly Mortgage Interest @ 4%: £200

£600 - £60 - £20 - £200 = **£320 profit per month**

Using the example above, an original investment of £26,200 with an annual return of £3,840 demonstrates a 14.5% return on your money. To put that into perspective, the highest interest rate offered with a savings account at the time of writing this book is 5.25% – so it's clear to see the instant attraction to investing your cash in property rather than leaving it in the bank. However, using this model you would need to be prepared to wait over six years before you made your money back, and that's my main issue with it. You would require a seriously big pot of cash to be able generate enough from your buy-to-let portfolio to replace a full-time income. The average salary in the UK is currently about

£30,000 a year, so essentially this means you would need ten of those buy-to-let examples to replace your income, which would require £262,000 of cash to be invested. That's a lot of cash to find, especially if you're only earning £30k a year!

A much more effective method of buy-to-let investment is to utilise the model known as 'BRRR' – Buy, Rent, Refurbish, Refinance. This is exactly what we do at REWD Group, and we do it on a massive scale.

This method involves purchasing the property with cash or with a short-term finance solution known as a 'bridge', refurbishing the property to increase the value, putting a tenant in and then refinancing the property on to a buy-to-let mortgage at the increased property value. A perfect example of this is 170 Quarry Street, Motherwell, ML1 4HJ.

Purchase Price: £35,000
Sourcing Fee: £2,000
Legal Costs: £1,000
ADS: £0 to pay, as purchase price was below £40,000
Refurbishment: £9,500

Total Cash Invested: £47,500

New Property Value: £70,000
BTL Mortgage at 75% of new value: £52,500

Cash Left-in: **ZERO**

This means that the total costs of the project above came to less than what the bank gave us as a loan, putting us in profit from day one of refinance. The bank lends against the property's market value, which was £70,000 after the refurbishment and therefore because our total costs came to less than 75% of the property's value, we ended up with £5,000 surplus cash in the bank – meaning not only do we have all of our money back, but we have actually profited straight away by owning this property. We are then paid every month from the property by renting it out.

This is how you create infinite returning assets. With our original investment now back in play and with an extra £5,000 on top, we can now simply repeat this process using the same original funds rather than having to leave over £26k tied up for six years.

Understanding how to use professional buy-to-let investment strategies, equipped with the correct finance solutions, can allow you to create a property portfolio that can change your life forever. This is how we managed to scale from 0 to over 200 properties in 2.5 years.

HMO: House of Multiple Occupation

Another option available to you is a further advancement on the buy-to-let strategy, and it's known as a House of Multiple Occupancy (HMO). This strategy involves renting a property to three or more unconnected people and charging rent on a room-by-room basis, as opposed to renting out an entire property on a single lease. This is an incredible strategy for cashflow, and can generate massive returns compared to a standard buy-to-let simply by operating the same property in a different format.

Key markets where an HMO works well are students, transient workforce, social housing and charities. These are certainly the main occupants of the HMOs in our portfolio and we currently have eleven of them that produce over £20,000 per month in rental income.

Although the cashflow is very attractive, it's important to highlight the strict legislation and compliance that must be adhered to in order to receive license approval to operate your property as an HMO. The legislation is different in every local authority, but you can check all of the relevant criteria on their website and ensure you tick all the boxes.

Our largest and most profitable HMO example is 60B La Porte Precinct, Grangemouth, FK3 8AT. This was an old Indian restaurant that we purchased at auction before converting it into a ten-bedroom residential property to be occupied as an HMO for oil and gas contractors who travel to the area to work at the large power plants and refineries in the local area.

Purchase Price: £60,000
Auction Fees & Legal Costs: £10,000

Refurbishment/Conversion Costs: £190,000

Total Cost: £260,000

New Valuation: £250,000
Refinance Loan @ 65% of new valuation: £162,500

Cash Left In: £87,500

Rent: £7,900 per month (10 rooms rented at £180 per room, per week)
Monthly Loan Interest: £677
Management Fee: £790
Insurance: £100

NET Monthly Cashflow: £6,333

That's an 87% annual return on investment based on the £87,500 we left in the deal. All money out in just over 12 months, creating an infinite returning asset and producing over £6k net income per month. Acquiring just one deal like this could change your life.

When it comes to lending on an HMO, it's a bit of a strange position that the lenders take. An HMO is classed as residential; however, it is much more of a commercial operation and clearly generates significantly more cash than a standard residential property would. Typically, a commercial valuation can be defined by the strength of the lease and it is not uncommon for a 10x multiplier to be used to arrive at the value of a commercial property. For example, based on a £94,800 per year income like 60B, this property should technically have received a valuation of £948,000! However, as this is not a fairy-tale world we live in, the valuer assessed the property under very different circumstances and arrived at a value of £250,000 based on a ten-bedroom residential property in Grangemouth. As it's not quite the same as residential, but also not fully commercial, the lenders tend to offer unique rates and levels of loan value. In this example, the lender gave us 65% of the property's value at 5%

APR; this meant we left cash in the deal, but the cashflow is so strong that we got all our money back in about 12 months. Although the cash-flow is incredibly attractive, it's worth noting that there does tend to be a higher tenancy turnover and void period with HMOs – but if you utilise this strategy in areas with significant demand, you can offset that risk as much as possible.

There are so many opportunities to create something special from absolutely nothing using this strategy. The restaurant had sat empty for years and served no purpose to the local community and now it provides quality, much-needed accommodation to the area. Combine this strategy with the BRRR model and commercial conversions and you can create a monster of a property business.

Property sourcing/deal trading

You don't always have to own property to make serious money from it. I have built my career on this strategy, and have become recognised as one of the best in the industry because of my approach to finding the best deals for my clients – deals that many people don't fully believe even exist.

Property sourcing, or deal trading as it is also known, is essentially where an individual puts in the leg work to secure an investment opportunity on behalf of a client and then charge a fee for providing this service. To really be successful at it, you must target property owners who have a requirement for a fast and secure sale, allowing the opportunity to negotiate an attractive discount on the property so that you can introduce an investor who can purchase cash and complete quickly. The beauty of this strategy is that when done correctly, everyone gains out of the transaction. The seller has a problem and needs a quick exit, the investor is looking for the next deal to wisely invest their cash and you're sitting in the middle pulling it all together – and getting paid handsomely for bringing the best deal you can to the table. It's a very straightforward concept, but – I'll be brutally honest – unless you have clients who are willing to constantly buy shit deals (which anyone with any experience and cash is unlikely to do), it's far from easy to implement.

There are plenty of property training courses out there who sell this strategy as a simple method to make £10,000 from every deal and claim they can teach you to become financially free within months using nothing else but their deal-packaging methods. Honestly, after doing this for nearly ten years I can tell you that you will not make £10,000 off of every deal, and you most certainly will not become financially free in a matter of months. This is by no means a passive investment strategy. It's a full-time graft, but it can be a very lucrative strategy to make money in property.

Before myself, Alex and Laurie got into business together directly, we had already been doing business together for a few years because I was actively sourcing deals for them. From single units to portfolios, I was bringing the guys the opportunities to invest in, and ultimately it led to me sourcing over 30% of REWD Group's core portfolio. That percentage is significantly higher now we're in business together, of course! But to be solely responsible for introducing a third of their rapid growth as an external supplier just goes to show the quality in the deals and service I was providing, and the solid relationship we had to get deals over the line – even when it seemed impossible!

Everybody wants to do this and believes it's an easy way to make money, but the harsh reality is very different. This is a professional skill, and those who are very successful in this space know exactly what they're doing and are usually spending an absolute fortune on marketing. One of the companies I used to work for are actively spending £200,000 PER MONTH on marketing. That's some serious f***ing spend, and that's what you're up against. It's a very saturated market; however, most people never do what it takes to be successful at it, and as long as you get clear on how you can stand out and deliver better results, you can definitely compete without the outrageous marketing spend.

It all comes down to understanding the seller's circumstances. If you get very good at understanding people, equipped with some technical knowledge on property, you can find great deals no matter the market conditions.

The biggest challenge you will face when working with sourcers as a property investor yourself is that many of them are looking for the best deals for themselves to keep. All of the stuff they look to sell on, is either shit they don't want or they're just trying to make a quick buck selling to an amateur, or what they typically call 'preferred investors'. If the deal doesn't meet their criteria, only then will they look to sell it on or use alternative exit strategies like auction or estate agency. By the time a 'deal' hits the open market, it's usually been knocked back by plenty of people already and loses a lot of its value. I've never operated this way, and we still don't; even though we are actively buying for ourselves, we are also committed to working with our training clients to grow their portfolios so we target multi-unit deals for ourselves, then trade single unit opportunities to our clients – plenty to go around, and everybody wins. That's good business.

1B Glencarin Square, Kilmarnock, KA1 4AQ

1 bedroom ground floor flat
Purchase Price: £10,000
Sourcing Fee: £3,000
Legals: £1,000
Refurb: £12,000

Total Cost to Investor: £26,000

New Valuation: £45,000
Rental Value: £450 PCM

Total Cost to Seller: N/A

Sourcing Fees Made: £3,000

The above is an example of a deal I sourced for Alex and Laurie before we worked together. An overseas client of mine got stung buying this property at auction. She had paid £20,000 for it, spent £15,000 on a refurb and her most recent tenant completely destroyed the place. She was heartbroken and needed rid of it. My original advice was that she should put it back to auction and try get more value, at least see if she could get what she paid for it. But she was so devastated with the situation, she just wanted me to get someone to take it off her hands. I explained that given the background of the property, the extent of damage caused and the risks associated, the best I could do was £10,000, but there would be no sales fee for her to pay. She accepted and I charged £3,000 to Alex and Laurie for the deal and within 14 days the problem was removed from my client, Alex and Laurie had added a fantastic addition to their portfolio, and I got paid £3k for making it all happen.

7 Allan Street, Aberdeen, AB10 6HL

2 bedroom first floor flat
Purchase Price: £65,000
Sourcing Fee: £5,000
Legals: £1,000
ADS: £2,600
Refurb: £6,000

Total Cost to Investor: £79,600

New Valuation: £100,000
Rental Value: £650 PCM

Total Cost to Seller: £2,000

Sourcing Fees Made: £7,000

This is another example of a property I sourced and traded to a client. The seller was based in Glasgow and had this property in Aberdeen occupied by family friends, covering the costs of his mortgage. Essentially, he became an accidental landlord and never followed any of the legal obligations, and there was no lease agreement etc. in place. His tenants were moving out and he was therefore going to be left with a second mortgage to pay, and if he wanted to rent it out again, he would need to spend money on refurbishing the property and registering himself as a landlord. He did not want to do this, and he couldn't afford any void periods as he simply couldn't afford the mortgage payments on top of his existing outgoings. He needed a fast and secure solution. I explained all of his options, but he was very clear that the only solution he wanted to look at was what I could give him as a cash offer to complete in less than four weeks. We agreed a price of £65,000 which included his legal fees to be covered and a sales fee to myself of £2,000. I needed a client I knew would have the cash and that I could trust to get this deal over the line within a strict timescale, so I offered it to an investor I had done five or six deals with previously. She made a quick decision, and paid a £5,000 sourcing fee as she recognised the quality of the deal. Win-win. Seller got the money he needed in the timescale he was looking for, plus the investor got an all-money-out deal to add to their portfolio and I got paid £7,000 for making it all happen. Good f***ing business.

The main point to highlight is the better the deal you can bring to your investor, the more you can charge. It's really just as simple as that. If you have access to a particular thing someone is looking for, don't be scared to recognise the value and put the appropriate price on it. Just please, for the love of god, make sure what you're offering is actually valuable. Too many f***ing people out there are charging wild fees for shit deals. If you're going to use this strategy to make money, make sure you do it right. Reputation is important.

Assisted sale

This is a fantastic strategy that can really accelerate the cashflow in your property business with very minimal financial input (if any at all). Not many focus on applying this strategy, but for me it's definitely up there as the best for making money from property without ever owning any. I've used this plenty of times, and could probably have built a business solely on applying this strategy correctly.

An assisted sale is simply when you assist in selling someone's property who does not have time, money, experience or wants the hassle of the entire process. You might read that statement and think to yourself, 'Okay…so you're basically just a good estate agent?' but that's not the case at all – far from it. There are multiple ways you can structure an assisted sale agreement; however, it all starts with agreeing a price with the seller. For example, you may agree with the seller that they will get £50,000 from the sale, but the property needs £10,000 to refurbish it and bring it up to a good standard. You would invest the £10,000 into the property, then let's say you sell it for £80,000 – come the day of completion, the seller would receive their £50,000 share and the £30,000 minus selling costs and legal fees etc would be payable to you. Seller gets what they wanted and you've nearly tripled your investment. The huge benefit to everybody of this arrangement is that you've essentially been able to take on a flip, but you've massively reduced the cash that would have been required to buy it – plus you've avoided the six month rule, as the property always stays in ownership of the seller. More money, less cash required, and done much quicker – that's what this strategy can offer.

Now, it can become a bit risky if you invest into refurbishing someone else's property and can't obtain security to protect your investment, or you lose control over the agreement. That's why it's essential that your agreement is watertight and that you have a rock solid relationship with the seller. Alternatively, you can look to employ this strategy without any cash investment. An example of this as follows:

Agreed Sale Price with Seller: £40,000

Purchase Price: £55,000
Sales Costs: £1,500
Legal Fees on behalf of seller: £1,000

Balance Payable to You: £12,500

No cash investment required. Simply an agreement with the seller that you can sell their property and they will receive £40,000 in their hand with no costs, and you deal with the entire sales process. You either sell the property off-market to a client or you put it on the open market with an estate agent who will allow you to defer all fees including surveys to the end. This literally allows you to do everything with no up-front costs and make £12,500 profit.

Game changer when you get this right, but do not underestimate your responsibilities within these arrangements. If it was easy, everyone would do it!

Commercial to residential conversions

The last strategy that I want to take a look at is more of a development strategy. It's not the fastest way to make cash, but it can be massively rewarding if you're willing to be patient. We currently employ this strategy as one of our core activities at REWD Group, as it allows us to create big lump sums of profit or create high cashflowing assets out of wasted space. This is known as commercial to residential conversion.

As the name suggests, this strategy is simply the process of converting a commercial property to change its use to serve a different purpose than what it was originally built for, i.e. converting old office space into apartments. As this is a development project and requires a lot more than just an internal refurbishment, you will be required to get planning permission and building warrant approval before you can proceed with any conversion. All up-to-date building standards must be met and this can have a serious impact on the costs of development, especially if the building you're converting is really old or in a conservation area.

There are endless opportunities to apply this strategy throughout the UK. Especially after the Covid-19 pandemic there are so many vacant commercial properties on our high streets and town centres. Architecturally stunning buildings that are just screaming out to be brought back to life and given a new purpose, but it's important that you take the time to identify whether a conversion project will actually be viable or not. If the value of the property once the conversion is done is too low compared to the costs to acquire the building and complete the conversion – then, as stunning as the building may be, it is not a solid investment opportunity.

We were committed to regenerating the town centre of Falkirk and had actually purchased five vacant buildings with the intention of creating over forty apartments, but unfortunately the end values were just too low and the costs to convert were far too high that we had to offload the majority of the projects. It's all a numbers game at the end of the day, and if there is no profit to be made then you don't have a sustainable business.

We have, however, completed a very successful development project at Temperance House, Lint Riggs, Falkrik, FK1 1DG where we converted a vacant office space into six luxury apartments that we sold on to make a £200,000 profit. This was a really challenging but rewarding project that had a lot of clever elements to it with regards to how we purchased it and funded the full conversion. We've done a short case study video on this development, which you can check out at ***www.makemoneyfromproperty.co.uk***.

Another example of a successful conversion is the 60B La Porte Precinct HMO that we looked at earlier. We transformed an abandoned restaurant into a ten bedroom residential property producing over £6k profit per month. Your exit doesn't always have to be resale when it comes to conversions; you can blend this strategy with many alternative exits and have very successful outcomes.

Some additional thoughts on strategy

Understand the benefit of having multiple exit strategies and use them to create multiple streams of income. I'm not for one second saying that you can only do buy-to-flip or that you must only focus on deal sourcing – do them all, just get very good at identifying when is the right time to utilise each one. Explore all options, and choose the one that makes sense to you and which ultimately makes a profit.

We built our business by focusing on buy-to-let because it gave us a foundation of consistent cashflow that provided stability and allowed us to feed our other ventures and expand into alternative strategies like the commercial conversions and flips.

The bottom line is that you must get educated to understand these strategies fully and use every opportunity to leverage your time and knowledge to make money through property.

Some examples of commercial-to-residential conversions undertaken by the REWD Group to date.

Chapter Four

Introduction to Property Tax

Alex Robertson

I N this chapter, I'm going to be taking you through an introduction to the wonderful world of property tax and will be discussing some of the different factors related to it. One thing you will find is that a lot of people leave tax to the very last minute when buying property. That can be a very dangerous strategy. There are some fundamental things you need to understand before you get into property. There are some vitally important decisions that need to be made about how you're going to invest and in the structure that you're going to use.

There is the question of how best to manage your business to make sure that you don't pay an excessive amount of tax, especially after 2015. Since then, the government is putting more of a focus on landlords and property investors in general; it is more important than ever that you structure your affairs in the right way to make sure that your taxable obligations are not excessive. So I think this is a really important section. The aim of this chapter is not to confuse you with technical tax legislation, but simply to give you an overview of some of the key decisions that you have to make so that you can start to understand some of the different classifications of property investing types, the effects that can have on your tax, and ultimately to arm you with some of the key knowledge that you need when you're picking the right accountant.

Tax in general is an important subject to learn for anyone serious about changing their financial prosperity. The UK tax system is set up in such a way that most people don't ever have to understand anything about tax. The PAYE systems deduct tax from your pay before you have even receive it; the only way you know you earned that cash is when you see it on your payslip. Conversely, many countries such as the US require that everyone submits a tax return at year end which leads to more people at least having a base level knowledge of tax. The set up in the UK is very dangerous for us as citizens, because when we don't understand the tax system we don't know how to avoid or minimize our tax bill and as we said in Chapter 2, "The Bascis", one of the key things that separates the rich and poor is taxes, as the rich use tax knowledge to legally avoid taxes by using companies. So, lets start with this subject: what do we mean when we talk about tax avoidance, and how is that different to tax evasion?

Tax evasion and tax avoidance

The first subject we're going to look at is tax avoidance and tax evasion. Firstly, we're talking about the differences between these two terminologies. If you know about tax, you may have heard of tax avoidance and you may have heard of tax evasion, but it may not be quite clear what each of them mean. So, it's important we understand the distinctions.

Tax evasion is very much illegal. It is essentially the illegal non-payment or underpayment of tax. So, it is not fully declaring your tax situation, or failing to declare it at all. And we see this quite a lot in property, especially with non-professional landlords when they have a couple of buy-to-let properties and maybe a day job as well. They're not used to having to file a tax return, because – as we mentioned earlier – it's not required for most people in the UK as your taxes are deducted before you receive your salary. You don't normally have to think about the taxman and don't have anything to do with HMRC. But after you've got this additional income from the rental of property, you are going to have to start to file a tax return.

If you're doing it as a sole trader – for example, through your own name, not in a company – you're going to have to start filing a self-assessment tax return every year. This not only highlights the income that you make through employment, but also highlights the additional income that you make through investment, less tax-deductible expenses. Then that will come to a level of profit that you will have to pay tax on, so don't avoid it. So many people don't realise that, or maybe they think they'll get away with that. HMRC is very good at knowing when some-one is due to pay tax. An example of this is when you're a landlord and you have properties generating rental income, and you think that HMRC won't know about the extra few thousand pounds you make from property – but that's not true! Do you have a mortgage on the rental properties? Do you have a first charge security registered against the properties? Have you registered as a landlord with the local council (which is a legal requirement)? Have you registered the property as a rental with the local council? Have you paid council tax on the property whilst it was vacant? Have you advertised the property for rent on a na-tional property website? Well, these are just some of the ways that HMRC can track you down. There can be serious implications for you if you don't declare your taxes due.

If you try to evade tax, the bottom end of the scale is fines. You have to pay tax on your income plus interest on top of unpaid taxes; the top end of the scale is where things get very serious and people go to jail. There have been a lot of cases recently, particularly amongst tradesmen who have been taking cash instead of putting it through the books, and they've massively understated their income and ultimately gone to jail. This is something the HMRC won't ignore. Tax evasion is a serious business; it is very much illegal.

Conversely, you need to understand that tax avoidance, on the other hand, is more of a duty. It's a moral duty, as I see it. Certainly, we spend a lot of time arranging our affairs to minimise our tax liability, and that's all we're talking about. With tax avoidance, we're talking about the arrangement of your financial affairs in order to minimise your tax liability. In order to do that, you need to understand what affects your tax liability. The key thing is knowing what your obligations are to HMRC before you even get to the point of doing a tax calculation and payment. We're going to cover those key elements in relation to property throughout this chapter.

Tax avoidance, in the sense of minimising your tax burden, is a specialist subject. It's not a topic for this section. In terms of the introduction to property investing, we do cover advanced tax avoidance strategies within some of our more advanced courses. These are more specific to certain strategies within property. For this chapter, the aim is simply to understand the sort of taxes that are likely to impact you in property investment and to make you aware of some of the key categorisations that HMRC will make relating to your investment, to determine what they'll be. The key here is to understand the difference between tax evasion and tax avoidance – and ultimately, if you arrange your affairs upfront and in the correct way before you start investing, you will have the opportunity to minimise your tax. If you leave it and just figure it out later, you will pay excessive tax.

The only other thing I think we want to mention in context of tax evasion versus tax avoidance is quite simply: ignorance is not bliss. We don't ignore the fact that there are taxes to pay. We can minimise them sometimes, but we certainly can't evade them. We need to understand how we're going to keep our money, and ultimately if you don't understand the tax system, you're likely to give more tax than you need to. A lot of people have accountants and say, 'I'll leave it to my accountant. He knows what he's doing.' But property is a very specialist subject. What you will quite often find is that accountants can do it, but really all they're doing is preparing a set of financial statements based on HMRC legislation and guidelines. They're not looking at any ways of tax planning or tax avoidance, because that's a very specialist subject.

A lot of accountants don't see their role as helping to minimise your tax. Their role is simply to prepare your tax reports in the quickest and easiest way, to keep HMRC happy and take no risks of your return being challenged; in this sense they are working for HMRC, not you! So don't assume the accountants are always going to take care of minimising tax. And finally, the only other thing I want to mention in terms of tax avoidance is that there are a lot of people out there that sell these models that you can invest through, which are deemed to be aggressive tax avoidance schemes. We've all seen in the papers when celebrities use tax avoidance schemes abroad, which can get them into a lot of hot water with HMRC. Now we have what they call the General Anti-Abuse Rules – or GAAR, as they have become known. That gives them the authority to get into the detailed analysis of any tax avoidance strategies that HMRC feel may be either circumventing official normal arrangements or which are arrangements that are solely for the purposes of avoiding tax.

Remember, you are only looking to avoid tax. Not evade it. There's no other reason why you've structured your affairs in that way. And in those instances, as you know, HMRC have powers to investigate you. Potentially this is one area where tax avoidance at the extreme end could cause you pain in terms of fees, and then there are issues caused by late payments, underpayments, recalculation of your tax, and so on. So just be aware that there are people out there selling aggressive tax avoidance strategies. When you look at the tax avoidance strategies that we talk about in some of our advanced courses, there are maybe two or three, out of ten in terms of how aggressive they are, we would advise that you avoid tax avoidance strategies at the higher end of the risk scale; after all, no-one wants to be the next Jimmy Carr.

Broadly speaking, that's an introduction to tax avoidance versus tax evasion – just to get a general flavour of the subject. The last thing I wanted to mention here was a quote by Lord Clyde in a tax legal case dating back to 1920. It's a very famous quote:

'No man in the country is under the smallest obligation, moral or other, so to arrange his legal relations to his business or property as to enable the Inland Revenue to put the largest possible shovel in his stores.'

So basically, he's saying that no man in the country must pay more than is legally necessary in tax, and if he can apply the correct legal arrangement to his business or his property to legitimately reduce their taxable liability, then that is not illegal.

Tax avoidance is to be applauded in the sense that we don't have to feel like we are being immoral by trying to avoid tax. You should take the steps that you can – those that are available and legal – in order to minimise your tax obligation. That's only to be commended. It's not to feel that you are under some obligation to pay HMRC as much as you possibly can. So that's tax avoidance, and why it's so different in principle from tax evasion.

Tax classification

Our next subject here is what classification do you belong to within the sphere of property tax? Now, broadly speaking, there are two types of property investing. Either you are a property investment business, or you're a property trading business. Property investment means they're looking for rental income – maybe through taking on a tenant, through leasing the property, and capital growth being the value that the property appreciates over time. So you're looking for the benefits of holding the property for the long term. And on the other hand, property trading is much more in pursuit of short-term profit. It's essentially for strategies like flipping property, where you buy it within a six-month period, you want to do a refurbishment and then sell it on to a third party for a quick profit. Those, broadly speaking, are the two opposite ends of the spectrum of property.

Why is that distinction important? Because they are taxed very differently, and it will affect the way that you're taxed. A property investor is taxed massively differently to the way that you tax the property trader. We're going to get into the details of what the implications are for each type of investor, and what changes – as well as why it changes. And that's how we'll come to understand how you fit in that framework based on your strategy.

It's important, and of course it doesn't mean that you can only use one of these strategies. What is generally recommended is if you are going to do multiple strategies, you separate the businesses. For example, our group has Real Estate Wealth Development Ltd. which is our main buy-to-let portfolio, and – in that particular one – we've got about one hundred properties that are solely for property investing as we rent out the properties and hold them for the long term. Then, separately, we have a company called REWD Development, which is essentially a property trading business. This is where a commercial property is converted into residential properties, and then we sell these new properties to third parties. In that instance, we're very much a property trader, and the way that those two businesses are taxed – and the way that their accounts are prepared, and those companies are taxed – is dramatically different.

We're going to get into the details of how these two approaches affect your ultimate tax bill. So the first question that HMRC is going to try to determine is: what kind of company do you have? And here are the things that they're going to look at when they're trying to determine how you do business. They're going to look at what the original intent of your investment was. An example of this may be, for instance, Mr Smith buying a property because his son has gone off to university. Mr Smith has bought up an investment property with intention of holding it for the long term whilst his son is at university for four years. Maybe he plans to sublet some of the other rooms, since it's very much an investment. He's expecting capital growth. This is at least the intent of it. But unfortunately, his son's time at university only lasts a couple of months. So now he's in a position where he's got this flat that is an investment, and that no longer makes sense as his son has left university, so he sells the property and makes a profit. So in this case, on the face of it, HMRC would look at this arrangement and say: you've flipped the property. You bought it here, you sold it there... that's trading. It's not investing. But you know, if he could support the fact that his original intent was to hold it for the long term, then it could still be classified as property investment, even although it has been sold in the short term.

Another question they will investigate is, how was it financed? There are different ways that property can be financed. And the key is whether its short- or long-term finance – for instance, bridging finance, which is covered in one of the other chapters. This kind of finance is really just designed for a 12-month period maximum while you're developing a property. And that would clearly be an indication that you had a short-term view on that property. The long-term option would be something like a buy-to-let mortgage, which typically ties you in for longer-term periods and has early termination fees; you have to pay to get out of that mortgage within the first three or five years, for example. This would be

• • •

a fairly good indication that you are a property investor, because you're looking at a longer-term view with that type of finance.

There are other factors HMRC will look at to determine if you are investing or trading, such as the frequency of transactions. If you're regularly buying and selling, obviously that is going to be a clear indication that you are running a property trading business, and you'll be taxed as such. But what if you're holding another 20 properties and you only sell the occasional property? Then again, you could argue that that those are just disposing of occasional properties within the regular process of a property investing; after all, as investors it would be normal to analyse our asset performance and offload underperforming assets occasionally. Really it becomes a matter of building up the facts, and that's how HMRC looks on it. Did someone live in it at any point, or was it vacant all the time? Did you renovate the property? Then again, that's going to lead to another indicator of whether you're an investor or a trader.

None of these things are absolute, and they would weigh up the evidence of many such factors. Ultimately, if you want to do a mix of both investing and trading then keep them separate for tax purposes. Say a property becomes available and I want to do this as a development. I want to sell on the units, because they are going to be higher-end, so it is not going to make sense to fit it into my buy-to-let portfolio. In that case, keep those things separate from a tax perspective. If you're working as a sole trader, you can manage your bank account separately. If you're working as a business through a company itself, a separate company for development, you can set up an SPV for your property development business. SPV stands for a 'special purpose vehicle'; it just means a company that's dedicated to that one activity.

Why does it matter? Trading versus investing

Now we've been through what determines the classification of investor and trading, you're justifiably asking, "Why does it even matter what classification I fall into?" Well, we're going to get into more about why these things matter. Ultimately, what impact is it going to have on tax – whether we're an investor or whether we're a trader?

Property investing

Let's start with tax for property investment. What type of taxes are we going to have to pay as a property investor? The common type of property investment is obviously buy-to-let. That is the most popular one, where you buy a property, you rent it out, and you want to benefit from the rental income in the long term the capital appreciation. So first, we're talking about rental property profits, because every year you're going to make a certain amount of rental income less your deductible costs. Those will depend on what structure that you invest in. But ultimately, you have rental income, less things like mortgage interest rates, your insurance, landlords, insurance, and your agent costs. If you're paying sort of a flat 10% rate to the agent, for example, that's a deductible cost and coming off your income.

So what type of tax are you going to have to pay on those rental profits if you are a sole trader? If you invest in property through your own name, and not through a company, then ultimately you're going to have to pay income tax annually on your rental income. Here's where it gets scary. If you're an investor and you already have a job, and if you're well-paid, you may find yourself in a higher rate tax band, which in Scotland would be 41%. So if you're already earning through your job and have an income that takes you to a higher rate of tax, any additional profits that you make from property rental will also be taxed at 41%. Which is a massive amount of tax. On the flipside, if you have no other income then it could be quite beneficial to invest in your own name, because you have an annual tax exemption which is just over £12,500 per year that you can earn tax-free. So you know, that £12,500 that you earn as a property investor is tax-free.

If you invest through a company, the rental profits that you make annually will be based on corporation tax. So your profits are currently taxed at 19%. The only other thing to mention here is that if you want to take those profits out of the company – if you want to put them into your personal account – then you're going to have to pay another level of tax. Now that could be dividends if you decide to distribute the profits based on evidence, or it could be income tax. Another option is to pay yourself a salary from the company, which may or may not make sense depending on whether you already have a job with significant income. Ultimately there are several different ways to take money from the company and you can structure that in the best and most tax-efficient way for your current circumstances. That's something that your accountant should be able to help you with. So, if you're paying income tax or paying corporation tax on your profits, really it comes down to the individual's personal circumstances to decide which is going to be more beneficial in terms of minimising your tax obligation.

> **EXAMPLE 1:** You have an annual salary from regular income of £50,000 meaning you are already a higher rate tax payer, you also have a net income from property of £30,000, calculate the tax payable on your property income for both investing as an individual and investing as a company (for the moment we will ignore the effects of Section 24 – that comes later):

> *Individual:* As you are already a higher rate tax payer your property income will be immediately taxed at the higher rate, so: £30,000 x 41% (Scottish tax rates) = £12,300 tax payable

> *Company:* investing as a company you will pay corporate tax in the first instance on your profits, so: £30,000 x 19% = £5,700, then assuming you want to take the cash out of the company the remaining amount (£30,000 - £5,700 = £24,300) will be taxable at the higher rate dividends tax, allowing for the first £2,000 of dividends tax free: £24,700 - £2,000 = £22,400 x 33.75% = £7,560. Total tax paid: £5,700 plus £7,560 = £13,260.

Whilst on the face of it the tax is higher for the company, the important point is that this second level of tax is not necessary to pay with a company if you don't want to take the profits, but simply reinvest them. In that instance, your tax payment goes down to £5,700.

The second type of tax we are liable to pay as a property investor is capital gains tax. Capital gains tax is a tax on the profit created by the increased market value of the property. However, importantly, this tax only ever applies when you sell a property. So as a property investor, maybe it's your intention to hold properties for the long term or indeed indefinitely, but – like all investors – you must analyse your assets and say, okay, these ten properties are performing really well, but these two aren't so I'm going to sell them. Clearly it's not our business as property investors to sell properties regularly, otherwise we would be traders, but a limited amount of property sales are expected as investors. And when we sell those properties, we will have to pay tax on the gains. As a sole trader (i.e. through your own name, and not through a company), then you have the ability to use an annual tax-free exemption of £12,300 (as per 2021), whereby the first £12,300 of profit you make on the sale of any property is free.

Currently for the tax year 2021 to 2022, where you can say, 'Okay, the first £12,300 independent gain I've made on the sale of that property is tax-free,' thereafter any residual profit is taxed according to the capital gains tax banding.

EXAMPLE 2: You have sold a property for £150,000. You bought the property 5 years ago for £100,000. When you bought the property, you had upgrade costs and legal fees of £30,000. This is purely an investment property. Calculate your capital gains tax obligation assuming you had no other gains in the year, and assuming you are already a higher rate tax payer:

Answer: Your taxable gain on the property sale is £150,000 - £130,000 = £20,000. The first £12,300 of that gain is tax free, leaving £7,700 to be taxed. This will be taxed at the higher rate of capital gains (as you are already a higher rate taxpayer) of 28%. Tax payable: £7,700 x 28% = £2,156.

If you have sold the property as a company and made a gain on that sale, ultimately that's going to be taxed at the corporate tax rate of 19%. So it's taxed ultimately at the same rate as your rental income profits. However, it's important to note that these two things are calculated separately. Whether it's a company or you are investing in your own name, the important thing to note here is that we only pay capital gains tax when we sell a property, but we pay tax every year on our rental income. Therefore it is not surprising that one of the biggest questions in property investment tax is whether any cost is capital (against the value of the asset), or revenue expense (against your rental profits). As revenue expense you get immediate tax benefit, and for capital expense you may never get a tax benefit if you don't sell the property.

Other taxes to be aware of as a property investor are the taxes that you must pay when you're purchasing the property. Whether you invest as a property investor or whether you're a property trader flipping property, you will still pay these taxes on the purchase of the property at the front end. The first one is LBTT (Land and Building Transaction Tax), which is the Scottish equivalent of English stamp duty (SDLT), as it's more commonly known. LBTT is a building transaction tax, and ultimately this tax is just based on the value of the property that you buy.

For instance, for residential property in Scotland, if the property is valued at £145,000 or less you pay 0%. So if you're buying a property in that range, you're going to pay zero LBTT. But if you were buying a property, for example, for 150,000, you would pay 0% for the first £145,000 and then for the additional £5,000 you pay tax at the next band, which is 2%, equal to a total LBTT tax of £200.

Ultimately the bandings and rates are different depending on whether you're buying a residential property or whether you're buying non-residential premises – a commercial shop, an industrial unit or an office. Something like that. The rates are different, and ultimately for commercial property you pay less LBTT.

Additional dwelling supplement is another type of stamp duty. Again, it's based on the value of the transaction and it only applies to residential properties. If it's a residential property and it's not your home (i.e. your principal private residence), you're going to have to pay 4% (in

Scotland) on the value of the transaction. So for instance, going back to our £150,000 purchase price, you're talking £6,000 in additional tax from that transaction. We will cover this tax in more detail later in this chapter.

Finally, another transaction tax that may apply is VAT (Value Added Tax), which you might have to pay on your purchase. If you are purchasing an existing residential property, that will be VAT exempt. But if you're buying a commercial property, it might be that you must add 20% depending on how the property is categorised. So that tax is something you need to be aware of, and if you're buying commercial property you need to be asking those questions at the front end because you don't want to find out when you're closing on the property that you need to find an extra 20% cash for VAT.

Residential property purchase and rental – just to be clear, when we're renting out property or purchasing residential property these are VAT exempt transactions, so you can't register for VAT as a property investor business on residential property, which means ultimately that you can't reclaim the VAT on any of your costs. The entire amount of the cost becomes available for tax deduction as a business expense, but you can't reclaim the VAT – so that's a key distinction to understand. That's because it's exempt. The only other distinction to make – that a new build residential property is not actually VAT exempt, it is zero rated for VAT, which is important for developers looking to reclaim the VAT on their build costs. But that's something we'll cover in a little bit more detail later.

Tax deductibility and Section 24

Perhaps the most significant tax change in the last 10 years for property investors is the introduction of section 24. This change effects mortgage interest cost deductibility when calculating taxable profits. For most of us property investors who want to maximise our "good debt" and use highly leveraged mortgages to maximise the amount of properties we have, then mortgage interest costs will be our biggest cost. In basic terms, Section 24 disallows the deduction of mortgage interest costs when determining your taxable profits. Yes, you heard me right: they have disallowed the deduction of your biggest cost. And instead, you get a 20% tax credit for the mortgage interest. Now, its important to mention that this does not apply to companies; only people investing in their own name, or via a partnership. For those who are already paying higher rate tax, the impact of this change is significant, and I think its worthy of an example:

> Here's an example on section 24 and how it can affect your tax calculation, just to give a bit more of a flavour of the impact and how this affects you. We've covered Section 24, which I've already mentioned has become one of the most significant tax areas – certainly the most significant tax change within the last four or five years when it comes to property. I'm going to give you an understanding of what the numbers look like before and then what they look like afterwards, and assess the financial impact of that.
>
> So let's start. Say someone has an income from employment of £50,000 in the year, so that's a salary from their day job that brings in £50,000. In addition, they have property income, and just to simplify it for this example we're going to say they also have a property income of £50,000 per annum. This property income is through their own name, so they are investing in properties as a sole trader. Essentially they are not an investor with a limited company or anything like that, so they are going to be subject to income tax and because as they are a higher rate taxpayer already, given the fact that their employment income is over the higher rate tax threshold, they will automatically pay tax on the rental profits at the higher rate of tax. Not a great situation, but certainly not a new situation, so let's work out what would have been the rental income tax liability before Section 24 and then afterwards.

Before Section 24

The first thing is to work out the profit levels on the rental income, so we said they had £50,000 of rent received and from that we need to deduct the associated costs. In this instance the costs consist of £35,000 of mortgage interest, £5,000 of letting agent costs and £5,000 of other costs, totalling costs of £45,000. This means they have £50,000 of income and £45,000 of cost, equating to a taxable profit of £5,000. With the current higher rate tax band (in Scotland) at 41% the tax is equal to £5,000 x 41% = £2,050.

After Section 24

As before, the rental income and costs have not changed: £50,000 of rent received and costs of £45,000, equating to a profit of £5,000. The tax calculation, however, does change as we are no longer getting tax deductibiity for the mortgage interest, meaning the new taxable profit will add back the interest costs of £35,000, thus meaning a taxable profit of £40,000; the initial tax payable is £40,000 x 41% = £16,400. We are not done there, as you also get a 20% tax credit for your mortgage interest which would be £35,000 x 20% = £7,000. So, the final tax obligation is £16,400 less tax credit of £7,000 = £9,400. This is a scary situation, when effectively you have only made £5,000 of profit in real terms and your tax bill is £9,400. So you are losing money!

Due to the significance of this change, a lot of people have left the property investing market entirely. So anybody that's been around the property world or started to get into it or has been studying it, has probably heard of Section 24. Section 24 was basically put in place by the government to discourage accidental landlords. Ultimately the way they viewed it at the time was that too many people were not selling the property when they moved on; they were holding it and renting it, maybe to boost their pension pots or whatever. The government didn't like this and decided that this was leading to less properties being available for first-time buyers – properties being available to meet the needs of the many people that were trying to get on or move up the property ladder.

Section 24 does not affect companies. So, the situation for companies is not so different than it was before. This creates significant benefits of investment to a company and in recent years there's been a big move towards that type of investment since these rules came in, and the tricky part is for those who maybe have 10, 20 or 30 properties as a sole trader through their own name. It's very difficult then to transfer them into a company to avoid this situation. It's not impossible – there are strategies to do it – but it's likely to be very costly and even with things like entre-preneurs' relief that will reduce the tax implications, you are still going to have challenges with your lenders. So if you're setting up a company to invest in property, it's quite a good time to do so because you have the benefits of these rules. You know them, and you can structure your af-fairs in a way to make sure that your tax impact is minimised as much as possible. For REWD Group starting out, thankfully we didn't begin until well after these changes were established. So in our case, we were able to structure our business through companies to avoid such a situation. But for many people who historically invested as sole traders, they were less fortunate. So that's led to a lot of people leaving the market. That's why, now more than ever, you must be very careful about how you set up your property investment business at the front end. For that reason, you need to understand property investment tax.

Property trading
Our next topic is tax for property trading. We've looked at the implica-tions of tax for property investors. So, what if you're classified as a property trader? How is that going to affect the taxes that you have to pay on the amount of profits you make? We said during the last section that tax on purchasing a property really doesn't change between property investing and property trading, so we don't need to cover that again here. Similarly, VAT implications are well aligned with property investing; for ex-ample, if it's a commercial property that's opted to be taxed, those things still apply whether you're trading or investing on the purchase.

Broadly speaking, if you're investing as a sole trader (i.e. through your own name to trade), then ultimately income tax is going to be paya-ble if you're investing through a company, then corporation tax is going to be paid on the profits that you make. The big difference here is that your business is buying and selling property, not holding it for the long term like an investor. How the does that change the tax you pay? For example, when you sell a property as a property investor, it's deemed to be a capital gain. And if you're a sole trader then with capital gains, you get the benefit of your annual exemption of £12,300, which you get tax-free. This tax-free allowance for capital gains does not apply as a property trader, as ultimately your job is buying and selling property, so this equates to your income, i.e. not capital gains tax but instead income tax. This is a big issue for anyone who does property trading in addition to a day job which pays more than £43,662 (2022/2023), as instantly this will mean you are being taxed at the higher rate of income on any profits from property trading. Not only are you losing out on the annual capital gains exemptions that investors get, but you are being taxed at a higher rate under income tax than you would be under the capital gains tax rates. This is not good news for traders. For property traders that choose to invest via a company, its much more straightforward as profits are still taxed at the same rate of corporation tax: 19% (2022/2023). This makes corporate structures much more attractive to property traders than a sole trader arrangement.

The next big change for property trading versus property investing comes down to whether a property represents inventory or an asset. Those are fundamentally different accounting terms and are valued in different ways. They are accounted for in different ways, with different tax implications. For instance, if you're a property trader, it's likely that your property is considered inventory – meaning something you bought that you'll then sell on for a profit. Whereas if you are a property investor, it's an asset that we hold for the long term, that we generate rental income from, and we get capital gains from its increased value over the long term. We only pay tax on those capital gains when we realise the gain, i.e. sell the asset. If you never sell the asset, you may have a profit and loss gain on your account of the year, but you don't have a taxable gain. So, you can end up making quite a lot of money in property investment year-on-year in your accounts on theoretical gains that haven't been realised, and which don't have to be taxable.

If you're trading in property, it's going to be classified as stock. The key difference there is that stock is valued at the lower of cost or net realisable value. So, the lesser of what you paid for the property or what you could sell it for currently. Assets, on the other hand, can be revalued at the current market value, meaning they are valued at the highest level. If you bought it cheap and it's now worth more, you could revalue that and recognise the gain on it. Those two things are valued very, very differently. So, if you have an asset, you can revalue upwards, while inventory is always going to be at the lowest possible value.

That's one of the fundamental differences between property investments and trading. Another major difference is that property trading gets full mortgage interest deductibility, unlike property investment under Section 24. That becomes very interesting, because you are trading the property – you're not holding it for investment purposes, even if you're a sole trader who is trading as an individual; you get the full benefit of interest tax deductibility. Unlike Section 24 for property investors, where you no longer deduct the mortgage interest costs when calculating tax, you only get the 20% tax credit. That's not the case for property trading, because you're not holding that for the long term.

The other key difference is that trading losses are much more flexible. With property investment, if you make any losses in a property investment business, you can only really apply those losses against future profits of that investment business. You can't apply against other trading activity profits that you may have in another business you own. So trading losses have become much more flexible, with the potential to take the losses back and apply them against previous profits; there is the ability to take them forward and apply them against future profits. There is also an ability to offset them against other types of trading activities, potentially. So the losses that you potentially make – and nobody wants to make losses – but it's good to know that you've got the tax benefit if you do. It's a much more flexible way of doing business.

Within investment companies, National Insurance is another big thing. Like I said earlier, in property investment National Insurance does not apply to the income that you make when you're a sole trader, when you're working as yourself. For property traders, it's very different because this is deemed to be income and would be subject to National Insurance. So you would have to pay National Insurance on your profits, essentially.

Then there is the matter of abortive costs. This is another one, and it means the tax deductibility of costs for projects that you've been unsuccessful with. So, for instance, if you spend a lot of money on legal costs for a property you were trying to purchase and then, for whatever reason, you weren't able to get that over the line. It wasn't a successful project. You weren't able to derive any profit from it. In property investment, that cost would be gone and it would not be tax deductible against any other income that you got within that business. However, for trading that's not the case. You can apply it against profits from other projects, i.e. the cost to evaluate a deal that never went forward. You can apply those costs against your profits.

Business structuring

In the next section of this chapter, I am going to be looking a bit more closely at how you should be structuring your business. This is the critical first step in property that you must get right. How are you going to structure? We've considered this to some degree already. In almost every instance, I'm talking about whether or not you're a sole trader, an investor yourself, or whether or not your company invests through a business – a corporate entity. Now, there are few models in-between, but ultimately those are the two main options which have significant impact on the type of property tax you're going to have to pay and how your business is going to be run.

Now we're going to look into that. Why would you put either option over the other? Remember that we are a business, and this is something that we try to get across. And a lot of our training makes the point that if you're going to do property investing professionally, it needs to be treated like a business. Many people do this, by the way, on a really amateur basis; they manage all the properties themselves. They've taken calls from angry tenants about broken boilers on Christmas Day, they spend all their spare time with a paint brush or fixing broken toilets; this isn't professional property investing. This is something that we ask people to think about at the start, certainly when we talk about buy-to-let on a massive scale. When it comes to professionals and buy-to-let, essentially we say that you need to get the systems and processes in place before you get to that stage of building your business to any scale, because it is a business. It's really hard to scale and manage your business if you don't have the systems and processes in place in the first place.

When you're thinking about your structure, you have to think about it in the terms of a business and where you want to take it, as well as the scale of it. For any type of sole trader, individual investing is going to be limited by the level of tax or the level of income that they can make before they are taxed at a much higher rate. In the UK, really beyond £50,000 you're in the range of a higher rate of tax payable. So you can earn a certain amount of money and then you're looking at 40% upwards of tax, and it can get very serious. It's a huge amount. A huge chunk of your profit has gone, whereas through a company's corporate structure in the UK you are currently paying a flat 19% irrespective of profit levels.

So if you know you're going to scale to a significant level, it really comes down to what your objectives are at the start and what skills you have. I know I mentioned this at the start, but ultimately there are several options for property, and for most types of businesses it's a limited company. So setting up a limited company is a straightforward process, and you do that with Companies House. It costs as little as something in the region of £13 to register a company. The costs of running a company in the long term are likely to be more, as a company must have an annual set of accounts created and submitted to Companies House, as well as an associated tax return.

Another type of structure is a limited liability partnership, which is essentially two or more people working together under a partnership agreement, but the partnership is formalised into a corporate body that limits the liability of the partners, so it's kind of a hybrid between working through a limited company and working through a partnership in your own personal name. Whilst there is a limit of liability like a company, a limited liability partnership still pays tax based on individual income tax for each partner based on their profit allocation.

The other option is obviously a sole trader, in your own name. Whether you are a sole trader on your own or working with someone else through a partnership, from a tax perspective, in both instances you pay income tax on any profits that are allocated to you from the business. The impact here is that if you're working through a limited company, you're going to be taxed through corporation tax. Then on every other type of investment – whether it's a limited liability partnership, partnership or sole trader – you're going to be taxed through the income tax and your share of the profits of that business. It is going to be taxed through income tax and, as I say, it ultimately comes down to a question of whether you're paying income tax or whether you're paying corporate tax, and which one of those scenarios works best for you. As I mentioned previously, with a business that you're trying to scale to a significant size, it's unlikely that the allowance that you have on income tax is going to set up a multi-million-pound business, for example. In that instance, a lot of people are going to incorporate and go through the corporate element of company structure.

So what are your goals, ultimately? That's what this all comes back to. What are you trying to achieve, and how does that best fit, if you're just looking to achieve maybe £6,000 or £7,000 from rent? For example, you're close to retirement and it's going to replace your income – in that case, doing it through your own name could make sense, to make the most of your personal tax allowances. You're just looking to get £1,000 a month coming in, or whatever you need to pay your bills. Then there is an argument that that doing it through your personal name avoids Section 24, because Section 24 only really starts to affect the amount of tax you pay when you are on the higher tax rate (i.e £50,000 a year income or more). That makes it the simplest and easiest way to do it. Under that scenario, you know you have at least £12,500 a year of tax-free money if you have no other income. On the other side of it, as soon as you start to scale you know it's likely that the overall tax implications would be such that a company would make the most sense. So it's really about weighing up what your goals are.

That's why we always recommend that before you get started, you should understand what you're trying to achieve, what your financial objectives are, and get advice as to the best way to set up your business depending on the objectives that you're trying to reach. This is not a one-size-fits-all strategy. As I see it, different strategies are taxed very differently, and your objectives in terms of scale, longevity, etc. could potentially be very different. There's no global answer. We wouldn't say that everybody should incorporate or everybody should work as a sole trader. It's very much specific to your circumstances and your objectives.

So take the advice, but have a clear picture of what you're trying to achieve through property investment before you take that advice.

Costs can be a big part of it as well. For example, if you just set up a company and you're only going to have maybe one or two properties in play within the first couple of years, you're not looking to grow in an aggressive way or scale it quickly. It can then be quite expensive to do it through a company, because you're going to have to pay for annual accounts and submit a corporate tax return. There are more obligations involved in running a company than there would be as a sole trader, which ultimately just needs a self-assessment tax return form to be completed and filed every year. So for instance, you know, a decent accountant to prepare company accounts can cost you about £200 a month, irrespective of the scale of your buy-to-let business or your trading business. If you had to return to them for additional services, it's going to go up to more like £400 or £500 a month depending on how much extra work there is involved. So the costs of running a company can be quite significant. If you're only going to have one property in your first year, for example, and you're only generating maybe £200 a month of net cash, that's all going to be swallowed up by your accountant and that's where scale comes in. You know, if you're not going to try and scale up your business in the long term, a company is not going to be worth your while.

Let's think about how a company is structured. Of course, this needs to be to be factored in, even when you may get tax benefits from investing through a company. It goes by your personal circumstances, and one additional thought is maybe about generational thinking when you're trying to understand what structure you want to put your business into. There are many more things you can do with assets in a company and shareholders of that company to pass on to your children in the next generation without paying significant amounts of inheritance tax. Whereas investing as a sole trader, as an individual on the properties or in your name, for the mortgages that are in your name it's not as easy to arrange your affairs to avoid inheritance tax. It can take a little longer. So those are a few things to think about in advance. You still need to get professional advice before you make a decision on how to structure your business. But this is a really important point – with Section 24, with different tax rules between property investment, property trade and wealth with different tax rates, it's very important that you get this right.

Take the time before you start a business to understand how you're going to structure it, because a lot of people would just start investing through their own name and say, 'I don't want to think about it'. So that's the easy option. But really, it's not. It can cause you a lot of heartache down the line. So I really urge everybody to get their advice at the front end and to think about what the plan is for the long term. There is no one-size-fits-all answer, so it really is critical to get tailored professional advice from a specialist accountant that deals with property.

Deciding between limited companies and sole trading

There are couple of other things that may affect your property investment structure. This isn't really so much about tax. This is just to make you aware of some of the diffrerent things that can affect you, depending on your decision. If you're going for buy-to-let mortgages as a company, for example, the interest rates will be higher than going for a buy-to-let mortgage as an individual. Now, on the other side of that, there's potentially a lot more products available for individuals than buy-to-let through a company, so it's relevant. The market for buy-to let through a company is fairly new, as there weren't a lot of people doing it pre-2017 and pre-Section 24. There are a lot more people doing it now. There are a lot more products than there were four or five years ago and the gap is closing, but BTL through a company remains at higher interest rates and on more restrictive terms than through your personal name. You're looking at about 4% APR on interest rates through a buy-to-let company mortgage, whereas it can be as low as 2.8% or 3% for individuals in some instances with personal mortgages. So the buy-to-let mortgages are more expensive through a company currently. But then, when you look at the tax benefits of Section 24, it is still advantageous for most people to do it through a company.

You've got many more options when it comes to lending through your name, because a lot of the high street banks are providing that type of funding; borrowers find that they have lots of options, and subsequently there are lots of products. Whereas when you do buy-to-let through a company, it comes down to only a few specialist lenders. It's non-traditional guys who know precisely how different mortgages work. There are a handful of them, maybe seven or eight, who offer products in Scotland. The criteria can be random, and they don't like certain types of properties and certain postcodes. Some will insist on a minimum property value of £60,000 and so forth. It's important if you are investing via a company to get a good mortgage broker who understands the market, and line up your lender before you commit to purchase a property.

It's not just the finance you need to think about; legal fees can change, generally within a company where there will be more legal work involved, and consequently it will cost a little bit more. Finding a good broker can be challenging because of the complexities of buy-to-let mortgages through companies – there are the ever-changing products, and the question of who's offering what. It's just often not worthwhile for brokers to be fully up to speed on all the products and how best to guide you. They can be quite lazy when it comes to that, at least for a lot of brokers. So you need to be aware that if you're investing through a company, it's better that you get to know the criteria yourself. If you don't and you're relying on a broker, it could be that there's something in the criteria that you've not read or not understood, and that could potentially break the deal down when you're just three months into trying to finance a project. Each lender will have their detailed criteria summarised on their website.

Generally when we are making a decision over what structure to choose, tax will be the driving force behind the decision. These are just other considerations to be aware of when making your choice. Mortgage products can be a little bit more complicated on the finance side for limited companies, and brokers don't always know them as well as they should do because it is a more specialist area. Again – and I've mentioned this a few times now – this is the recurrent theme in your structural planning, and the way that you want to do your business is going to be largely based on your goals. If you're just trying to get a little nest egg for your retirement and you're quite close to that retirement, you're not going to have too many income tax years before you retire, it might be best just investing in your own name. If you're looking at massive scale, on the other hand, you're more likely to need to go down the route of incorporation. Otherwise the income tax rates get very, very high when you start to get into serious numbers of profitability. As I see it, understand what you're trying to achieve before you make a decision on which structure you will choose for your property business.

Key taxes in property

The next subject we're going to cover is all of the key taxes in property. A lot of these we've mentioned already, but we're going to go through them in a little bit more detail. In particular, we'll look at some of the specifics about these types of taxes and how they affect property investing.

Income tax

The first tax we're going to cover is income tax. Income tax is applicable to anyone who is an individual earning an income, essentially. If you're operating as a partnership, you're still subject to income tax based on your percentage of the profits of that business, even if you're working under a limited liability partnership that's going to be subject to income tax. It's very much a personal tax you have to pay, and most people will be familiar with this because if you've got a job, you're paying income tax. Some people might not even know the ins and outs of that, really, because ultimately your employer takes care of the income tax from your income before you even receive your salary. You receive a net income less tax, and they pay that over to the government on your behalf. That's a PAYE (Pay As You Earn) scheme, as you are only paying tax on what you are earning. But when you start having multiple sources of income, the game changes somewhat and you need to start submitting tax returns. You need to get an understanding of what your income tax liabilities are, based on the income that you have.

The first thing to understand is that income tax is determined based on the amount of income that you receive. You should always be aware of the current rates of income tax payable in Scotland. These change very slightly between Scotland and England, but now if you're earning anything over £12,570, which is your tax-free allowance, anything between £12,570 up to £14,667 is paid at the starter rate of 19% tax. For the next amount, between £14,667 to £25,960, you're paying 20%. Then for the next band, which goes up to £43,662, you pay 21%. You can see it just escalates and escalates. Anything over £43,660, depending on the higher rate, is taxed at 41%. The maximum rate is 46%, and that's for earnings over £150,000. So if you had an income and you were fortunate enough to have an income from a job where you had £150,000 of salary, then you're already in the top rate of tax. Any income that you had for property investments in addition to your job, assuming you are investing in your own, would be taxed immediately at 46% – so almost half of your profits are going immediately to the taxman and that's before the impact of Section 24 is applied. Please note that income rates and bands change annually, and the latest rates can be found easily on the Internet.

Your rate of tax, and which band you're in, very much depends on what your income is. You would normally apply your personal income to your main source of income, being employment if that's the case, and then any subsequent income would be taxed based on the rate of the band that you're in. For instance, if you earn £43,662 from your day job, your additional income from property would actually fall into the higher rate tax band because it takes you over that threshold of £43,662 and you're going to be paying 41% on that extra income. So we're going to go through some examples of this just to give you a flavour for calculating your income. It demonstrates how to calculate an income from employment and how it's likely to affect the tax that you pay on your income from property.

Just to understand that, as I said before, there is a tax-free allowance of £12,570. Everybody gets that tax-free allowance. An additional income is higher, as I mentioned, so if you have a single source of income from employment and then you have a second source of income from rental, for instance, the rental is going to be immediately taxed at the same rate band following your employment salary.

The way that the PAYE system is set up in the UK makes it so most people don't have to understand anything about income tax; they do all the leg work for you, which is a very dangerous scenario as you can't manage what you don't understand and ultimately tax is the biggest cost most people have. So it's good to understand tax, because then when you start to add multiple sources of income you are in a position to be able to minimise your tax and maximise the cash going into your pocket.

A note of warning here, which comes back to the issue of tax evasion. If you're aware that you have this extra income from property, you need to pay tax on it. There's no point in avoiding it; HMRC are going to pick up on it. They will generally find you and when they do, you will be investigated for tax evasion. It can get very messy.

Corporation tax

The next tax we have is corporation tax. Again, we've covered this briefly earlier. But just to put a bit more detail into it, corporation tax is payable by a limited company. If you plan to set up a company, as I have said, it can be straightforward. It costs around £13 to register a company. You then must submit accounts at the end of your first year of trading. So for accounts, you will have something like 12 months to submit them following the end of your first year. From that, you will then make a calculation of your tax payable and submit a CT600 form for corporation tax.

If your company is liable to pay corporation tax, it's currently 19% of your taxable profits. This is currently a flat rate of 19% (not banded) and represents a much lower tax percentage than the higher rates of income tax. There is no tax-free allowance when it comes to corporation tax; it's not like income tax, where you get £12,570 free. With a company it is clear you are running a business, and therefore there is more flexibility in terms of how you can deduct expenses when determining your profit versus operating as a sole trader. So that can be one of the biggest benefits. Ultimately a lot of the tax avoidance strategies that are available to you technically within property are through, or maximised through, the corporate structure of your companies. We discuss that in some of the other sections, where we show the corporate structure that we have, and the fact that the company owns other businesses; they're all companies, but are owned within a group structure. This allows us to maximise tax-efficiency, because it means we can move assets to or from one company to another without huge tax implications. That wouldn't be possible if they weren't part of the same group. There's some really big stuff to consider, but ultimately companies just provide a greater level of flexibility when you're looking at tax avoidance strategies and ultimately structuring your tax affairs.

Every year you must produce a set of annual accounts. As I said, you'll have your first accounting period and then you'll have a period of 12 months from then to submit your annual accounts. At the same time you're going to need to complete a corporation tax form, which essentially calculates how much tax you have to pay. Now, most people don't know how to do this themselves. As a specialist, I suppose, you could do it, but usually you have to hire an accountant to do that. This is likely to cost you around £200 per month. It depends on the scale of your plans for your business, and whether or not that cost is too much to justify running a company. If you're looking to buy property but are only anticipating one profit or whatever, it may not stack up to go through the cost and the obligations that come with running a business.

Value Added Tax

Our next tax to consider is VAT. You may be VAT registered, especially in a trade, and particularly if you're looking at commercial properties. VAT would normally be reported quarterly, and unless you're a specialist you will have to instruct an accountant to prepare a VAT return for you.

VAT is a very complicated topic. As I said earlier, depending on which type of deal you're doing – especially when you start to get into commercial residential conversions, and particularly when you start to get into commercial property generally – VAT can be very complex. So here we're just discussing the basics of how VAT can apply in property, because a lot of people think it doesn't apply.

Obviously you have an exemption when it comes to existing residential property and whether you're leasing it or buying it, it's VAT-exempt. But there's this whole other world of property in terms of commercial property conversions, land development and residential conversions that does have a VAT element to it. You need to have a broad understanding that there are questions to be asked, albeit that you may be asking them to a specialist. So yes, VAT is very complex.

Take the subject of existing residential properties, for example. I said that whether you're buying a property that's already been built or whether you're buying in order to lease a property, know that it is subject to VAT exemption. The only distinction is new residential property. Newly-built residential property is not VAT exempt, but it is zero-rated for VAT, which is fundamentally different because it means the build costs associated with the creation of that new residential property have the ability to reclaim some of the VAT on the costs. It is an important distinction that one is exempt and one is as zero-rated for VAT. It depends on whether you develop or build on how that will impact you. Given that the rental of residential property is exempt, this fundamentally means that you cannot reclaim any VAT on your expenses associated with making that property available for rent, such as agent fees.

Commercial property may attract VAT. It depends on whether or not the building is applicable to the tax, and then there is something called a transfer of going concern (TOGC), which is a way to apply for a VAT exemption. So even if the building is opted to tax, you may be able to get a VAT exemption when you're purchasing it to avoid having to pay tax on it. However, these are complex, advanced things. You may know about them, but more than likely you will need a specialist to discuss them. Just be aware of them, especially when you're purchasing commercial premises.

Understand that there are more complexities in commercial property around VAT than you might be used to in a residential property deal. That can apply to both the purchase of the property and the ongoing rent. We have within our development business a few commercial units that we bought as part of a conversion, but we would only convert the upper floor. So we were left with the commercial properties and the bottom ones, we rent those out to businesses. Some of the buildings are opted to tax and we charge VAT. Some of them aren't opted to tax and we don't charge VAT. So you need to understand the difference between the two and manage them appropriately.

Residential rental income is VAT-exempt. Again, I brought that up earlier. But ultimately what this means is that you cannot register for VAT as a residential property investment business and you can't reclaim any VAT on costs. For instance, refurbs where your building contractors charged the entire cost inclusive of that will be tax deductible in terms of how you calculate your profits. However, you obviously can't reclaim the VAT element.

Service accommodation is where the line between commercial and residential starts to blur, especially from a VAT perspective. Serviced accommodation is a weird dynamic that exists between residential and commercial, because it's almost like a hybrid between rental and running a hotel. For example, we own a ten-bed HMO and we charge rent on a weekly basis. If those ten beds were fully occupied, we would generate more than £100,000 of rent in the year. So it would take us over the VAT threshold, meaning revenue over £85,000 per annum then requires a business to VAT register. Now, if we are renting a residential property and it's completely self-service – we don't pay the utilities, we don't we don't provide cleaners, we don't provide services to them like wi-fi and all that sort of stuff – then you can justify that it's a residential rental arrangement and not subject to the VAT rules. However, if you are servicing it, there is an argument from HMRC that that HMO is serviced accommodation and, because you're providing a service there, it's no longer strictly investment. Therefore, you have to be VAT-registered and essentially charge VAT on your rent. So the reality in that scenario is that you can't charge any more rent than you're already charging to your tenants, as you're at the market rate. That's what the market will sustain, and what you have to do is essentially just deduct VAT from your income. So essentially the £100,000 that you thought you were going to receive as revenue in the year becomes your gross number. Once VAT has been paid your net income now becomes £83,333, which represents a fairly big drop in your profits.

So there is some limitation, but it's just another thing to factor in when you're looking at potential investment opportunities. That's just an example which shows the difference between serviced accommodation and residential leasing. Various rates of VAT apply for new builds, commercial, residential, etc. So for instance, the build cost on a commercial to residential conversion project – assuming that you've got a main contractor and you've been through all the due diligence – would only be charged at 5% instead of 20%.

When you get into more complex types of property investment strategies, you need to understand the VAT rules that go along with them. We do more advanced courses where we talk about scale, specific tax implications for property investing, and tax avoidance strategies which outline how to minimise your tax obligation. There is a huge tax element to that which you need to understand, but it is very specialised – so not under the remit of this chapter. I'm just trying to give you a general flavour here of some of the VAT elements that you're going to have to consider throughout your property journey, depending on which strategy that you're going to employ.

Dividend tax

There is also dividend tax. If a company is distributing its profits to its shareholders, the share-holders receiving the cash have to pay that extra level of tax, generally as dividend tax. There are other ways to structure cash extraction from a company to minimise your tax. If you don't have any other income, you could pay yourself a salary from the company up to the amount of your tax free allowance. If you invested in the company start-up using a director's loan, there could be interest, and there are ways to manage that to maximise tax efficiency. It all just comes back to a much higher level of flexibility investing through a company than you have investing as a sole trader. If you do have a double layer of tax, you can repay 19% at the corporate level and then you have to pay tax when funds are distributed to yourself. But there are more tax strategies to minimise the effect of that.

Dividend tax is very much about what happens if you have shares in the company and the company has profits they want to pay out. They pay their corporation tax on those profits, but then you also have the right to distribute those profits to the shareholders. That distribution is done via a dividend. That dividend would have to be taxed, so it is paid by individuals on profits distributed to them by a company. Basically it's a second level of tax for shareholders. You invest into a company, pay a corporation tax, then you may also have to pay dividend tax. You have, as an individual, a tax-free allowance of £2,000 for dividends. That means you can receive up to £2,000 in the year without having to pay any dividend tax. Interestingly, you might want to include your partner in the company because then you can both receive up to £2,000 tax-free every year. It's essentially doubling the tax-free allowance, on profits being distributed by your company. So, it may be worthwhile adding your partner to the company shareholder structure.

Dividend tax reliefs are in addition to your personal tax-free allowance, where the personal income tax is £12,570 as of this financial year, 2021/22. The £2,000 dividend allowance is in additional to that income tax free allowance, but only for dividends. If you don't use your entire personal income tax allowance on other income, this can also be used as relief against dividend tax. So for instance, say your only income is £15,000 worth of dividends. In the year you could use your personal allowance of £12,570 tax-free of income tax because you have no other income. If you use that, you can also use your tax-free allowance with dividends of £2,000, giving you a total of £14,570 tax-free. This leaves only £430 of income to be taxed. If you're a high-rate taxpayer already – so you have a job, and you're earning over the £43,667 limit at a higher rate tax on the 41% you're already paying in income tax – then when you receive a dividend, it's immediately going to be taxed minus your £2,000 dividend tax-free allowance at the higher rate tax level for dividend tax. Albeit it's not 41% like income tax – it's a lower percentage – but you're still going to go straight into a higher rate band.

Dividends are taxed at a lower rate than income tax, but they are banded like income tax. The band would depend on the level of other income that you already have, and that will set you in a par-ticular band. You can find the latest dividend tax rates at www.gov.uk.

Land Building Transaction Tax

We'll now go on to the subject of stamp duty, essentially Land Building Transaction Tax (LBTT) as it's called in Scotland, though better-known as stamp duty in England.

Rates of stamp duty are banded; the rates that you must pay depends on the value of the property you are purchasing. For instance, purchasing residential property up to £145,000 is 0% rated, meaning no stamp duty applies. Thereafter, between £145,000 and £250,000 is 2%; above £250,000 up to 325,000% is 5%; above £325,000 to £750,000 is 10%. And then over £750,000 it goes up to 12%. For non-residential LBTT or commercials, the rates are different. Up to £150,000 is zero rate; beyond £150,000 to £250,000 is only at 1%, and above £250k is taxed at 5%. The rates are lower for non-residential properties than they are for residential. Those are the rates for property LBTT at the time of writing; however, they do change, and the latest rates can be checked at *www.gov.uk*. It's important to note that these are marginal tax rates, meaning that you are only taxed at the higher rate for the amount that is over the band threshold, not the entire amount of the value.

We'll look again at some examples of calculating those transactions. But as I said before, the solicitors would normally calculate those, as when you're analysing the deal it's good to understand what costs are involved. Because ultimately these are the costs of your business and the costs of the purchase. It's usually the property investor's job to minimise those costs wherever possible, and to know the terms of the type of asset that you intend to buy. In our residential portfolio, we generally don't buy premises anywhere near £145,000 and value most of our assets below the £100,000 mark. So stamp duty doesn't generally apply to any of our acquisitions or residential buy-to-let properties. There is also the additional dwelling supplement, as I said earlier, which was an extra tax brought in 2017 for any residential property that is not your principal private residence. For any qualifying property, additional dwelling supplement is charged at a flat rate of 4% in Scotland (3% in England) and is chargeable on the full amount of the transaction value. Additional dwelling supplement does not apply to commercial property or residential transactions with a value of less than £40,000. So, for additional dwellings we're only talking about residential property that is not your home, essentially. Obviously if you're investing through a company, because you can't have a home through your company, the whole purchase price is charged at 4%. So if it's a £200,000 house you're buying, then you're going to have to pay a rate of 4% on it. The one get-out clause is that if the property is worth less than £40,000, you are exempt from this – and there are properties on the market for under £40,000. On a lot of REWD Group investments you'll see that we bought them at just under the £40,000 mark, and the value will rise to maybe £65,000 to £70,000 once the development's been done. You know, there's a reason why that's the perfect dynamic, because generally you usually get the highest yields on those types of properties, but you don't have to pay that extra fee additional dwelling supplement of 4% of the transaction value. It's a significant number, and if you can avoid it then obviously it's in your interest to do so.

EXAMPLE 3: You are buying a residential property for a price of £300,000 in Scotland. This property is not your principal residence. What is your total stamp duty tax bill:

LBTT
0 - £1450,000 @ 0% = 0
£145,001 - £250,000 @ 2% = £2,099.98
£250,001 - £300,000 @ 5% = £2,499.95
Total LBT = £4,599.93

Additional Dwelling Supplement would also be chargeable in this example:

ADS = £300,000 x 4% = £12,000

Total Stamp Duty = £16,599.94

Multiple dwellings relief
In residential property, there is a tax relief called multiple dwellings relief which is a complicated subject and really for more advanced tax teachings. Simply put, multiple dwellings relief effectively means that if you're buying more properties – if you are buying more than one property in a linked transaction – you wont be charged stamp duty based on the entire

transaction value; allowance will be made for the fact there are multiple properties involved.

If you are buying six or more properties in one transaction it becomes a commercial transaction, which means you can avoid a significant amount of tax, especially as Additional Dwelling Supplement will no longer apply to the transaction. It's essentially like if you're buying a portfolio: you could avoid the Additional Dwelling Supplement because it's deemed to be a commercial transaction when you when you buy multiple properties. That also affects the rates of stamp duty because you go into a non-residential property, so there's a whole multiple dwellings calculation that needs to be done. We're not going to talk about that topic here; this is just to cover the basics.

Inheritance tax

Inheritance tax is a tax that people don't like to talk about. They don't want to think about their own mortality. They don't want to think about facing their own death. But, as you know, we've always been about generational wealth. It's much more about the legacy that we're leaving for our kids and family going forward, so inheritance tax planning is really important. You can do a lot at the front end to manage it, but the important thing is not to ignore it. Don't avoid the subject, because it can be very costly for your family going forward if you're not willing to think about this stuff at the front end.

Just to understand what I mean by this tax, it's a tax on your estate when you die. 40% of the value of your estate is taxed. Yes, you heard me right! The figure is 40% – and it's a straight 40% – but the only thing you do have is a couple of exemptions. Everyone gets a tax-free exemption of £325,000. So, the first £325,000 of your estate is not taxed. You also have £175,000 of residential residence exemption. For example, if you have a house that's maybe worth £200,000 and that's part of your estate, you can apply for £175,000 not to be taxed. So ultimately, combine these two – assuming you do have a residence within your estate – and you can go up to £500,000 of that estate's value being tax-free. Everything beyond that will be taxed at 40%. So it is a significant tax and, if you have a lot of assets – if you generate wealth in your lifetime – you need to plan ahead. If you've set up a business for a massive scale and property, and you know you want to you want to scale up significantly, then you have to start thinking about business in the front end.

There are so many ways and so many different strategies to mitigate inheritance tax, again outwith the scope of an introduction to property tax. All we're doing is introducing you to the concept of inheritance tax here. But just know that it's not an inevitable tax, and there are ways to manage it. As I said before, companies have a lot more flexibility in how you can arrange things to protect them from these types of taxes in the long term. We do cover some of that stuff in some of our more advanced courses, so just be aware of that.

Pensions, property and tax

This next subject is to give you a flavour of what you can do beyond the realms of the normal systems that people work with. Pensions, property and tax – how do those three things come together, and how can you use them to your benefit?

Pension funds can be used to invest in property. That's the first, most fundamental thing to understand. That pension funds can be used to invest in property. Now, what most people understand is that they can set up a type of pension that would allow them to buy a commercial property. That's quite widely known. So you can invest directly and with pension funds into commercial properties. Residential properties are a more complex issue, but there are strategies to allow you to use your pension funds to invest in residential property as well. A lot of people will say you can't do that, and that may be very true in terms of a direct relationship. However, there are ways to invest those funds indirectly into property and indeed through real estate investment trusts (REIT). Many pension funds invest directly in real estate on a much bigger scale. So, you know, it's not impossible and there are ways to do it, but this kind of topic will be covered in more detail in a future book.

Obviously, the benefits of that pension environment apply – especially, for instance, if you are buying a commercial property to rent out for the long term. You wouldn't have to pay tax on the profits that you make, because those profits are within your pension fund. Annually, you can contribute up to £40,000 to your pension and not have to pay tax on that income. So, for instance, if you earn £80,000 in the year then you're going to be a higher rate taxpayer, because everything over £43,667 is taxed at 41%. If you want to avoid having to pay tax at that 41%, everything over £43,667 that you've earned in that year can be contributed to your pension and you won't have to pay any tax on that money as it will go into your pension. You get the tax relief on that, so you won't have to pay the 41% on it.

Once you've contributed to your pension and you can access those pension funds, you can then use those pension funds to invest into property. That is a massive benefit, and yet a lot of people don't know about that. Obviously if you're making pension contributions through your work, that counts towards a £40,000 allowance, so you must understand how much you've made there before you can see what other additional contributions you can make. There's really no tax benefit beyond the £40,000, so it's not necessarily that you're interested in more than that. Corporate profits can also avoid tax via pension contributions. There are also ways to manage and avoid paying corporate tax so that you contribute money to your pension. Again, this can be a complex and more advanced strategy, so it tends to be something that we teach at an advanced level.

I just want you to be aware in this introduction that these things are out there and available to you, and there's so much that you can do with a pension: pension funds to minimise tax and maximise the benefit that your business can gain from your pension funds. There are so many tax avoidance strategies which use pensions. So it's something that's worth investigating further. And if you go forward on your property journey, as you start to advance your knowledge then that is a big area to focus on, because it can massively accelerate your growth. That's been one of the key areas that have led to the serious growth of Real Estate Wealth Development, because we've used these pension strategies effectively.

Income and cash extraction

If you operate your property business through a company, then this topic of how to extract cash from that business tax efficiently will be of great interest to you. You will remember we said earlier in this chapter that companies have two levels of tax; corporation tax, and then a second tax when you extract cash personally, mainly dividends tax. This second level of tax isn't inevitable, and you can be very efficient in the way that you extract cash from a company. You know, we talk about dividends and you immediately think about a salary from the company which is subject to income tax. It depends on your personal circumstances, what you're trying to achieve, and what your long-term goals are. But ultimately, this is an area that you really should get guidance on. Don't just take money out of the company and think that you can worry about the tax implications of that later. You want to take the money out of the company in the best, most tax-efficient way possible based on your personal circumstances. Ideally this is where your accountant should be adding the value, especially if you're a high-rate tax-payer on your main employment and you're already paying maximum tax on your income.

One of the best ways that we recommend to a lot of people is how you manage your initial investment into the company. So if you put money in as a director's loan, the company still owes it back to you. It's not equity you've put into the company – it's just a loan. You can charge interest on that, so a certain amount of interest can be received by yourself tax-free, and moreover the interest payment is tax deductible for the company. When the company pays you that loan back, it's not subject to tax because it's just a repayment or a loan. If you had put our initial investment in as equity, however, there would be profit distribution, and dividend tax would be payable. Those are things to think about. But ultimately, the point really with this is that you must put a plan in place. Talk about it with your accountant, and discuss how best to structure cash extraction – especially if you've got a company.

If you're invested as an individual, there's not a lot you can do about it. You're going to have to try and minimise your tax with as many tax-deductible expenses as is legally possible. But you must pay your tax annually. And that's where, as a company, whilst you must pay corporation tax based on your profits, this second layer of tax may not have to be paid if you don't need to extract the funds from the company and you chose instead to reinvest those funds. If you do want to extract the funds, there are multiple ways that you can do it to try and minimise your tax liability, depending on your personal circumstances. So there is important tax planning to be done there, and that's something that your accountant should be able to guide you through.

Working with accountants

If you have a company, you're going to have to prepare a set of accounts annually. You must prepare a tax return, and to do that you're going to need an accountant – unless you are an accountant, of course, in which case you probably wouldn't be reading this section! But you're going to have to prepare a set of accounts, possibly even as a sole trader, depending on the complexity of your business and the level of property and income, etc. It may just be easier to prepare a set of accounts for your property investing activities or your property trading activities.

I think the important thing to mention about choosing an accountant is that you need to make sure that they are a specialist in property. Because, as a specialist subject, many accountants don't see themselves as tax planners – they just see themselves as tax compliance experts. So they're really just looking at making sure that your accounts are correct. They won't challenge any of the norms. They won't look at any sort of serious tax avoidance strategy, and they won't question things to a higher degree to try and minimise your tax. Literally they will just prepare your accounts in the easiest, most plain vanilla, almost HMRC-benefiting way. So you need to be very careful with your choice of accountant. You want to fully understand the implications of the key differences between property investing and property trading. It could cost you a lot in tax, so consider your plans carefully. We had to change fairly quickly and regroup because we almost paid at least an extra £15,000 in tax that we didn't need to. So get to know some of the important strategies involved in property tax, and make sure that the accountant you're considering comes recommended. Always ensure that they have other clients they can point to in the property industry before you pick an accountant.

● ● ●

Some final thoughts

It's important you understand the basics on property tax. We've given you an overview of some of the key taxes and key implications. As I see it, once you pick a strategy that you want to focus on then get more detail on the property tax implications of that specific strategy. When we do our advanced courses on buy-to-let at massive scale, we talk about property tax implications for buy-to-let investment but also tax avoidance strategies for buy-to-let to minimise your tax on the front end for commercial residential strategies. It would be the same for any other strategy that you want to follow; know the specific tax avoidance strategies that are available, and some general ones as well. You know, pension investment startegies work well no matter what you're investing.

So, understand the basics and maybe even some of the more advanced tax avoidance strategies, just so you can question accountants and make sure that they're delivering on what they need to. You know, this isn't about becoming a tax specialist or a tax expert, but rather making sure that the guys that are working for you know what they're talking about. The only way you can do that is by having a broad understanding of it. It's key to understand tax basics. You can lose all your profit without the right structure in place from the start. I think we've demonstrated that through our discussion of Section 24. You must get educated. You've taken the first step by doing this introduction of property tax, to give you a broad overview. That's a great start.

You should seek specific mentorship on your chosen property strategy, or at least the one you want to follow. Actually, there's no harm in looking at different strategies, but it's best to focus your time on one of them to begin with. Once you've chosen that topic, try to get as much mentorship as you can from people who are in the industry – people that you know, and who can offer guidance not just on the tax side of things or corporate structure, but more broadly. Why not take advantage of any mentorship that's available with professionals, where you can get recommendations from anybody that you're working with? Make sure that there are people within the industry who are also working with those people. They can give you good references.

The final thing to consider – and I hope I've made this clear throughout this presentation – is that understanding tax is fundamental. It's a foundational element. You need to understand it before you even get started. It's too late to leave it to the end of your first year, when you need to submit your finances and you realise you've not structured yourself in the right way. You're going to be hit with a big tax bill, and by then there's nothing you can do about it. Now is the time to sort that all out before you get property investing in a big way.

This has been an introduction to property tax. As I said at the start, please familiarise yourself with the type of taxes that you're likely to see as a property investor, and we wish you all the best with your investment strategies.

REWD Group management on location at existing and renovated properties throughout Scotland. (Images Copyright © Sara Amelia Photography, all rights reserved.)

Chapter Five

Due Diligence

Conar Tracey

WELCOME to the next chapter of *Fast-Track to Property Millions*. I've designed this chapter to equip you with all the tools necessary to correctly analyse a potential investment opportunity, identify any issues, limit the risks and create an accurate budget that will increase the probability of a positive outcome. By getting comfortable with the process of gathering evidence to support your investment decisions, you will have better results as a property investor and will commit to opportunities faster and with much more confidence that will ultimately support your growth.

Geographical location/area

Having the ability to assess any location in great detail – even if you've never heard of it before – could turn a dead end into a deal. Some of the key questions you must ask yourself are as follows:

- What kind of properties are in the area?
- Who is likely to occupy the kind of property you're considering?
- Are there good transport links and local amenities?
- Can your power team manage a property in this location?
- Is there a demand for what you're looking to offer to the market in this area?

Don't limit yourself to a specific geographical area purely because you're comfortable with it or you know it. Learn how to correctly assess a location and you can eliminate this 'goldmine area' concept. Not considering opportunities in all areas only has one outcome – limited growth. Build a team that can support you on a larger scale and optimise the skills they have wherever the deal exists.

A key consideration to make note of is that some lenders will actually remove certain locations from their list of 'approved areas'. Usually this has been a case of where the bank overleveraged themselves in a specific location when the market was strong, and they ended up getting burnt further down the line. Aberdeen is a prime example of this, where in 2015 – as the market peaked – everyone could only see the market in the Granite City continuing to grow. But unfortunately it's one of the rare places where the property market actually correlates with another commodity – in this case, oil – and when the oil industry took a hit, so did the property market in Aberdeen. Always check with your mortgage broker or directly with the lender that they will definitely lend in the location you're considering investing in. Oh – and to prevent yourself getting burnt by buying in a location at the wrong time – do your research and run analysis on the number of properties available on the open market and how long they are taking to sell.

This quick calculation can give you a brief understanding of the strength of the market:

- Go to Rightmove or the main advertising platform for properties in that area
- Search properties for sale within one mile of the location you're looking at
- Click the filter that says 'show sold/under offer'
- Then simply work out how many properties are currently for sale compared to how many are currently sold or under offer and calculate that as a percentage

For example, if there are 20 properties for sale and 10 of them are sold/under offer, that means that 50% of properties in this area have sold which demonstrates a good demand. Typically, a good rule of thumb is that anything above 40% demonstrates strength in the market in terms of demand. If it's less than 20%, demand is slow and it should trigger a red flag to ensure you consider an aggressive price.

Home Reports (Scotland)

Everything we talk about in this book applies to the property market in the UK; however, there is no hiding the fact that our core business is focused on Scotland. Not just because we live there, but also because there is an abundance of opportunities in Scotland with significantly higher returns than alternative locations in the UK. With that being said, there are certain things that are only relevant to the property market in Scotland, and I did debate with myself whether to include this in the book or not. But I feel it's important for everyone to understand how the Scottish system works, because it genuinely is a fantastic place for investment and you will be hard-pushed to find better returns anywhere else in the UK.

A Home Report is a survey that is a legal requirement for property owners who wish to sell their property on the open market. This includes sticking a sign in the window saying 'FOR SALE'! It is not legally required if you agree a private sale where the property has never been advertised or promoted as being for sale.

Home Reports are divided into four sections:

- **Single Survey**

    The single survey section of the home report is essentially like an MOT on a car. The surveyor will apply a grading level to sub-categories to rate the condition of the property – 1 is equivalent to a pass, 2 would be like an advisory on an MOT, and 3 would be a failure as it's something that requires immediate attention. It also includes details of construction type, any alterations that have been made, age of the property, heating system, etc. All relevant information that you will need to determine if a lender will actually lend on that property.

- **Energy Performance Certificate (EPC)**

    Exactly what it says on the tin. This section provides an assessment of the current energy efficiency of the property. Very important if you're considering BTL as your investment strategy, as legislation states that all properties must have a minimum D rating in order to be compliant. It also provides an internal size of the property which is really useful to use when looking at comparable sales evidence. You can find a property's EPC in Scotland by using *www.scottishepcregister.org.uk.*

- **Mortgage Valuation**

  This section is probably the area that most people are concerned about. It's where the surveyor will advise the banks what they feel the property is currently worth and apply a value. A bank will base all of their decisions regarding how much of a loan they will give you off of this figure and, if you agree to purchase for more than this valuation, the extra cash will need to come from yourself. They will also apply a reinstatement value, which is essentially the figure you need to provide to your insurer.

- **Property Questionnaire**

  Provides information such as how long the current owner has owned the property, what Council Tax band the property comes under, who the utilities provider is, who the factors are (if applicable), and also if there have been any alterations made to the property or if there are any works scheduled to the building.

Home Reports can be a very useful tool to extract information, but I must highlight that these are produced by surveyors and their opinions of the property are what is documented. You may have another surveyor visit the same property and assess it very differently, so it's important that you extract the information from it but that you don't rely solely on the Home Report. Run your own analysis and find evidence to support your conclusion.

Viewings

Where possible, it would be beneficial for you or a trusted contact to view the property you are considering. A lot of the time if you're fully systemised and operating based on where the deals arrive, you need to rely on alternative sources of information as opposed to a physical viewing. Use photographs, video tours, Google Maps and surveys.

Key factors to maximise the benefit of viewings:

- Always prepare for the viewing and take a checklist. Make sure you have reviewed all information before you view, and make note of specific areas of concern that you want to check out further. Ensure you have a look at the local area on Google Maps and understand the local area before you go. For example, there shouldn't be a surprise that the property is next to a prison if you've checked it out in advance!
- Take photographs and videos for your own reference. People will always try and hide the bad parts when selling!
- Take a trusted tradesmen or builder with you if possible.
- Trust your instincts. If something seems off, explore it further. Ask questions or have a professional review for peace of mind.
- Get a good look at the externals and the expensive internal parts such as kitchen, bathroom, heating system, electrics, etc. These are going to be the areas that make or break a deal, as they will be the most expensive part of any refurbishment.

Comparables
Understanding how to anticipate the value of a property is critical. You absolutely will not be successful if you cannot do this accurately. If you don't know what something is worth and have evidence to support the value, you cannot buy it. Simple as that.

- Use property portals that will allow you to gather data to provide accurate information to estimate the value of a property.
- Rightmove price comparison report is one of the best tools I use when carrying out my due diligence process. I'm baffled at the amount of 'professionals' in the industry that don't know this report exists. It gives you full information on all the properties currently on the market for sale, properties that have been recently removed from the market, previous sold prices, properties for rent and a link to Google Maps of the area – all on one report!

- Learn to navigate all of the property platforms such as Rightmove, Zoopla, OnTheMarket, etc., to build a clear picture of what a property will be worth so that you can deduct all the costs of purchase and refurbishment, add the profit margin you want to make and deduct from the end value to produce the price you must pay for that property to make it a good deal for you.

End Value: £100,000

Refurbishment & Running Costs: £30,000
Buying & Selling Costs: £5,000

Desired Profit: £10,000

EV £100,000 – RRC £30,000 – BSC £5,000 – DP £10,000 = **£55,000 maximum purchase price.**

Using the method above gives you a clear starting point for negotiation and clearly identifies that if you can negotiate and secure below £55,000, you've got yourself a great deal.

An effective way to run detailed and consistent financial analysis is to use a deal calculator with prepopulated formulas that allow you to complete this process much more efficiently. You can download the quick deal calculator we created for running analysis on potential BTL deals by going to **www.makemoneyfromproperty.co.uk** – simply input the date based on the numbers of the deal and the criteria you want to set and voila. Financial performance analysis in seconds: you just need to make sure the information you input into the formula is accurate. If you say the property is worth £100k when it's actually only worth £80k, it's not going to pan out the same way as the spreadsheet in real life!

Become a property detective

Correct due diligence is genuinely the most important step within the process, in my opinion. There are so many sources of information available to you online these days that you can literally deep dive into everything to find the important details you're looking for. If you can master the art of due diligence and find out everything there is to know about a deal – and do so quickly – there will be no nasty surprises, and you can commit to the deal in record breaking time with no hesitations. It's actually pretty addictive once you get into it; if you've ever fancied yourself as a detective or private investigator, this part of the process will be right up your street! (Pardon the property pun.)

Key sources of information:

- *www.rightmove.co.uk*
- *www.zoopla.co.uk*
- *www.onthemarket.com*
- *www.scottishepcregister.org.uk*
- *www.propertyfactorregister.gov.scot/PropertyFactorRegister*
- *www.openrent.co.uk*
- *www.lha-direct.voa.gov.uk*
- *www.google.co.uk/maps*
- *www.earth.google.com/web*
- *www.scotlis.ros.gov.uk*
- *www.gov.uk/government/organisations/companies-house*

A selection of examples showing residential home refurbishments under-taken by the REWD Group.

Chapter Six

Finance

Laurie Duncan

G ENUINELY, this is my favourite topic of all the different things we teach. I love finance, mostly just because of the endless things you can do when you know how to use it – and there are many, many different types of finance. Combining these is a game changer, and we wouldn't be doing all of the different things that we are doing now if it wasn't for our creative thinking around finance. So I'm really excited about this section of the book, and I really hope you enjoy it.

Please take note, one of the biggest realisations that we ever had was that there is unlimited money everywhere. There is never a time where finance should ever be a stumbling block. It should never be a barrier to moving forward, because there is just so much money everywhere. And anything that you want to acquire, you just need to go out and get it. We would love to get your feedback, where you tell us about all the awesome deals you'll be doing after learning all the education that's to be found in this chapter.

Types of finance

Let's get down to finance. There are lots of different types of finance. I'm going to talk you through some of the finance solutions that are out there. I guess some may be more obvious than others. Firstly, high street banks. These are banks that you will find traditionally on the high street, though maybe not so much anymore. Generally, you still find these guys based around the high street, though. We're talking about places like the Bank of Scotland, which is part of the Lloyds Group. Lloyds now includes Lloyds, Halifax and Bank of Scotland. Then you've got the RBS, which also includes NatWest and Ulster Bank. There is the HSBC, Santander, Nationwide, and others. This is literally just a handful of these high street banks. But I want you to understand the category of high street banks and realise the kind of benefits of working with them, and equally the limitations.

We have a relationship with Bank of Scotland, for example. They are our bank of choice. We have contact with the bank manager, so we have a one-on-one personal relationship. Working with them is very good when it comes to getting things done. You can just phone the guy and he will take care of things for you. There's none of that endless call centre bullshit that so many of the other banks seem to operate by these days. When it comes to lending with these types of banks though, you'll get better rates of interest from working with these guys, but it's unlikely they're going to lend to you if you don't have any company structure. You will likely have a lower LTV, which means you will have to put more money in upfront to buy the deal. Or if you're refinancing, you'll need to leave more equity in.

For example, at time of writing, Bank of Scotland's LTV ('Loan to Value') is about 65%. It might be say 60% for HSBC, or 50% for Santander when it comes to a portfolio lend. As far as I'm aware, they still focus on individual residential buy-to-let single purchases – that type of thing. You can get access to these types of deals, these types of mortgage products through your mortgage broker. That also includes TMW (The Mortgage Works), which you may or may not have heard about depending on what kind of level you're set up for. I think you can only take a loan for up to six or eight properties before you need to start looking elsewhere for other solutions. So, high street banks: a very basic take, but the rates can be good or bad depending on what kind of stage in your journey you're at. They offer lower interest rates generally, but equally lower LTVs.

The next batch of lenders I'll mention are specialist buy-to-let mortgage lenders, but you may also have heard these referred to as the 'challenger banks'. There are different levels of challenger banks, and these particular guys here are more kind of entry-level challenger banks. And what I mean by that is they will support you if you have a limited company and you're operating your business that way. Now, again, all of these companies have their own different types: their criteria, different loan values, different interest rates, a lot of restricted criteria as well. In terms of their type: the house, the size, the council, the number of levels and the postcode – these are all different restrictions considered by these guys. But if you're buying as a limited company and you're going via a mortgage broker looking for buy-to-let, lending on a normal residential buy-to-let but just as a company, then these are the types of guys that you're going to come across.

Next we have TMW, which is The Mortgage Works – part of Nationwide. And then there's TML, which is The Mortgage Lender. There's also Kensington and LendInvest. Now, that list is not exhaustive; it's just to give you an idea of the names that your mortgage broker is going to put forward to you if you're still buying single units. You might be just getting started, and these guys are good to deal with when you're in phase one. Be aware that there's a lot of admin as you're going through your refinancing process. There's a lot of paperwork and a lot of signatures that are required. There are a lot of documents to fill in and file, though most of them you can do electronically now. So make sure that you've got access to a copier/scanner. They are absolutely essential for dealing with all this paperwork, because if you don't have one, you'll be messing about trying to find one and that can really delay your applications.

You want to be able to act effectively and efficiently when you're going through these processes, because you can also get stung at the very last minute. Deals can fall apart, refinancing can fall apart. You need to start all over again. Then it can be maybe another eight weeks from that point; you've maybe already been in the process for seven weeks, then the lender pulls the plug on you. There are a lot of different reasons why these lenders will pull the plug. But just for the sake of awareness, these types of challenger banks or specialist buy-to-let lenders are the guys that lend to you as a company, because the high street banks I was talking about before are unlikely to want to lend to a company – or if they do, it would need to be at a certain scale in terms of the number of properties, asset value and also equity position. Because your LTV is going to be lower with high street banks, you will get higher LTV from challenger banks for specialist buy-to-let products from them. But again, you're paying higher interest rates usually depending on your LTV. It's currently around 4% APR for these types of guys.

Assets and liabilities

Now when it comes to finance, you also have your own liquid cash. Interestingly, this is something that we are asked quite a lot. What do I do if I'm sitting on liquid cash? People really limit themselves by their own liquid cash position. So even if you've got a couple of hundred thousand – say £250,000 or something like that – you could go ahead and buy maybe five units at £50,000 each. Something like that. But that being said, you're not going to continue to expand with that strategy – what we usually see with people is if they have their own liquid cash, they might need to use it. You might have a refinance go bad, you might have a refurb, you might need to put more money in. It might go over budget. There are lots of different reasons as to why you might need to tap into some kind of cash buffer. So just be aware that you shouldn't be using your own money to buy properties. Ultimately, you should be using other people's money. And whether that's the high street banks, the challenger banks or some of the other methods that we're going to talk about a bit further on in this presentation, you shouldn't be using your own cash to purchase your properties.

The main thing about it is, you can't scale massively. Whether you only want five units, ten units, twenty units... whatever it is, you can't scale up and you can't scale rapidly unless you use OPM – by which I mean, 'other people's money'. But if you've got your own liquid cash and you want to use it, by all means use it. It's pointless just sitting in the bank. However, it probably makes sense for you to have a buffer zone, just in case something comes up unexpectedly. So ask yourself the question, how much cash are you sitting on and what can it do for you? Whether that is buying more properties, or it's for a refurb, or it's covering some fees, or it's maybe contributing towards a purchase. Maybe if you're buying a property for £50,000 and you've got £40,000 from an investor, for example, you may need to cover that £10,000 yourself. So think about how much cash you're sitting on and be aware of what you're spending that cash on if you're spending it. One of the biggest hurdles when we were getting started was to keep spending money on assets. It's a good thing if you can do that, right? But what I mean is, you don't want to be spending money on liabilities if you can avoid it, because liabilities take money from your pocket. However, the resulting profits can put money in your pocket and the more you do, the more assets you buy, the more cash for your investments, and the bigger your business becomes.

It's very tempting. Naturally it's tempting, because you deserve it. You've worked hard. You should spend your money how you want to. But ultimately, if you're just buying liabilities, you're wasting your money. It's going to be different for everyone, but you want to get to a point where the assets that you've built up can pay for your liabilities comfortably, because we are always going to have liabilities, right? Most of us want a fancy house and a nice car. Your house isn't an asset, by the way. It could be, if and when you sell it – if you make a profit, then it's an asset. Otherwise it's a liability until that point. Don't get confused by that. We all want the nice house, the nice car, all the holidays... but you want to make sure you get to a point where your asset position and cash flow allows you to pay for all that. Take note of this stuff; then you can live your life of abundance, which is what we all want for you.

One book I would recommend is *Rich Dad, Poor Dad*. Read it, because that's the catalyst to every successful investor's journey. It massively changed my life, and it's changed the way we think. The story that they put across is excellent, and I've never heard anyone say a bad word about this book. It's only ever positive stuff. That is quite interesting, actually, because Robert Kiyosaki – the guy who wrote it – initially created a game called *Cash Flow 101*. It was all about teaching people how to manage their cash flow, buy investments and sell stocks... and all that type of stuff. But then nobody was buying the game. So he wrote this book called *Rich Dad, Poor Dad* which told the story. Then everybody bought the book. Check out that fundamental book – you really must, must read or listen to it.

So buy assets, not liabilities. I've mentioned that already. But if you are buying the liabilities, like I said, then pay for it using the cash flow from your assets. We talked about the buffer zone, and that buffer zone value is going to be different for everyone. You don't necessarily have to have one. You don't need your own money. But if you've got some liquid cash, you could use it wisely.

Home equity and mortgage repayments

Now, the subject of home equity. I've done this myself. It can be a great strategy. You can borrow money against your own home at one of the lowest interest rates out there; currently at the end of 2021 it's among the lowest that have been recorded. Interest rates on your own home can be around 75% LTV at approximately 2% APR, or maybe less. So you can borrow money at 2% APR if you've extracted it from your home. Now I don't know anywhere else you can borrow money at that kind of level. Using bridging finance, you could pay 1.25% per month; that's versus 2% APR in this example rate. So your home equity, if you've got any, is an excellent way to access liquid cash from your own home.

One of the biggest mistakes that everybody makes – and I've done this in the past as well – back when I was 30, I was aggressively trying to pay off my mortgage. I was trying to pay it down, trying to get mortgage-free by the time I was a certain age. I soon realised that I might pay off my mortgage, but what difference was that going to make to my life? The amount of cash I was having to put away to aggressively drive down this balance was significant, and it was impacting on my lifestyle because of the amount of money I was putting into the house, reducing the mortgage. I never had disposable income to go and live off, so it's a really interesting thing that everybody wants to clear off their mortgages – myself included. At some level I think it's just what we're taught; like get a job, buy a house, clear your mortgage, be mortgage free, live free. Well, the reality is that you're still in the rat race. Even if you've paid off your mortgage, you might still hate your job. So paying off the mortgage isn't really going to get you anywhere.

But back to the point about cash extraction from your home equity. You can really use that to your advantage. So buy more assets with the liquid cash that your equity position releases. Then, if you're recycling your cash properly – like we teach you how you do – then you're only using the cash short-term. If we build up an asset base and you want to pay off your mortgage, you can get that mortgage paid off, but use the cash in the interim to build up your asset base. I mentioned that it can provide access to the cheapest lending, and you can't get cheaper than say 2% APR. So at the highest leverage you can get up to maybe 90% to 95% or something like that on your own home, whereas currently you can get up to 80% as the highest rate of LTV on buy-to-let mortgages. You might get 85% somewhere, but for most of the lenders it's around 75%. On investments against your own home, it can be much higher. So, what we're trying to get you to do is think about things differently.

Some of the things we're talking about here might be changing your perspective on finance, your mortgage and your home equity position. We want you to think like an investor, which is why you're here. You wouldn't have bought this book if you didn't want to think like an investor! So, you have a £100,000 mortgage on a £200,000 house, which means your loan to value is 50%. So, you've got £100,000-worth of equity. And in this example, currently you're on a 15 year term and you have a mortgage cost of £650 a month, and that's capital and interest rates. On buy-to-let it's a bit different. Most people would operate on an interest-only basis on buy-to-let. So now, if you were to increase your borrowing from 50% LTV to 85% LTV, that would mean your new mortgage would be £170,000. This would result in a net cash release of £70,000. Right? That £70,000 is the difference between £170,000, which is your new loan, and £100,000, which was your original loan.

By doing this refinance you can have £70,000 liquid cash in your bank ready to build your asset base. Your debt values has increased from £100,000 up to £170,000. You're also doing this over 20 years now in terms of your repayment profile, compared to the original 15 years in this example. So then your monthly mortgage payments go up from £650 a month to £840 a month. That's an extra £190 per month that you need to find, and you need to factor that in. A lot of people would be concerned about that, but if you use the £70,000 liquid cash to buy five buy-to-let properties, as in this example, what we're seeing is that if you're buying properties at £50,000 and you're buying at a purchase price of £50,000 per flat, then each time you buy a flat at £50,000 you'll need around £14,000 cash to put into that purchase. That's based on a 25% mortgage, which would be £12,500 at a rate of 4%. It's 4% in Scotland and it's 3% in England currently, plus legal fees.

So, for the net cash flow per property generally, we talk about £250 per month per property. The cash flow is equal to rental income less mortgage interest, less estate letting agency fee, less insurance. This means perhaps £250 to £300 per month per property, and in this example we're using £250. So the net cash flow is then going to be £1,250 per month. Because the income is now £1,250 and you've got your mortgage to pay £840 per month, if you use a buy-to-let strategy and come to pay off your home mortgage, that'll take care of itself. Not only that, but you still have over £400 a month of liquid cash by refinancing your own house and by using that liquid cash wisely to buy other investment properties.

Now, this is gold, all right? Yet it's confusing for a lot of people. A lot of people don't understand this, but if you invest wisely then extracting the capital from your house and increasing your monthly mortgage payments can actually be a very good thing. It can pay for itself. Not only that, but you've still got your own home that's worth £200,000 and you've got five buy-to-let properties that are worth £50,000 each. That's another £250,000. So your asset value goes up from £200,000 to £450,000. And remember, you will achieve capital growth on your total asset value. The more assets you have, the higher this capital growth is going to be over time. Make sense? I love that stuff.

Loans and security

Now, on the subject of bank loans. A lot of people don't think you can use bank loans to buy properties, but you can – again as long as you know what you're doing. If you log into your banking app right now, what you would see is: 'Welcome – would you like a bank loan? Click here to see your options and you can do the pre-checks. We can already tell you if you're going to be approved or not before you even apply, so you don't have to affect your credit score.' Now, anybody can log into their own banking app and should see this type of information. If not, then you can go out and try various websites like MoneySupermarket.com, MoneySavingExpert.com, CompareTheMarket.com, and others like that. On there, you can see all the different types of bank loans. Based on your name and your address information, these websites will usually tell you automatically what you can expect to get in terms of a loan on value as well as the interest rate you would need to pay and over what kind of timescale.

It's worth checking, just to be aware of how much you can get. Do you want to try a bank in the first place? Because bank loans are different. Remember, you need to factor in the monthly repayments, and they could be a bit more significant because you have to clear them and then there's a cap on interest, maybe over a five year period. So you need be aware of that. But how much of a loan can you get? How much of a loan can your mates get, and what are the rates? Because again, these personal loans can be cheap, cheap money. You can have anything from 3% up to maybe 7% or 8%, depending on the lender, depending on whether it's secured or unsecured. But it's quite cheap money as long as you can factor in the monthly repayment, and then it's a decent way of getting some liquid cash into your bank account, secured or unsecured.

If you're not sure about security, we teach a bit about this in our courses. We're actually going into more detail about security but, basically, if in simple terms you have your own home and you have a mortgage on your own home, if you don't pay the interest to the bank then the bank will repossess your home. So the home is the security for the bank. If you're borrowing on an unsecured basis, there is no security. That's the concept of security in simple terms. So, for bank loans, really you can go onto a website, go click, click, click and then you're done – you can have the money in your bank account more or less immediately.

It's incredible, depending on your objectives and depending on if this is right for you or not – we're not here to advise on that. We're just making you aware of these different options of security and finance. Maybe that's the right way for you? So check with your bank about commercial lending. This is what we do. What we do is work with specialist commercial lenders because of the scale and the complexity of some of our transactions. It's necessary for us to deal with commercial lenders. Now, I mentioned earlier in the presentation that we also have a relationship with a high street bank, the Bank of Scotland, and the Bank of Scotland could be included in a commercial lending setup in this kind of case.

Commercial lending

Once you get past maybe something like 20 properties, something like that, the high street banks, the specialist buy-to-let lenders and the challenger banks all start to have some issues with your size. They don't like you having too many properties or having too much debt, or whatever it might be. So then we step into the world of commercial lending, and commercial lending is a lot more flexible. You don't have the same types of restrictions as you do with any of the high street banks or the challenger banks. It's a much more personal relationship; when there are issues, you can discuss them, you can talk them through, and it's much more of a business relationship. Commercial lenders want to help you to try and get deals over the line.

We've got some very decent, established relationships with our key lending partners and, again, they've been fundamental to our growth. We wouldn't be doing what we are now if it wasn't for the support of our commercial lenders. I want to just give you an outline about some of the commercial lenders you might come across now. Some of them could also be in the specialist buy-to-let lender or challenger bank category. There is a bit of crossover between all of these lenders. But again, depending on what stage you are at, it might make more sense for you to look at the likes of these commercial lenders that we mention here rather than the challenger banks. If you've got less than ten properties, or you're only getting started or whatever, the challenger banks are usually fine.

You might have heard some of these names before: companies like Shawbrooke, Selina Advance, Redwood Bank and the Cambridge Building Society. This is just a brief sample, and the list is not exhaustive. These guys will still have criteria, but they are somewhat more relaxed than others. Take, for example, Selina. If you have equity in your home with Selina, you they will get you a pre-approved funding line, but they will also take a second charge over the asset. So if you've got a house worth £500,000 and you've got a £200,000 mortgage on the property that you're paying off with your residential mortgage lender – probably one of the high street banks on your own home – then Celina will allow you to basically borrow, say, another £150,000. So your second charge could go up to £400,000 in this example, which would be on 80% LTV. I don't know if that LTV is strictly accurate; this is just an example to explain how it works. So if you then needed £150,000 liquid cash, they will already have pre-approved you on a bridging loan facility. So it's quite expensive, but it allows you to borrow money immediately should you find something that you want to go and buy. You can just call them up and say that you need that cash, and they will go click, click, click. Within a couple of days, the money will be in the bank, and then you'll want to go and use that £150,000 to do whatever it is that you want to do with it. So really it's quite an interesting process.

There are a lot of different types of products out there, but be wary if you're dealing with mortgage brokers – whoever you choose to use – as not all mortgage brokers really understand things to the same degree that we do. They're used to dealing just in usually residential matters, and the scope of that isn't so technical. We know a lot of this stuff because we're involved in it. But I just wouldn't expect the mortgage brokers to know these products the way that we do because of our experience. Mortgage brokers' experience is very different. They're usually just reading off a criteria sheet, and a lot of times they can get it wrong. We don't really use brokers anymore. Instead, we go direct to the banks. I mentioned we have direct banking commercial relationships. I have key partners, and there we just find the solution rather than going through brokers. We prefer to deal directly, but again, depending on the stage you're at, you'll probably be using mortgage brokers yourself. So just be wary of what information they feed you, because it might not be as accurate as it could be.

Bridging loans

The bridging loans I mentioned earlier can be quite expensive, and we're going to just talk a bit now about bridging loans and how they are different from the other types of loan that we've talked about so far. Some of the names that you might see in the marketplace are lending on anything; so you can arrange a loan and you can secure against that. Bear in mind, these are secured loans, not unsecured loans. So they will take securities, and they might take personal guarantees too. They might take bond and floating charges depending on the structure of the deal, but the rates are a lot higher compared to other rates that you can get with the likes of the challenger banks, the high street banks, the commercial lenders – and some of these guys are involved in commercial lending as well. Again, there's a bit of crossover, but if you pay only half a percent per month, that's the equivalent of a 6% APR rate. Just multiply by 12 to get the difference between the monthly rate over 12 months, which is the annual percentage rate, or APR. That's quite a cheap bridging rate at half a per-cent per month, and they do go up – even above 1.5% to 2% per month.

It could be dependent on the loan, the value, the security, the cir-cumstance. But in this example, we're looking at 0.5% up to 1.5% per month. Now if you're paying one and a half percent per month, and you have that loan for 12 months, then you're going to be paying 18% APR – a very high interest rate. Not only that, but this is just the interest rate analysis. You can have entry fees, you can have exit fees, and you can have broker fees. You need to pay all the bank's legal fees too, as well as survey fees, so that total cost of finance can be really quite expensive. You need to factor all that into the deals. You can use bridging funds to secure against most types of properties. But what you'll find is if you're looking for them to lend against a property with four walls and no roof, they will very likely reduce the loan to value. So, you may only get say 50% LTV against that type of acquisition. All that means is that you need to put in more money upfront. Don't be distracted by that, because if you're working with private investors or if you've got a bank loan for other cash, you can combine all these types of things to acquire properties if you want them. Don't be limited, because finance should not be a bur-den; I said that at the start of the chapter.

You can buy what you want. Really you just need to be creative and structure it correctly from a financial perspective. I mentioned earlier about the extra fees we need to think about. So the first is the actual cash advance that you will receive. If you're going to borrow £100,000 gross, by the time they deduct all the fees and everything else and the interest – and whatever else you might have to factor into that loan – now you'll be paying them back £100,000 because that's the loan that they've given to you. But the net cash advance may only be £75,000. So basically the cash that you get is £75,000, but you still pay them back £100,000. It's just a very rough illustration. Whoever you're dealing with, they'll keep you right. I would advise you to be very, very aware of these terms, because they're very different from a normal property loan. They are commonly used, but are just quite expensive ventures.

Joint ventures

We are very, very lucky to be working with some fantastic people. In October 2020, with our joint venture SPVs – Special Purpose Vehicles – together we acquired 82 units in Lanarkshire with an asset value of £3.7 million, a gross monthly rental income of £35,000, and a net cash flow of £20,000 before maintenance costs, voids and arrears. It was a significant portfolio acquisition for REWD Group and our joint venture partners, as at the time we only had 40 or so properties. This allowed us to more than treble our portfolio size and our asset value in just this one transaction, albeit split between three different joint ventures. So that acquisition has allowed us to grow massively.

We all have to bring something to the table in a joint venture situation. So you've got to ask yourself, can you help each other? The way we structure things at REWD Group, we provide our own joint venture agreement which is between us and our joint venture partners. The way we structure things is that the joint venture partner brings the commitment and the cash, and we organise everything else. That's the way we're structured, and we can help the joint venture partner with their aspirations to be involved in property, property investment, and to own a property buy-to-let portfolio. They can help us with acquiring more and more units, and it allows us both to grow. So that's how we structure things. It's not to say that that's how everybody should structure things. You will have your own reasons for structuring things the way that you do, but can you help each other – and how can you achieve some mutual benefit for everyone involved?

That might be you plus one other. It might be you plus two of us. In fact, it might be you plus three of us – who knows? But whatever middle ground you can find between the people you're working with, if you can both help each other then that's a beautiful thing for a joint venture, and it can allow you to do a lot more than you could just do on your own. Even if you look at us when we started, effectively we were a joint venture, and it was obvious to us early on that working together was so much more powerful than working alone. Definitely we would not be doing what we are now if it wasn't for us working collaboratively with each other. Each was helping the other out, and we bring different values and different experiences to our business.

So have a think about that for your own business, and consider what you and others might bring to your venture. Do you have deals but no money, or do you have money but no deals? It can be very common. These things can be as simple or as complex as you want, but really you want to write things down for clarity. You want to make sure everybody's aligned. You want to have something written up and signed by whoever is involved, in case you need to refer back in terms of duties, obligations and responsibilities for down the line. That can and will happen. So as important as it is to have things written down, think about who's bringing what to the table, where the strengths are, and be open and honest about your weaknesses. If somebody else is stronger in a particular area than you are, allow them to manage control of that area of the joint venture. But definitely write things down. Don't just do things alone, because that can get messy at that early stage. But look, don't just get into a business with any Tom, Dick or Harry. A lot of people come and want a joint venture with us. Obviously it's an attractive scenario, but we will only do business with – or get into business with – people that we know, love and trust. Because if we do not know you, love you and trust you, then why would we why would we ever get into business with you?

A fundamental aspect of our partners' journey as well is to ensure that they've done the right training, because we go into a lot of detail about all the intricacies of the way everything works through our joint venture agreement – the way we acquire properties – and it's important for anyone that we have any business with to fully understand that. For anyone that is serious about a joint venture with us and who wants to make that proposal, we insist that you do the training first to ensure you understand what you're getting into. Look, you might find that it's not going to be right for you. It might not be right for us. But if it's right for both of us, that could be the start of a beautiful thing.

Credit cards and private investors

If you don't get the cash, I find that credit cards are one of my favourite strategies within finance. I use this myself, and it's awesome. You can buy properties using credit cards, despite something like 99.9% of people telling you otherwise. Because many people will say that you cannot do a lot of the different things I'm talking about here. People will tell you that you cannot do what I'm telling you that you can do. But credit cards are very, very effective – and not just *your* credit cards. It could be *your friend's* credit cards. It could be *your partner's* credit. You can use credit in so many different ways.

I've made the point here to name-check MoneySupermarket.com, because it's my favourite website to analyse the credit potential on credit cards before I actually make any commitment. Now, to put this into personal perspective, I've got around £60,000-worth of credit on credit cards in terms of available credit. And my wife Emma has about the same. So at any one time, we can click a few buttons and then we have £120,000 in the bank, ready to go and do whatever it is that we want to do with whatever it is that we want to acquire. It's a very powerful position to be in, obviously. Knowing your way around the website, knowing how to extract that credit if you want – that's something that you can see value in, and it's a really powerful thing.

And you've got to ask yourself, do you like what is essentially unlimited free money? Do you? I do, and I guess you do too, otherwise you wouldn't be reading this book, right? But there is lots of unlimited free money to be had out there on credit cards. My favourite thing about credit cards is that you can borrow at 0%! I go into a bit more detail about that in one of our more advanced level courses, but if you have a balance transfer credit card that you can transfer at 0% APR for two years, there's no interest to pay. The fee for doing the transfer is 0%, so for two years you can have no cost on that money. It's just insane. Now obviously you need to transfer a balance into that card from another credit balance. Knowing your way around credit cards can massively increase the amount of available cash that you have. But then, it's not just you; we have we have investors that use this strategy with us as well, and they borrow money on credit cards too.

We pay 10% on unsecured loans. So they're benefiting by 10% APR interest, and when they lend money to us at 10% APR, they are borrowing at 0% APR. In other words, they've got free money for their holiday, or to pay for the car, or to pay for whatever they want to use that money for. But again, don't limit yourself by your own credit or your partner's credit. Think about your wider circle and who would be interested in working with you on this basis. I like having lots of unlimited free money, and I believe you do too. So do you believe you can buy property using a credit card? Well, it's free money, and you can buy it for nothing. There might be some minimal fees that you need to factor in, but yes, you can borrow at 0%. You can have multiple credit cards, all at a 0% rate that can cost you nothing apart from some of these small fees, which is usually like a 3% transaction fee or something like that. But for two years, you can have use of that cash at 0%. So how much cash can you bring in, and how many properties can you acquire with it? Now, you might even use that cash as deposit cash rather than buying something outright, but it brings a lot of flexibility should you choose to use this method.

Think about your wider circle. How many people do you know that have good credit and don't even use it? Maybe they don't even have a credit card, and their credit is immaculate. So if you educate them on the strategy and it works for them as well as working for you, this could be something that would be very useful. It's something that we have used in the past. It's something we still use to this day. And in all honesty, it's fantastic. It's very quick and very cheap, and it can be massively beneficial to your growth. Some of us are very lucky to have the bank of mum and dad, but some of us don't have that opportunity. So this is just another potential finance solution for you.

If you don't ask you don't get, so bear this in mind. You ask yourself, are your folks loaded? Do they have lots of cash? Do they have some spare cash? Could they help out – and would they want to help out? If they have their own liquid cash, then whether it's your mum or dad or an aunt or uncle somewhere, you should be talking to them about your vision, your aspirations, your goals, your dreams. If they want to support you, you might just find that they have some extra cash available to support you on this journey you're going on.

As long as you know what you're doing, as long as you use it wisely, this is an excellent, excellent method of securing some finance. Do you have friends who are loaded if your mum and dad aren't loaded? Who is the rich friend that they know? Perhaps they may already be involved in property, and they might want to get involved in a joint venture with you. If you're not talking about these things with all these people, then how can they possibly know about how to get involved with you? Some might want to lend to you. They may want to do a joint venture with you, or they may not be interested at all. But ask the question because, if you don't ask, you don't get.

Then you've got the credit card strategy to bring in as well. How is their credit? Most folks like mums and dads have good credit, though that's a separate issue. But if you're trying to convince them to take out credit cards and then do money transfers and balance transfers, lending you the money, it's up to you to give the sales pitch around that and see if that's something that you can use and they're willing to do. The more people that you tap into that are interested in this type of strategy, the more you're going to benefit. Ultimately, all these things have the capability to finance your dreams. It's really a question of how badly you really want to achieve those goals. Are you going to do whatever it takes? Are you going to have these awkward conversations to get what you want? Or are you going to sit on the side-lines and not take any action? Because if that's the case, you're not going to grow. That's the long and the short of it.

You will tend to find, however, that your mums and dads, aunties and uncles, grandmas and grandpas... they will want to support you. They would love to support you as best they could. Being a recent father myself now, my son Daniel is just one year old, and I have an undying passion and love for Daniel. I cannot wait to see him grow up and get involved. I definitely want to support him. My mum and dad – his granny and grandpa – and Emma's mum and dad, they would all of course love to support him too because he is just so special to all of us. So you've got to ask yourself about how you approach your own family and friends, because there are people out there who love you dearly. They will care about you, will want to see you succeed, and will love the fact that you're making business moves. They will love the fact that you're energetic, driven, charismatic, passionate – all of those things.

If you don't ask them, then you're never going to know. The likelihood is that is there will be people out there who would love to support you. So you really want to tap in to that network and ask yourself how you can incentivise them to help you. Because they might just loan you some money, they might even give you some money – whatever it might be. But equally, they might want to loan you the money and you can pay them back. You can pay them whatever interest you agree. We generally use 6% APR for secure loans and 10% APR for unsecured loans. You can agree whatever it is that you want with these people, but if you incentivise them somehow, then it might just be the turning point for them. Maybe the family sweetens the deal; they help to get a deal over the line for you. It can literally be gold. These people have unlimited money. So ask yourself, who do you know that has some cash sitting in the bank? Really, if you put a focus on private investors and working with people that will work with you, you can consider all of these different strategies that we're talking about here. If you put a focus on it, you can literally buy whatever you want.

No, we can't get over 200 properties in two and a half years. We can't get five or six commercial residential projects on the go at the one time – we can't do all of that. We can't run the building company, we can't do any of these things without focus on bringing more cash into the business at all times. Now, I cannot emphasise this enough. This has been the game changer for us and everything that we're doing. If it wasn't for private investors, we wouldn't be able to buy these multiple things and keep growing. Really, you need to get comfortable being uncomfortable about these conversations. They are the conversations you're going to need to have, because they provide unlimited money, unlimited growth potential, unlimited cash flow. You need to get at that goal and go after it passionately. Even in your little circle in your home town or amongst your family and your friends, you need to build a network and talk about all these different things.

Think about social media posts and publicity, all that type of stuff. You can find more and more investors to buy into all these different methods. Even in your own circle, I guarantee you will have people that will have money in the bank who will be very happy to at least discuss the options with you because they are getting nothing from the bank. Zero. So you can provide a very attractive solution for them by loaning the money for 12 months or a couple of years, whatever it's going to be. You pay them the interest once every six months, 12 months, at the end of the 24 month period – whatever you agree – it's a commercial arrangement between you (the borrower) and them (the lender).

Working with private investors is going to be a game-changer for you. You need to tap into this. I guarantee you will sell your idea very well, but you definitely need to understand the securities and the risks. The securities in particular, like I mentioned earlier, can be a bit more detailed. There are a lot of different types of securities: the first charge, second charge, bond and floating charge and personal guarantees... various different things. You need to understand these securities and risks. You need to make sure that you're conveying that to whoever you talk to, as you have to present this information to them. But look, these private investors do not need to have pinstripe suits, top hats and canes – that type of thing. It's just a case of asking yourself, who do you know that may have some money in the bank that could support your growth?

Convey the securities and risks clearly. If it's secured, the lawyers will be involved anyway. Make sure you also factor in anti-money laundering regulations and all the compliance stuff you need to do, because there is legislation around this type of thing. Make sure you understand these issues, and make sure you convey them properly to your investors as well. But what is it that you want to offer? I've given some examples of what *we* offer, but of course some of the commercial projects are a bit different, and depending on the motives, your own plans could be different as well. At the end of the day, it's your business. Think about what you want to offer and then put that across to your private investors. But really, if you put a focus on this, it can change your life massively. It has done for us.

Always remember to seek professional consultation as you need it, for all aspects of your property business, to ensure you remain within the legislation at all times. What we are writing in this book is not advice – we are simply teling our story of what has worked for us, and what may also work for you.

Pensions

Now, the wonderful world of pensions. Pensions are a controversial topic generally, and many people tell you that you can't buy residential property with pension funds. We live in a different world. Of course, there is legislation in place that we must adhere to. Nobody's doing anything untoward, but you definitely can buy residential property with pension funds. There are different methods of doing it. Now we work with SSAS pensions, which stands for 'small self-administered scheme'. It is important to point out that we are not pensions advisors. We're not advising you on anything here to do with pensions. We're just making you aware of what we do, and explaining how it works in our business. You must have a sponsor to set up a self-administered personal pension, and the SSAS is, for us, just a bit more flexible and less restrictive.

You can only do certain things with those assets. You can buy commercial property, you can buy land, you can loan those funds to your own business and help your business grow. You can loan the funds to external businesses on your own commercial terms, to allow those businesses to grow and pay your interest back as well. So it's a very useful vehicle and, I guess, one of the other benefits of the SSAS is that you can order or combine all of your pension funds into this one location. So whether it's a separate SSAS, if you have multiple pensions – because you've maybe moved companies over the years – you may have £100,000 here and £50,000 there, so wherever you can combine all of these funds into the one SSAS it just gives you a larger pot of cash to then go to work and do whatever it is that you want to do.

We have a SSAS administration team that takes care of all our compliance with legislation on our behalf, and of course we pay them for that service. But our SSAS has allowed us to do a lot of different things along our growth journey. I'm not sure of what the outcome would have been if it wasn't for the SSAS and its flexibility; it's been great. We've bought commercial property, we've developed some properties with loan funds and have done a lot of different things. It's a very flexible product. So if this is new to you, check this out because it can be a very powerful thing to use. Especially if you're the owner of a business or a one-off property investor, the utilisation of assets can be very, very powerful.

Be careful who you take advice from, however. Because even if they are very experienced professional pensions advisors, they don't necessarily know the ins and outs of SSAS technicality. They might be corporate pensions advisers rather than looking at pensions from a business owner perspective. So just be very wary of that. We found through posts on social media that there's a lot of resistance and frustration around what we see regarding pensions, because many people believe that it cannot be done. Even if they are very experienced people, like the ones I'm talking about, there is reluctance. But what we do definitely *can* be done. We do it ourselves, and we continue to do it on a regular basis. In fact, we're looking at even more advanced pension products above the level of the SSAS. So form your own picture of this, speak to different people, get different feedback, and if you feel that this is something that could help you along your journey then check it out.

It definitely has helped us, but so many people out there think that you cannot access, use, or even touch a pension until retirement age. And it's just not true. We are using these funds. We're not extracting the funds, we're not spending the funds, but we are in full control of our own pension funds. Yet we use them to do different things. At every point that the pension fund is drawn on, it is always adding interest; it has its own commercial interests which continue to grow. But so many people just think that you can't do that, and it's just comes from a lack of experi-ence. It's probably bad advice from people that just don't know SSAS and don't understand it as a technical product. If you think this can help you, that's fantastic.

Summarising finance

Just to finish up the finance section of *Fast-Track to Property Millions*, you need to start thinking about which methods of finance you will choose. I've given you a lot of different types and different options here, and I want you to think about which one is right for you. One look at these many different things can show how you might use them and com-bine some of them, because the combination of these can be very powerful.

How big are you thinking? Or are you thinking that you'll just use the challenger banks or just use private investors or just use the credit card or just use a joint venture. Come on! Use them all; they are right there at your fingertips, ready for you to tap into if you take the action to move yourself towards that goal. Do you think small, or alternatively, do you think big? We always think big with our Group, and that's a huge difference compared to some of the people that we speak with. If you're thinking small then you're going to get small results. If you think big you'll get big results. So don't just use one of these methods. Use every single one of them. We do, and look at what we've managed.

Do you really want to achieve your goals? Are you going to go af-ter them, and are you're going to do whatever is necessary? Or are you going to make up bullshit excuses time after time? We hope that you will achieve your goals. How badly do you want to create that extra cash flow? What do you want it for? The house, the car, the free time – whatever it may be for you. All these finance solutions are the key to you changing your life. They are the key to achieving your goals. You really need to go and hunt them down. It's essential.

Some people look at our growth and they say it's unrealistic. Or it's not possible or it's against convention... or whatever. But we don't have an infinite magic money bag. What we have done is implement all of these financial strategies and combine them all in wonderful creative ways, always following the legislation. And we've used these financial solutions to allow us to acquire more and more properties. But we don't have any magic money solution. It doesn't exist. We have built what we've built through professional investment strategies, professional finance strategies, professional acquisition strategies, and all the things that I've shared with you in this chapter. They are what we use in our business on a day-to-day basis.

So please let the thing you take away be that you can have whatever you want if you go after it and implement all of these strategies. That's very important: not just *one* of them, but *all* of them. The big question is, will you take action after reading this? Well, you should take action. So many people read the content, make all the notes, and then take no action at all. This baffles me. We are action-takers. Are you? Because if you're not, you're going nowhere. If you are, I'm very excited for you and I can't wait to see what's next for you.

I really hope you've enjoyed the finance chapter, and that the content has been helpful for you. I cannot wait to hear about all the people that go off and take all these amazing actions and achieve all these amazing things, and ultimately make the changes in the lives that they desire. That's why you bought this book in the first place. Please take some action. Please make a move, and let us know how you get on.

REWD Group management overseeing property refurbishment and renovations. (Images Copyright © Sara Amelia Photography, all rights reserved.)

Chapter Seven

Understanding the Numbers

Alex Robertson

T HIS next section in *Fast-Track to Property Millions* is all about
teaching you to understand the numbers. At the end of this
course, the objective is that you're going to understand some of
the key metrics that we use in analysing property investment opportunities. We're going to look at some real examples where there are various
strategies that we have employed, and we're going to give a few examples
of deals that we've actually done. More broadly, we will give an overview of all the various different things that are involved: the strategies
and the numbers associated with those types of strategies. We will look
at how to analyse them, how to understand them, and how to compare
them against other types of investments.

Really, this is all about giving you the tools to understand some of
the financial jargon that comes along with the numbers. That should help
you in understanding general investment analysis and appreciating what
makes a good deal on any type of investment, because the idea is that we
can stack up the returns and some of the key metrics against other types
of investment – not just property. So, it does go bit more broadly beyond
just property investing.

Calculating key metrics

We're going to start in the first section with an overview of a comprehensive example that allows us to calculate all the key metrics. And then

in the second section, we're going to look at numbers associated with various types of strategies we've covered. An earlier chapter of this book outlined all the various different strategies that are available for property investment. Here, we're instead going to look at some of the numbers for those specific types of strategies. Where REWD Group actively employ the strategy, there'll be an actual example of a deal we have done to illustrate that strategy. It will be a pure example of what the numbers look like, and some of the things that you need to consider when you calculate your numbers. That should give you a good overview of how to calculate the financial aspects of property investing.

Let's get started. Profit investing numbers can be a little bit scary if you've just moved into investment. You may find some of the terminology is quite confusing. You may be scared by analysing the numbers, or just not really understanding what they mean. So we aim to clear all of that up for you through the course of this chapter. We want to make sure that by the end of this section, you are very clear on what they mean – not only how to calculate these key investment strategies, but also what they mean at the other end. This will give you the opportunity to then be able to create your own investment criteria, your own targets, for each one of these metrics. Ultimately, it's not about any one individual metric; it's about looking at it holistically with all the various different metrics, and making a holistic decision of whether or not the investment stacks up. You also need to understand some of the key costs involved. If you're analysing the deal, it's not enough to say, 'Okay, this is the income.' You need to understand what costs you're going to accumulate through the process of employing that particular property strategy. We're going to give you a good flavour of some of the key costs associated with that. Probably, if you do a web search, you can find a property investment calculator and some very structured strategies, and all that's good to think about as well.

There really is no substitute for understanding what your cost drivers are, and just being able to lay out the calculation yourself. We're going to look at several examples and work through the calculations with you, and we're considering each one of these examples. Like I said, when we do the strategy then you're going to have a lot of real life examples that we've done.

Just before we get into any live examples, I should say that I like to cover mortgages, because I'm going to be referring to mortgages quite a bit during the process of some of these key calculations. It's important that you understand the fundamentals of mortgage calculations and how we are calculating these things, and some of the basic options that we take. Fundamentally there are two different types of mortgage. There's one that covers the original capital amount plus the interest cost, which is what we call a repayment mortgage, and there's an interest-only mortgage where all your payments are solely for the interest costs of the borrowed capital. A repayment mortgage payment will be assumed over a period where you're going to pay down the capital as well as covering the interest costs. When we're looking at property investing, we're only generally looking at mortgages on an interest-only basis. There's a whole host of good reasons for that. Ultimately, it's just the most comparable way to assess the investment. Now, I'm not going to go into that in any more detail here. But like I say, there's a whole host of reasons why we look at interest only. That's the way that we're going to be analysing the numbers going forward for the rest of this presentation.

When we talk about LTV, or loan to value, it refers to the percentage of the loan that the bank will give you based on the value of that property. So an example could be a property that's worth £100,000; if you get a 75% LTV, it means you'll get a £75,000 loan against your £100,000 purchase. That's all we mean by LTV. We use that terminology regularly, and generally it is used for the purposes of refinance; we assume that the bank will give you 75% of the loan, which is 75% based on the value of the property. The only time we would maybe see a smaller LTV would be in the instance of an HMO house, which I'll talk about a little bit later in the chapter.

The interest payments that we're going to assume on our mortgage calculations can be anything from 2.5% to 7% on a standard mortgage, depending on which lender and depending on the way that you invest. So if you invest through a limited company, generally interest rates are higher versus whether you invest through your own name as a sole trader.

Although for a sole trader the rates will be lower, you're likely to pay much more tax. So it's a balance; if you invest through a company structure, generally your finance cost will be between 4% to 4.5%.

You need to understand when you're looking at a safe investment option. When we're talking about mortgages, you need to understand what your likely interest rate is going to be when you finance any particular property investment. A broker can help you understand what products are available. But the other thing to mention is that the lender that you use may also be highly dependent on the property and the specifics of the property, because so many lenders don't even consider certain types of property. They don't like certain types of postcodes, which can limit your options if you are looking to invest there for any reason.

Looking at repayment mortgages? As I mentioned, that's not something that we consider in this chapter; we're looking at interest-only mortgages. They are very easy to calculate by just applying the percentage to the overall loan value. If you need to calculate a repayment mortgage, it's more complicated, but you can do that using a mortgage calculator. Some websites have a very easy, quick mortgage calculator that will tell you what the monthly payments are. Given the parameters for any repayment mortgage arrangement fees apply on the loan, they're usually about 1-2% generally. The mortgage company will add that 1-2% to the loan to cover the arrangement fees, so its not necessarily a cost you have to cover with cash upfront.

Early termination fees apply between two to five years, so it depends on the type of product that you pick. But if you want to terminate the mortgage before the end of the the introductory rate that you've been given, there will be a fee associated with that and it's normally between 2% to 5% of the loan value.

Working example

In order to explain the key metrics, we're going to do an example. Now, the reason why we're using a buy-to-let example is because it gives us a more comprehensive view of all the key metrics that we that we use within property. Now, we may not apply all of these to every type of strategy, and we'll cover that when we look at specific examples for each type of strategy.

This is a broad example where we can start to try and teach you the key metrics. It's based on a buy-to-let example. So, you're buying the property you purchased, with the intention of holding it long term, renting it out and benefiting from the rental income and capital growth over a period.

In this example that we're going to do the numbers on, you're buying a property for £50,000; you buy it with cash. You're not using a mortgage at acquisition stage, based on the condition of the property being poor. The rental income is £500 PCM. (PCM just means per calendar month.) If you are to renovate that property to a decent standard, you would be able to increase the rate to £575 per calendar month, and that is standard.

The property needs, in order to achieve its maximum market value, around £5,000 of work done to it. That won't be an extension. It could be about decorations and carpets; no significant investment, probably mostly cosmetic at that level. So, once you've done this £5,000 of work, you've done your cosmetic refurb and it looks all nice and shiny. Now that you're at the higher rate of valuation, it's reasonable to expect that because you got a good price when you bought it and because you've added value through the refurb that when a valuer comes in to reassess the property, they're going to value it at around about £65,000.

So, this is the basis of a buy-to-let investment example. Let's go through some of the key metrics based on these numbers. The first metric we're going to be looking at is cash for net cash. Now before we do this, I just want to mention that we're looking at initially the base numbers, which is the numbers on acquisition numbers at the time that we buy it, which is the purchase price of £50,000 range or £500 in your account every month, etc. We're going to be analysing key metrics based on the base numbers. Then we'll reanalyse these key metrics after refinance. We'll see the difference once you've done the refurb, once you've taken on the new mortgage, once you've got the higher rents etc., and then we'll compare the two. So, we're looking at the base numbers.

Net cash flow

Net cash flow, or cash flow – let's talk about what that means. Essentially, it's the monthly rental income, less the direct costs of providing that rental property. Direct costs, as per industry standard, include mortgage interest, the cost of your letting agent's fee (assuming of course that you have an agent managing the property on your behalf) and finally landlord's insurance. Agent fees for managing your properties would normally charge at least 10% of rental income. Landlord's insurance is a fixed value per month per property that you would normally pay. Now, there are other costs you may think about – things like council tax, utilities, all those sorts of things. Those are things where the tenant pays the cost directly. Obviously if the property's vacant, there might be a level of cost, although council tax exemptions usually apply for vacant properties in that instance depending on where you live. The Direct costs we have mentioned, however, are the core costs. We don't include maintenance within this calculation; we will talk more about why that is soon. You will find when people are talking about their cash flow as an industry standard, they consistently only look at Direct costs when calculating the number. Essentially this becomes an indication of profit; an indication of the amount of cash that you're going to receive in your bank every month. It's a strong indicator of profit.

In terms of Net cash flow, we normally look for about £250 per calendar month per property. That's a good broad basis of a reasonably decent investment, given the standard investment level of our buy-to-lets are around £40,000 to £80,000. We don't have many £300,000 houses, for example, and I will explain why that is shortly. So, it's a good basis for us to start with, and what we will learn throughout the course of this chapter is that it's about being able to take a holistic view of all the key metrics and avoid over-focus on one element of the investment.

We'll talk a bit more about the holistic view towards the end. But £250 is a good metric of where you want to be in terms of net cash flow. So, why don't we like £300,000 houses? Well, lets talk about interest rate risk. If you've got £250 per calendar month coming from a £300,000 property where you have a £250,000 loan against that, that is very different to having a £250 per month cash flow on a £50,000 property that has a £40,000 loan on it. For example, if interest rates go up 1% on your £250,000 loan, that's going to wipe out your entire cash flow. On the other hand, if they go up by 1% on your £40,000 loan on a smaller property, it's only going to have a marginal effect on your cash flow (£33 per month). Understanding how these things affect your overall investment is important. That's why we don't go for high-value properties; we normally stick towards the lower end of the market.

Maintenance costs

I mentioned earlier that we don't include maintenance costs in this calculation of cash flow. Why is that? Well, there are quite a few reasons why we don't. Firstly, maintenance costs can vary significantly by property. Say you've got a property that's of a certain age and it's going to require significantly more maintenance. Surely that's an important factor to be included within your investment, and ultimately it will depend on what type of strategy you're using with them, generally. For the property we're talking about, we need a strategy. So the intent to buy, refurbish, rent and refinance the property is a strategy, as is to renovate the property and then refinance, and extract as much of your cash as possible. So under that instance it sort of levels the playing field in terms of maintenance, because the intent in the long term is that you have a property that is fully renovated up to a good standard and maintenance costs are going to be broadly similar going forward.

Estimating the maintenance costs can be very subjective. People can have vastly different views on what the monthly average maintenance costs could be. Unlike Agent fees or mortgage interest, maintenance doesn't have a reliable percentage to apply; there's no market rate for maintenance, because it's generally determined by the property or tenant type.

You know, some people may estimate 5% of rent as a maintenance costs (on the low end). Some people may say 10%. Some people may be at 3%. It's too subjective. If you're someone who's a bit of a penny-pincher when it comes to the everyday stuff and, when a tenant asks for something, you say no – perhaps you've got some damage on the property and they want to fix it, and you don't do it, or you only deal with high priority, dangerous types of maintenance and you're not maintaining the property passionately, effectively or to the standard that it should be at. At the other end of the scale, you may have someone who wants to keep the property in very high-quality condition as well, and who spends a lot more on maintenance. It depends on the individual and the way that they manage the buy-to-let business. Ultimately there is little value in including a provision for maintenance in your investment calculations.

Finally, and this this is one that is actually quite important from a tax perspective: maintenance is not always an expense. Maintenance to a certain classification can be a refurb, it can be innovation, it can be improvement of the property. This would mean ultimately a capital expense. For instance, if you buy a property that doesn't have a kitchen, it would equate to capital because of improvement; the property didn't have it before, or it wasn't rentable in that situation. It's going to improve the property. That wasn't technically maintenance in that instance; it was it was capital expenditure. There can be a fine line between what's improving the property in capital expenditure and what's maintaining the property. There are types of maintenance that could be classified in either bracket. So it's not always a given that maintenance, or your view of maintenance, is definitely an expense. That's another reason why we don't include it within that cash flow calculation, because it's not necessarily fitting into an expense bracket.

Cash flow

Going back to our example, let's run the calculation for this specific example based on the acquisition numbers. The base numbers are for cash flow. So you're going to start with your rental income, which is £500. We said this was the rent prior to any reasonable mortgage interest; you bought with cash in this example. So, there are no mortgage interest costs to consider. You have an Agent cost, which is assumed to be 11% – a standard level. That's £55 per calendar month, and insurance costs £10 per property every month. Now, the insurance can cost from £7 per property, and some of the portfolio was up to £15 per property. So generally, a standard outlay is going to be between £7 to £15 per month, depending on what you want. And your insurer is just providing standard landlord insurance. If you start on things like loss of rental etc., it can get very expensive. But a standard landlord insurance coverage with general cover will be at that level. So, in this instance we're talking about £435 of net cash for now. As we said before, there are still other costs to come off that, but we don't factor them in within the industry view of net cash flow. Also important to mention is that it's a pre-tax profit. So, your tax will also play a part in your actual final net profit after tax.

Gross yield

The next formula that we're going to look at is gross yield. What do we mean by gross? Your gross yield is a percentage return on investment before expenses. But generally, we are looking for 10%+ gross, which is used as standard throughout the industry. What do we mean by the investment before expenses? It means that we're just looking at the gross rent. We're not deducting mortgage interest, the agents' fees or the insurance. We're just looking at the gross income divided by the value of the property.

Why do we want to do this? Because ultimately, it's not always just the gross income before we adopt the investment and expenses. That's why it's compatible across multiple property investments. The cost of capital can change the cost that you must pay for a mortgage. It can change significantly. Some of the expenses that you have can change substantially. If you're invested as an individual, maybe you're only paying 2.5% or as low as 2% interest on your buy-to-let mortgage. If you invest through a company, it can be 4.5% or more. If you've got a unique property, where it's hard to find a lender that will lend on it, you might be paying upwards of 7% for a specialist lender. That can change dramatically across investment, unless this eliminates all of that and just gives a high-level, compatible view of things.

A lot of time when people are talking about yield, if you watch TV programmes like *Homes Under the Hammer*, generally they will be talking about gross yield, because their interest is in what your rental income is in relation to the price of the property. There's an industry standard calculation, so you're looking for 10%+ across your entire portfolio. At REWD our average gross yield is 10%. That is a very important figure to remember. It's harder to get those yields when you get into very expensive property down in London, for example, because the rent prices don't go up proportionally in relation to the value of the property and you can find the yields start to get very, very low. But then, they're focused more on the capital growth of the asset rather than the gross yield rental income.

The gross yield calculation is simply annual rent divided by property value. As I said, this gross yield terminology is something you'll see everywhere, and it's very easy and quick to calculate. It's always good to have these high-level quote calculations that you can do. So, let's look at gross yield – gross monthly rental income multiplied by 12. So, in our example, £500 per calendar month – which is our rent, which equates to £6,000 per annum then divide by £50,000 (the property value), to reach your gross yield figure of 12%. That's quite a strong yield, because it's a cheap property at £50,000 and we've got a good, solid rent.

Net yield

So how does net yield change from gross? Well, ultimately the biggest difference is that instead of looking at your gross rental income, you're looking at your net rental income –which is essentially rental income less the rental costs. As with net cash flow your rental costs would be mortgage interest, agent fees and landlord insurance. Simply put, net yield is just your net rental income divided by property price. It's less comparable than gross yield, as rental costs may vary from person to person depending on costs of capital, and their specific agency costs for example. Maybe someone pays 9% Agent fee, maybe someone pays 12%. Maybe someone manages the property themselves. All these elements could change an individuals calculation of net yield. Although this measure is less comparable as certain elements are specific to the individual, it gives you much more comprehension of your profit over the investment that you've made. It's going to give you a better understanding of your real returns. So then you can compare that with other investment vehicles, such as stocks and shares and see where might be the right place for you to be investing your money.

So, let's calculate the net yield for our examples. Net monthly cash flow times 12. So, the monthly net cash flow times 12 over the purchase price. We're £435 per calendar month, net cash, and that's because there's no mortgage. That's normally your biggest cost: mortgage interest. We have £435 times 12 which is £5,220, divided by the purchase price of the property, which was £50,000, meaning a net yield of 10.44%. Compare this level of return to 0.5% interest rate that you can get from the bank, and you can start to see why proper investment is so attractive. At the 10.44% net yield this is a really good rate of return, and that's without using that leverage. At the acquisition stage we just put in cash, we're getting a high percentage return. That is the complete return, before tax is deducted. You know, you might have other costs to consider like maintenance, etc. But it does give you a much closer understanding of the real rate of return.

Return on cash invested

Let's look at the key remaining issues. We had gross yield, which didn't include any of your costs and was just a high-level industry standard. For net yield, we have seen that factor includes some of the key costs, so it was closer to your real return for the investment. Debt leverage really is one of the most powerful tools in advancing your property journey, given the fact that we can take a relatively small deposit and leverage a large percentage of debt against the property to create an investment situation where you get the benefit of full rental income and the full capital gain, less a relatively small finance costs. Even though you've only put in a relatively small sum of money to the investment, you get most of the gains. So this metric is about understanding the return you get based on cash that you've personally invested in the property. This is what we're looking at with return on cash invested. Ultimately, that'll consider any debt, the cost of the debt, and the deduction of that from the overall investment.

When we're looking at other industry terminology for return more generally – that is, looking at a return on capital employed – that's something you'll hear a lot when you're looking at big companies and when you're looking at share investments. It's very much a term that's used to explain what they make for the overall working capital that's been employed within a company, though it's a more complicated metric and it doesn't quite fit right with property investing. With return on cash invested, we're focused more on how much cash we earn for the cash we invest. It's a more simplistic way to look at it.

This return on cash invested will give you the closest understanding of how much money in percentage terms you can make from your money in property and use that to compare against other opportunities. So, if you can make a 15% annual return on share investments and you have a 25% return on cash invested in property, the likelihood is you will be picking property as your investment vehicle. Assessing your own investments, your tax situation can change considerably. In order to avoid that complication, we generally do not include tax within any of these investment metrics.

That's a broad overview of return on cash invested. Let's consider a particular example. Say we look at only cash invested; that's the net monthly cash times 12. So we've already calculated that I was £435 per month times 12 over the total cash that you've invested within this deal. A total of £5,220 annually. The value of the property was £50,000. However, our total investment would also include all fees associated with acquisition. So, in this instance we're probably going to be looking at about 4% additional dwelling supplement, which is the extra stamp duty, which is £2,000 in this example, plus another £600 of legal fees. A total investment of £52,600. If there was a mortgage – which there is not in this case – we would be deducting the value of the mortgage from our investment, as that's not cash we had to personally invest. In this case there is no mortgage, so return on cash invested is £5,220 divided by £52,600, which is is equal to 9.9% return.

Compared with other types of investment like shares, equity, etc. 9.9% is a good return; the important point to mention here, though, is that this return does not include the capital appreciation of the property over time. That will ultimately increase your overall return for property. On the flip side, the return on cash invested doesn't include absolutely every cost; there may be costs for maintenance, and on the commercial side there might be the odd fee here and there for things like the land-lord's registration, etc. There might also be some other small-cost basics. There is also tax to consider, but on balance the return on cash invested calculation gives you a good estimate of the real return from the invest-ment to compare with other investment vehicles.

Re-calculate the formulas after refinance

Now we have completed all of the key formulas for the first example, let's look at how things would change if we were to refinance this prop-erty deal after adding value. Say we were running the strategy on the aim of refinancing and then aimed to pull out all our cash. So, we bought the property for £50,000. There were fees associated with that. We spent £5,000 on the refurb and we've waited our six months, which is what most people must do, and we're now going to take out a mortgage on it. We're going to go to our mortgage broker to get the property financed. They'll value the property and, as we said in this example, £65,000 was expected in valuation. They'll give us a loan to value over that property at about 75% of value. So, we're going to get a new arrangement; we're going to get a bundle of cash back on it, and in this example the refinance value would be £65,000 x 75% = £48,750.

What changes?

Let's have a look at that. Refinancing changes all the formulas, as I said. There is an investment increase, because we've had to put in another £5,000 for the refurb. But then, a lot of that money comes back to us when we do the refinance because we're getting this new loan based on the higher value, 75% LTV. I said at the start that the cash flow would go up to £575 per calendar month once the renovations were done. Once we get a higher quality of prop-erty, we can increase the rents. It may well now be that generally.

We also now have a mortgage, so we have to calculate the mort-gage costs. In this example, it is £163 cost per month. Now how did that calculate from the new value of £65,000, based on the values we know have already been done? A surveyor said okay to the upgrade, so the property is now worth £65,000. The bank said they'll give you a 75% loan to value, and on the new loan they're going to charge you 4% interest per annum, which we then need to bring back to a monthly amount. So £65,000 at 75% is £48,750. So that's the new loan: £48,750. The annual interest on that is 4%, so it's going to be £1,950. And we want the monthly cost, which is £162.50, or £163 if rounded up. That's just to give you an overview of how we got to that number.

Your letting agent cost is still 11% of your rent, and as rent has increased so too does your cost of agent fee. So that's gone up from £55 to £63. However, your insurance costs have stayed the same. They're unlikely to change dramatically, because effectively the cost to rebuild the property – which is usually the biggest factor on calculating your insurance cost – hasn't changed.

New Calculations

Summary of changes:
New Property Value: £65,000
New Rent: £575 PCM
New Mortgage: £48,750
New Mortgage Interest: £163 PCM

1) <u>Net Cash Flow</u> – this is monthly rent less mortgage cost, agent fee and landlord insurance = £575 (rent) - £163 (mortgage) - £63 (agent fee) - £10 (insurance) = £339 PCM.

2) <u>Gross Yield</u> – this is gross rent divided by property value = £6,900 divided by £65,000 = 10.6%. The big change in this formula's being the increased rent and the new property value post refurb.

3) <u>Net Yield</u> – net cash flow annually divided by property value = £4,068 divided by £65,000 = 6.3%. This percentage has dropped from the post refinance net yield of 9.9%. The reason for the drop is the cost of the mortgage interest. The upside of this drop in net yield is that the refinance has released cash to reinvest on more assets.

4) <u>Return of Cash Invested</u> – net cash flow divided by cash invested. Cash invested in this case needs to be calculated due to the
refinance. We originally bought everything on a cash basis of
£50,000 property plus £2,600 of purchasing fees. In addition to
this, we spent £5,000 on the refurb. However, we then received
£48,750 back from the bank on the new mortgage. So, the net
cash invested in this is £50,000 + £2,000 + £600 + £5,000 -
£48,750 = £8,850. You now only have £8,850 of your own cash
invested in this property. Return on cash invested therefore is =
£4,068 divided by £8,850 = 46%. That's a 46% percent annual
return on your investment. Now we are really starting to see the
power of the Buy, Refurb, Rent, Refinance (BRRR) model.

Infinite returns

We're going to continue with a new calculation. We're going to look at
calculation of infinite returns. What do infinite returns mean? Ultimately,
all infinite returns mean is how long until you get back the cash you have
left in the investment via the rental net cash flow. So how long is it going
to take you to recover the cash that you've left invested, which in this
example is £8,850? We just calculate the money that you've got left in the
deal. How long is it going to take you through the net cash flow from this
property to get that money back? How many months? So it's simply
£8,850 divided by the net monthly cash flow, which is £339, and in this
example it is 26 months. So another way to look at this investment is in
26 months' time, through the net cash flow you've received from renting
this property, you have no money left in the deal, so thereafter returns
are infinite.

This kind of deal is where people start to talk about 'no money
deals' and that sort of stuff. No money deals normally means that you've
used investor finance, but the broader strategy is aimed at pulling out all
of your cash and being left with a free asset which generates returns. So,
that's all people mean when they are referring to infinite returns; it's having a free asset, because you've got all your cash out of the deal. We'll
look at some examples later when we look at deals that we've done ourselves, where not only do you get all your cash out of the deal because

you've done such a good deal but you also get cash back, plus this free asset; the returns on an infinite basis.

Therefore, you know, when you hear anybody from REWD Group talking about buy-to-let, we're always going to be massively biased towards buy-to-let because you can't recreate the investment dynamic in many other investment vehicles. With strategies like flips or property sourcing you constantly have to keep doing projects to be able to generate returns. You can't just do this one-time deal and then have an asset that continually returns cash month-on-month with no involvement from you, especially when it's managed by an agent; only buy-to-let can offer that.

Example summaries

Finally, we're going to look at a summary of these examples. What we're going to be looking at is each of the key metrics: cash flow, gross yield, net yield, return on cash invested and infinite returns, which was the last one we discussed. We've got the base numbers; the original numbers. We looked on the refinance numbers just to compare them, and ultimately the point I'm trying to get across here is that no one particular metric is a silver bullet. You have to look at things holistically. And when you're trying to decide on what your investment criteria should be, you're looking at a balanced view of all of these things in the story and what they suggest.

With the base numbers, we're still looking at a relatively modest investment. You know, £435 of net cash flow per month when it's a £32,000 investment with a gross yield of 12%, which is strong. You know, as I said earlier, 10%+ is a really good wheelhouse. That's because this is a fairly cheap property at £50,000, and the rent proportionately is quite high at £500 for the month. On the initial numbers, the net yield of 10.44% is again really solid, and there's not much difference between gross and net here because we're not using a mortgage. We bought with cash, so there's not much mortgage interest to bleed out of your yield, but your return on cash investment is 9.9% which, whilst it's still strong, is not dramatically stronger than other investment vehicles.

You know, you can probably go into stocks and shares, and if you have the right market at the right time with the right company, then you may be able to achieve similar levels of result. Whether that's sustainable in the long term is a different question. You know, if you look at year-on-year returns and currency markets, you may look at a much higher return on your cash invested, but ultimately it's not massive. It's not until we get towards refinance at the heart of our broader strategy with property where the numbers start to get really cool.

Okay, so cash flow has gone down. It goes down to £339, and that's because of your mortgage interest. But that's been partially offset by an increase in rent, because you've got better property gross yields which are still above 10%. Still solid, even with that higher value on the property. Net yield at 6.3% is still a good rate. You know, 6.3% is interesting, but remember net yield does not include the debt leverage. It's only when we get to return on cash invested we see how phenomenal the impact of that leverage can be with these types of deals. 106% return on cash invested – which we often refer to as our ROCI – is phenomenal. It's a great result, especially to get all your money out of a deal in 11 months – less than a year – because we normally look for less than 24 months as a maximum.

If you can't get all your money at the front end, you know this still really does represent a great deal with these dynamics. And this is not an atypical example that we've shown you here. The important thing is to not only look at one, but to look at them holistically. You know, is your cash flow sufficient enough to avoid too much interest rate cover risk? If your interest rates go up by 1% or 2% and the net cash flows are going to be at an acceptable level, your gross yield will be at a different rate based on the industry standard. You can compare that to various different other types of property investment opportunities. Net yield is a function of gross, but it's taken at a cost. If you are making sure that your costs aren't overly burdensome, this will go down to a lower figure of 3% or 4%. You know, anything above 5% is still within a solid wheelhouse. But really the core number you're looking at, especially off the refinance, is that you're out to see how much cash you're getting back in your pocket for the cash.

That is only the cash that you've got left in the deal by the end of the refinance process. And 106% return is a no-brainer. It's a great deal on 11 months at once. And within that period of time, 11 months till all of your money is out of that deal again, to get your cash back that quickly, is fantastic.

Applying metrics to different investment types

That was a broad overview of buy-to-let. We're now going to look at how these various different metrics can be applied to other types of investments as well. This next section is really a laundry list of examples, many of which are real examples of deals we've done for each different type of property strategy that you can employ.

So just before we move on to give you examples of each of the strategies, I want to show you a bad example of buy-to-let. That is, I will show you an example of where the investment numbers just didn't stack up. This example that I'm going to take you through was was my first investment property. And it was a house I used to live in. It was a £250,000 house, and I was working abroad at the time so I decided to rent it out. I thought, okay, I'll just rent it and keep hold of it. You know, this should be a good investment. The rent that I could get from it, was £800 per month, which was just about enough to cover the mortgage, given the mortgage was a capital and interest mortgage. My plan was basic that in 20 years' time the mortgage will be paid off, I'll have a free asset, and I wouldn't have paid much towards that.

On the face of it, that all sounds good. But, when you start to look at the metrics and understand this as an investment, it becomes very clear that this wasn't a great investment at all. I'd like to talk you through why that was. I'm going to take a little bit of time to explain this example, run the numbers, show you the metrics, and explain why – on the face of it – this might have seemed like a good deal, but really it wasn't.

Let's look at that right now. We're going to do a quick example. So, as I said, my first investment property was a £250,000 house that I had bought previously. On the face of it, it seemed good because the £800 a month rent came in every month and it covered the mortgage payment. My thinking in basic terms was that over the next 20 years that mortgage is going to be paid off. You know, someone's effectively paid the mortgage every month for me, and I've got the asset. That was the basic understanding.

Now let's look at that as an investor, in investment terms. So, the price was £250,000, though at the time the mortgage that I had outstanding was around about £175,000. This means effectively the cash that I had to invest was £75,000. So, I've invested that £75,000 and the main return that I'm going to get from it is a rental income. So, as I said, the rent was £800 per calendar month. Now incidentally, the mortgage was about £850 a month, and that was a capital repayment mortgage. So not just the mortgage interest costs; it was also a capital repayment. In simple terms approximately £400 a month was interest payment, and the rest was repayment of the original debt. To calculate net cash flow on this house we are looking at £800 (rent) less £400 (interest) less £80 (Agent fee) less £25 (insurance) equals net cash flow of £295 per month.

So in reality, the cash generated every month was basically under £300. That was £300 per calendar month, which equates to £3,600 per annum. That's my return on cash invested. So I'm getting quite low return on cash invested, which would be your net cash position divided by £75,000 investment. If so, the ROCI is going to be somewhere in the region of 4.8%. It's not a horrendous investment. You know, if you take ROCI, i.e. the cash on cash return – which is an example of real returns – it doesn't look too bad. You know, if you compare it to – for instance – having £75,000 sitting in the bank earning 0.5% per annum, it's a significant return. What we need to be aware of is that I've got this big loan of £175,000 where, if interest rates start to go up, there is the risk that my net cash flow will start to disappear.

Let's look at that very quickly. Imagine interest rates go up by 1.5%. I've got a £175,000 loan, I'm already paying £400 a month of mortgage interest, and I'm going to have to pay another one and a half percent per annum on that mortgage. That equates to another £2,625 per annum or, per month, an extra £218 off my cash flow. So if I go back to this net cash position of £300 per month, it would go down from £300 to only about £82 per calendar month. So with these higher investments, you've got a much bigger interest rate risk.

If we go back to the original examples that we looked up throughout the course of this initial part of the presentation, we looked at a £50,000 value flat. You know, when you have a mortgage of around about that level and a similar cash flow – because, as I said, we're aiming for about £250 to £300 per calendar month from every property that we have – but your property is only worth £50,000 or £60,000, so you've maybe only got a £50,000 loan on it. If that interest increases by 1.5%, that's a much smaller impact. So if you take a £50,000 loan at 1.5%, that's only about a £60 change, so your interest rate risk is significantly lower. That's one of the reasons why that larger investment property wasn't a good investment.

The next thing we need to consider in analysing this bad buy-to-let example is Section 24. Now I covered this in the introduction to property tax chapter, but let's just look again at the impact of Section 24. In this example, I had invested in the property through my own name. Ultimately what that means is that I'm paying income tax on the rental income. If you look back, I've got £3,600 per annum coming in on profits from this investment. Based on the current numbers I need to pay tax, and because I'm a higher rate taxpayer – because I already had an income above the higher rate tax threshold – I'm immediately going to have to pay 41% tax on that which equates to £1,500, and that's even before the consideration of Section 24. Section 24 basically says that the mortgage interest that I used to come to that profit is no longer tax deductible. So that £400 per calendar month of mortgage interest that I have now cannot be deducted when we come into this profit. What you get instead is a 20% tax credit, and ultimately that means you're going to have to pay much more tax.

Effectively what I would have to add back into this profit is the mortgage interest. So, adding back £4,800 to my profit figure of £3,600, means a new taxable profit of £8,400 at 41%. This creates an initial tax bill of £3,400 less that 20% tax credit on the interest. You're going to get £4,800 and a 20% tax credit. This gives us a £960 tax credit which comes off the £3,400 tax bill. Effectively your net tax position now with Section 24 – keeping in mind that your tax deductibility of mortgage interest is restricted – goes up to £2,440. That is now your new tax bill. So, when you consider that we're only making £3,600 profit on this investment and we now must pay £2,440 of that profit out in tax, you're not left with very much. You're basically left with around £1,100 per annum of profit on a £75,000 investment.

I've still got £75,000, but in terms of return only about 1.5%. So to summarise, we've got a huge tax bill because I was investing through my own name at a relatively low profitability level, and a significantly high interest rate risk because the value of this property is so high. Those are some of the reasons why ultimately this property investment doesn't really stack up.

Strategy examples

The next section involves giving examples of each strategy. We're going to look through the key numbers and the calculations, of course, that kind of run through the calculations of return. We're going to run through the calculations of some of the key metrics for the various different property strategies that we've looked at. Now, if you've already read the chapter that covers property strategy, it should be very clear to you what I'm talking about when I refer to each of the strategy types. If you've not done that, then it may seem a bit less clear, but we will work through it regardless. You can always refer to what you've read once you've finished the strategy chapter.

As I said before, the next section runs through several examples where we look at the finances and the calculations for each type of strategy. If we implement the strategy at REWD Group, it will be a real example. 100% real. Just know that these are real deals that we've done over the past few years. If we don't do a strategy, it's purely an example, and I'll make that clear when we're going through each section because, as we've said previously, we don't employ all the various property strategies, although we do several of them.

As we're going through the numbers, I will apply some of the key metrics where applicable. Some of them may not be applicable for certain types of strategies. I will discuss the numbers and look at the story that the numbers tell us; that's ultimately what it's all about. What story do the numbers indicate, and how does it help us make investment decisions?

Example: Buy-to-let

The first example we're going to look at is a buy-to-let. It's by refurb, rent, and refinance. We talk about this still quite a lot, because it was one of the first deals we did. This is ultimately the deal that led to the eventual formation of REWD Group. The property was an ex-local authority 4-in-a-block, and it was a lead I got through Facebook. I remember it because it was the night before I was due to get married, and Laurie agreed to go and negotiate the deal for me because I was busy with all that wedding stuff. I told him that if he did the deal, we would split it 50-50. He did a fantastic deal for me and, at the pub that night to see that deal was done, we had £25,000 to find because that's the price that he agreed on. The next day we found a private investor during a conversation at my wedding, so that was a cool start because this was a phenomenal deal.

The source of this deal, as I mentioned, was Facebook. It was a couple who had inherited the property, and they were just looking to get rid of it quite quickly. They didn't want to deal with all the old family memories and that sort of stuff. The flat was purchased for £25,000 and the refurb cost was £7,500, and that was mostly a cosmetic refurb. We put in a new kitchen, we put in a new bathroom, and we replaced carpets and repainted. There was nothing wrong with the flat other than the costmetic stuff. When those were sorted out, the roof was fine, so it was mostly cosmetic. There was no stamp duty in this instance because it was below £40,000 (so no ADS).

In addition to the legal costs and the arrangement cost of refinance, there are some types of other costs that you're calculating here. All in all,

our total costs were £35,000 in this investment. Then, at the time of re-finance, we went to get it valued and the value came back at £65,000. The bank as standard will give you about 75% loan to value, which meant a loan of £48,750. That's the money we got back from the bank. This meant that we only had £35,000 of cash invested and the banks were giving us £48,750. It basically means we've got all of our money back, plus an additional £13,750. So we've got an extra £13,750 of cash in the bank, and we've now got a free asset that returns rent every month despite the fact that we've essentially invested nothing. We no longer have any cash invested. The monthly rent on this property is £495, which means the net cash flow is £250 per calendar month.

So, let's summarise the numbers on this investment:

1) <u>Net Cash Flow</u> – this is monthly rent less; mortgage cost, agent fee and landlord insurance = £495 (rent) - £182.50 (mortgage = £48,750 x 4.5% APR divided by 12 months) - £49.50 (agent fee) - £13 (insurance) = £250 PCM.

2) <u>Gross Yield</u> – this is gross rent divided by property value = £5,940 divided by £65,000 = 9.1%. The big change in this formula's being the increased rent and the new property value post refurb.

3) <u>Net Yield</u> – net cash flow annually divided by property value = £3,000 (£250 x 12) divided by £65,000 = 4.6%.

4) <u>Return of Cash Invested</u> – Net cash flow divided by cash invested. You have no cash invested in this property any more; the bank has repaid you and provided additional funds. We therefore call this an infinite returning asset.

Example: HMO

Rents for the HMO properties are much higher, because you rent by the room – usually per week, rather than renting the entire building as one as a single unit. So you essentially multiply the amount of rents that you can charge from this one property. If there are three beds or four beds, there are potentially three or four rents coming in, plus charges for general services. So there are additional costs that you have to consider that, as standard, the tenant would normally cover themselves within an HMO. Whilst the rent is considerably higher, it is expected to be an all-encompassing rent.

As the landlord of an HMO, you are going to have to provide cover for council tax and cleaning. You're also going to have to cover utilities and wi-fi. So the tenants will be able to benefit from wi-fi and maybe, depending on your clientele, you might want to offer Sky TV or other subscription television services. These are the sort of things that you would also have to cover, because rental by the room is usually quite a flexible arrangement.

People living in HMO properties are generally not looking to be there in the long term. For instance, they can be popular with students (normally during term-time) or maybe contractors, and again it's transient in that they are offered a job and then they leave. Your market is maybe on the lower end. With a council, it might be longer-term tenancies. If it's a professional market, then you know you're likely to see more of them in the major cities for that type of market; the properties will be more expensive. But you know, professional tenants are likely to be a little bit less transient than others might be within an HMO. There are a few things to compare with that. But generally, because of the nature of

the tenancy you have, you may have a lower level of occupancy. Thus, you're likely to have more voids than standard.

We can take on tenants that stay in our standard rentals for ten years plus, and we never have to think about another tenant for a long time. Whereas with each HMO property, someone may only be renting the room for a period of one or two or three months and then you have someone else, and then maybe a gap depending on the state of the market. In terms of our own HMO properties, we've been quite fortunate because we generally rent them to companies who are there long-term for projects. Where we're based in Grangemouth – a port town in Forth Valley, in the Central Belt of Scotland – it's mostly the contractor market. So, these are things that you need to account for when you're looking at the numbers on your HMO.

As mentioned, you're going to have a lower level of occupancy, and occupancy basically needs to be factored in when you're looking at the risk of loss to your investment. So, you get more costs, you've got less occupancy, and you've got a higher front-end investment. There are standards that you must achieve in terms of fire regulations and fire safety, and you must abide by rules and regulations (which can and will change). Councils are much more stringent on HMO, because there are more people living there than most other properties. For instance, each room would have to have a fire door instead of a regular door. It must have a lock. There can be a certain requirement for minimum space levels. If you want to have double occupancy in the room the size requirements increase, you need to have a certain number of toilets, a certain amount of cooking facilities, and so on.

There are many more boxes to be ticked with an HMO. The investment is inevitably higher on the front end. As I said before, you must consider the occupancy rates first and foremost. So, with those things in mind, let's look at an example of one of our own moves before we look at the numbers. Our most recent HMO project, which is just finished, was a restaurant that we bought at auction a couple of years ago now. Between the planning process and the refurb, you know, it was a longer project; obviously conversions can be like that. This has been a fantastic investment for us in the end, although there have been significant challenges along the way.

I think this is a good example of the numbers on an HMO project. Now, the first thing I want to point out is that we are showing the numbers based on 100% occupancy. So, please realise, if you are reviewing your own HMO numbers or if you're assessing any HMO deals, I would look to a sort of best- and worst-case scenario and occupancy to maybe understand how you can break even. What is the minimum occupancy required to break even with all the costs that you have? And then look at the best-case scenario, which is 100%. The likelihood is that you will find somewhere between those two numbers. The reason why this example is at 100% occupancy is because we've been at 100% occupancy on this HMO, and indeed our other two, for quite some time. In fact, from day one, this one has been at 100% occupancy because a company has taken on the entire property, and they've been renting out long-term for a project. So, we've been quite fortunate. But the numbers on this HMO were phenomenal even at lower occupancy rates.

We purchased this property at auction for £60,000. The price of converting this into a ten bed HMO cost around about £190,000. So, it was a significant cost to turn the empty shell of a restaurant into a ten

bedroom property, all en-suite, with a massive kitchen in the HMO. We had a total cost of around £260,000 and the market value at refinance came back at £250,000. Because these investments are highly driven by the amount of income that they can generate, it can be quite hard to value them, and generally in Scotland you get a bricks-and-mortar valuation. They're just looking at the value of the property irrespective of the amount of money they can bring in every month, which means you sometimes get quite low valuations. Because of the cost to establish these properties, the investment costs of HMOs are generally quite high. It can be hard to get a market value that's in line with the cash you've spent.

That's not the case in every market; it's probably more of an issue in Scotland than it is down south, but what quite often happens is at the end of the day is that you have quite a lot of cash left in the deal as extracting all your investment at refinance is unlikely. It's also important to know that, with HMO properties generally, you can't finance them at the same percentage LTV as a standard buy-to-let. Standard buy-to-lets may go 70%, 75% or 80% LTV, whereas for HMO they're normally as low as 60% or 65% because they're seen as a higher risk. Because we have a good relationship with a lender, we can get 70%, but that's not always normal. Over £250,000 valuation, we're able to get a 70% loan, which is £182,000. So, we have a loan of £182,000 on this property. We spent £260,000 and got £182,000 back from the bank, meaning £78,000 of cash is tied up in this deal.

Normally with buy-to-lets we're getting all of our money out, or at least in a very short period of time until we get the cash back via rental income. So, to leave some of the money in isn't something we do very often. However with the substanitial cash flow that this property generates we will recover this cash left in the deal quite quickly.

Rent on this property at 100% occupancy is £7,900 per month – with ten rooms that works out about £175 per room per week, on an average of 4.4 weeks – which takes us to £7,900 per month, and we got paid three months in advance from the company that took over the home. The mortgage interest cost is relatively low at 4.5% APR, so we're only paying £683 per month. Our agent costs are 10%, so £790 a month. As far as insurance is concerned: because it's an HMO, this is slightly higher than the standard property, but still only £55 for the month. Then we've got all the other running costs which include council tax, utility costs, wi-fi and between those we make up most of the £550 per month of other costs. In this example, we don't service the property, so all the cleaning and that sort of stuff is done by the company that leases the property. So that's not included. Let's look at the rental numbers on this property at 100% occupancy:

1) <u>Net Cash Flow</u> – this is monthly rent less: mortgage cost, agent fee and landlord insurance less other costs = £7,900 (rent) - £683 (mortgage = £182,000 x 4.5% APR divided by 12 months) - £790 (agent fee) - £55 (insurance) - other costs £550 = **£5,822 PCM**.

2) <u>Gross Yield</u> – this is gross rent divided by property value = £94,800 divided by £260,000 = **36.4%**. Be careful on this formula if your investment is higher than the value. In this instance the investment was slightly high and is a better yardstick for gross yield formula.

3) <u>Net Yield</u> – net cash flow annually divided by property value = £69,864 (£5,822 x 12) divided by £260,000 = **26.8%**.

4) <u>Return of Cash Invested</u> – Net Cash flow divided by cash left invested = £69,864 divided by £78,000 = **89%**.

5) <u>Time until infinite return</u> – Cash left in divided by monthly net cash flow = £78,000 divided by £5,822 = **13.4 months** until all cash out.

Note: These HMO returns are unrivalled in terms of return. It is however important to adjust for your expected occupancy rates, keeping in mind that only a few of your costs will reduce when the property is empty; costs like mortgage interest, council tax, insurance are likely to be the same whether empty or full.

Example: Assisted sale

Our next example is assisted sales. This isn't a strategy that we implement at REWD Group; so this is purely an example to give an idea of what the numbers look like, and to outline some of the key points on the strategy itself. As you know as per the strategy chapter, an assisted sale is essentially where you agree a price with the seller which they're happy with, and you guarantee them a price for the property. Then you take the property and essentially refurbish it, improving its marketability with the aim of selling it for a higher price and pocketing a profit between the agreed price and the sale price. The more you can realise in terms of the sale price to the market, the better. That could normally include a refund cost to you to improve the marketability of the property, so if for example you have agreed the sale at £155,000 and maybe the market value in the current condition is about £160,000. If you spend a further £20,000 then it could be worth considerably more – or at least slightly more; say £190,000, for example. So, by spending £20,000 you you've basically increased the market value by £30,000, which means between the discount you agreed with the sale in the first place versus the current market condition and the value you have generated through refurb, there's a £15,000 profit.

You would also need to consider aspects such as legal fees on selling, which may have an impact on your margin. Or maybe you must pay the selling agent for marketing the property, so that would potentially come out of your £15,000 gross profit. Let's look at the numbers:

1) <u>Net cash flow</u> – Not applicable as no rent.
2) <u>Return of cash invested</u> – Net profits (i.e. net cash flow from the deal) divided by cash invested = £15,000 divided by £20,000 = **75%.**

In terms of an annualised return, 75% is quite substantial for a relatively small investment. So assisted sale is quite a good strategy if you don't have a lot of cash, because you don't need to buy the property as such. You just agree on a sale price with the vendor.

Obviously, this needs to be tied up by contracts to make sure that you're not just refurbishing someone's property and then you're going to lose out. But it offers relatively low investment, a reasonable return, and a good way to get involved in property when you don't have a lot of funds, as you don't own the property. You don't have to worry about your credit history or anything like that, if for whatever reason you've got issues with getting mortgages or trading activity. Be aware, of course, that you'll have to pay income tax on the profits from this activity. Depending on how much of this you do in the year, there may be other tax implications. So, there is short-term profitability and not a lot of investment, but you are going to have to pay tax very quickly. That's just a summary.

Example: Rent to rent

The next numbers we're going to look at are rent-to-rent. Again, this isn't a strategy that we employ at the REWD Group, so the example that we're giving you here is purely just that – it's simply an example. It's not a real-life scenario, but it does give a good flavour of how the strategy works and how the numbers attach to the strategy. Effectively, we're talking about a situation where you don't own the property; you rent it from a landlord on a guaranteed rent basis. That means you guarantee the owner landlord a certain amount of rent every month, if you can reach an agreement that you can sublet that property. The aim really is to try and get more rental income by renting out a room. So as we said with the general strategy, if you have multiple rooms, ideally at least a rebate property where you could rent a spare room and receive a significantly higher rent, you could essentially create a margin while still paying the landlord an original rent on a three-bed flat.

We're guaranteeing rent at £500 per month. There will be a conveyancing cost, and there will be some costs associated with creating a three-bedrooms HMO. Now, we're not necessarily talking about refurbs or anything like that. We're talking about things like having to put fire doors on rooms that would require upgrades to meet licensing legislation for the property. There are other requirements and, to make sure you get an HMO license, we'd also be talking about things like furnishings, fixtures and all that sort of stuff. You know the kinds of things: blinds, appliances, etc. Normally when you're renting property to the buy-to-let market, you wouldn't necessarily need to provide all that, whereas with an HMO type of service accommodation model, you would be expected to do it. So, there's going to be a bit of investment involved in the property to get it up to a standard where it could be an HMO or serviced accommodation, so essentially there's a way to add value to that property and create additional rent.

In this example we have spent £7,000 on this to convert it to an HMO, including all the furniture and everything. You'd also had to pay around about three months' worth of rent, because we'd have been empty during the period that you were working on the property. So that's a total investment of £8,500. Your gross rent per month would be £1,900, and that's based on renting each one of the three rooms at £150 per week. This is about reasonable for an HMO, though it obviously depends on location. But based on these numbers, £150 per week is about right.

From your rent of £1,900 per month you have to pay your rent to the landlord and possibly money to an agent, because you want these investments to be passive. You don't want to be involved in the direct management of the property and the running costs, which would include the likes of council tax and utilities – the sort of running costs that we've already discussed within our HMO example. Cost for this deal will be: Rent to landlord £500 PCM, Agent costs at 10% meaning £190 PCM, Running costs including utilities and council tax at £500. So, let's look at the numbers:

1) <u>Net cash flow</u> – this is monthly rent less; rent cost, agent fee and landlord insurance plus other costs = £1,900 (rent) - £500 (landlord rent) - £190 (agent fee) - £500 other costs = **£710 PCM**.
2) <u>Return of cash invested</u> – Net cash flow divided by cash left invested = £8,520 divided by £8,500 = **100%.**
3) <u>Time until infinite return</u> – Cash left in divided by monthly net cash flow = £8,500 divided by £710 = **11.97 months** until all cash out.

Again, the important thing to remember with these numbers is that this is based on 100% occupancy, assuming you can fill these three rooms all the time. So what you need to do is walk back and say, 'Okay, well, if I've only got the rooms filled for half the time, my total rent goes down from £1,900 to £950 a month and I still have the rent to the landlord to pay of £500.' The agent costs will go down to £95 based on 10%. So that goes down by £95, but your running costs such as council tax aren't going to go down. Utilities will go down slightly, but those running costs are not going to diminish significantly. So, you could find that if you're running at £950 – i.e. 50% occupancy – it could see you losing money.

> Net cash flow – this is monthly rent less: rent cost, agent fee and landlord insurance plus other costs = £950 (rent) - £500 (Landlord rent) - £95 (agent fee) - £385 other costs = **-£30 PCM**.

If you have a strong market and you're confident on 100% occupancy, this is a solid cash flow for relatively small investment. With net cash of £710 per month, your original £8,500 investment will be returned to you within 12 months. That's the infinite return calculation. And your return on cash employed is 100%, which means over the course of the year you've got net cash of £7,200 on your original investment, which was £8,500 of your return on investment. Ultimately what that means is that your operational investment is again highly dependent on occupancy. Any of these HMO-type serviced accommodation strategies are going to be heavily dependent on the occupancy rate that you can achieve and what comes along. If you're constantly having to market rooms because there's a lot of turnovers, it can involve a lot of management. Your agent may not be happy with 10% if they constantly must put effort into keeping the rooms full.

Example: Property flips

The next strategy we're going to look at the numbers for is a flip. This is buying a property to sell on for a profit where, essentially, we're looking at short-term profitability. We buy it, we refurbish it and we sell it on. You need to think of the end client with flips, so a higher standard of refurb is required; people are always going to have a much higher standard of expectation for somewhere that they're going to buy and live long-term versus somewhere that they're going to see as a potentially short-term rental, so the standard of refurb must be higher.

The roof may need to have tiles replaced, there's a higher expectation of interior decoration, and maybe more expensive kitchens and appliances. These may be things that we may not do on rental properties; we may just line them with paper and paint them, instead of a full plaster and repaint in a flip. Whereas trying to get the absolute maximum value for a property may mean that you must take these extra steps that that you wouldn't otherwise do for rental.

There will be legal costs as well. You not only have the costs associated with the purchase; you also have the legal fees to sell it as well. You must factor in the cost of the sale with the selling agent. You've got the financial costs, and it's more likely that you're going to have to use short-term finance rather than mortgages. There are short-term finance solutions out there such as bridges or development loans. However, finance can be very expensive. You know, it can be anything from 0.75% a month upwards depending on the product you use. So, you need to be aware of your financing options. If you do use a mortgage, then you're going to have to factor in early termination charges on that mortgage. The costs of going for a more expensive product like a bridge, as I said before, must be factored into the sales costs of the agent who is selling the property. If you need an agent to sell it, then you know you're going

to have to factor in the 1% or whatever the going rate is.

The other big consideration is if you are doing a flip in your own name (i.e. not through a company), as it's a trading activity, you're going to be taxed on it as income and not capital gains as many people assume. This means you're also going to have to pay National Insurance on that profit too. This causes serious issues if you are already a higher rate tax payer in your day job as you will be immediately taxed at a much higher rate.

Let's look at some of the numbers associated with this example. Again, this is not a strategy that we employ at the REWD Group. We don't do individual flips of houses. We obviously do much larger-scale developments like commercial residential, where we'll do seven or eight flats as part of a building redevelopment and then sell them on. It's a sort of a flip but, you know, more of a flip *en masse*. So, in terms of individual houses or flats, we don't really do flips. We prefer to hold our stock and keep it for the long term. So this is purely an example of what one would look like.

The purchase cost in this example is £80,000. Say you purchased a house or a flat with it. Legal costs would be around about £1,000 and the additional dwelling supplement would be £3,200, which is 4% of the transaction value. It's at 3% in England. There'll be no stamp duty or Land Building Transaction Tax because it's under the £145,000 threshold. You need to factor in the interest costs. It's probably going to be at least six months now, generally, when you buy a property – whoever you're selling it on to won't be able to get a mortgage on it unless you've held it for at least six months. So that six month rule applies here. Normally any project that takes less than six months, you're still going to have to wait until the six months are up.

In this example, we've taken the refurb cost to be £28,350. It's a significant refurb. Again, it's all about the standard that you must achieve. Since you're going to sell it, you need to factor in the legal fees to sell the property again. So that's about the same as when you purchased it: about £1,000. The selling agent assumes 1% of the sales value, meaning £1,450. Total costs of this flip so far excluding finance costs are: £80,000 (purchase) + £28,350 Refurb + £4,200 (purchase fees)+ £2,450 (selling fees) = **£115,000**.

Normally for finance costs it's not just the interest you have to factor in. There's an arrangement for when you start and there's an exit fee when you come out, all of which depends on the product. But normally it will be 1% or 2% of the loan amount that you need to factor in. We can assume that's the total investment, so suppose you're able to get a bridge or a mortgage for around £60,000; that's going to be largely based on the value of the property or a smaller percentage on the value of the gross development value. But £60,000 in this example is probably a fair analysis of how much money you will be able to get the bank to support. If you're lucky, you'll be able to get most of that at the purchase stage. If you're unlucky, you may have to get part of that as an advance, and then you may have to get a surveyor to do a value of work done assessment before they release the final funds.

So in this example we've got to spend the £115,000 with £60,000 coming through finance from the bank, plus £55,000 of it funded by yourself. This is quite standard with flips, where you must put in a deposit essentially to buy the property and then you must put in all the refurb and fee costs, especially in small developments. As you get the larger development, you can transition to development finance and you can probably get more towards the refurbishment. But it's not so easy to finance these smaller projects with finance because you're really just looking at a percentage of the front end value and then the rest of it you need to finance. So you can end up with flips, finance, and quite a lot of the development yourself. Finance costs on your £60,000 bank loan would be a round 1% per month for an estimated 8 months, which factors in the six month minimum ownership rule plus another two months to conclude a sale thereafter. In addition to the interest there is a 2% arrangement fee, so finance costs are £60,000 x 10% = £6,000. Finally, the end value of this property at completion is going to be £145,000 based on similar properties in the area. Let's calculate the return from this deal:

1) <u>Net cash flow</u> – Cash flow from the deal = Sales value less total costs less cost of finance - £145,000 (sales price) - £115,000 (total costs) – finance costs (£6,000) = **£24,000.**

2) <u>Return of cash invested</u> – Net cash flow divided by cash personally invested times annualised factor = £24,000 divided by £55,000 = **43.6%.** It's important to mention that return on cash invested is an annualised figure and our flip return was made in 8 months, so we have to annualise the return = 43.6% divided by 8 times 12 = **65.45%**

As in the context of other investments and property, also be aware that this doesn't factor in tax – which could be quite substantial in the year, depending on what your income is.

The bigger challenge with flips versus buy-to-let is you need to find the next project to make the next return, whereas buy-to-let yields a constant annual return once the property is rented. This is very much a short-term strategy.

Example: Commercial to residential

The next strategy is commercial to residential. We're going to have a look at the numbers for a commercial residential project. This is a strategy that we very much employ; in fact, REWD Development is all about commercial residential projects. So we've got a good example, and in this one the numbers and refurbs are much more complex. Now, I've been asked a few times about how easy it is to transition from the likes of buy-to-rent or flips to commercial residential, and I've always said this: this is a completely different animal. It's a much more sophisticated business, because of all the costs and the various elements that can affect the commercial residential project which are much more unreliable than a standard project. I mean, you're changing the purpose of a building. It's not a simple undertaking, and it shouldn't be taken on lightly. This is a flavour of some of the additional things you must consider in these types of projects.

Firstly, professional fees are a significant part of this process. With these developments, we're dealing with significant sites which come with a whole host of regulations. There's a lot of health and safety require-ments and, as a director, you are legally responsible for a whole raft of things. We're essentially now running a site, which means there are a lot of professions that need to be involved in the operation of that site to ensure that it's all done safely. So, you're talking about health and safety advisers. You're talking about principal designers. You're talking about architecture. You're talking about site supervision. You know, it's no longer a small domestic refurb. We're looking at a much more significant development. There are a lot more professional fees involved, plus build-ing requirements.

If it's in the middle of a town centre, it's at least likely to be in a conservation area. What restrictions you have on what you can do with the building can impede things even further. Of the five developments that we have on the go, four of the five are listed and all of them are in a conservation area. So, as you can imagine, that has quite a significant in-fluence on what we can do and what we can't do in the course of the construction, and those project planning contributions. If it's a bank de-velopment, you may have to provide certain facilities and you may also have to contribute towards the council's servicing of those facilities.

The specifics all depend on the area. But you know, if you're doing a development – say there are 25 flats – the chances are it's going to involve some planning contributions and complex reno-vation budgets. So, you're trying to essentially repurpose that building, and the budgets can be complex. The renovation budgets are quite often significantly more challenging in town centres. The logistics of trying to manage a major renovation in a built-up town or city location will add significant time and cost to your project. There can still be significant costs on bringing the appropriate utilities into the building (water, gas, electricity). Even if there are existing facilities, they are unlikely to be sufficient enough to support the multiple residential properties you are creating. I could talk for weeks about the various things that might impact on a commercial residential development. The long and the short of this is that it's not for anyone who's just getting started out to do this as their first project.

Business rates may apply, as commercial properties are subject to business rates. It's not like a buy-to-let property, where it's empty and unfurnished and you can claim an exemption on council tax from the local government or local council. When a commercial asset is empty, the landlords are responsible for the business rates. There could be a significant cost. The one benefit of all our properties being listed is that you can get a listed building exemption when it's empty against the rates. Business rates will need to be factored into the budgets if applicable.

On completion you are selling multiple residential units, all on their own titles, which means there's a lot of legal work involved in it. A commercial unit would generally have one title and as you sub-divide this, multiple titles will be created with detail on shared access and rights of each property. This can be a significant cost to factor in your selling legal fees.

Just to re-emphasise: if it's not already clear from what I've said, this is a complex strategy. It requires significant knowledge, and it's not something that I would advise anybody to get involved in lightly. We do offer a specialist commercial residential training course for those who want to learn about that strategy. But, you know, given that this is an introduction to property investing, to start your first

deal with commercial residential would be a very, very risky strategy.

Nevertheless, let's look at the numbers on one of our deals. This is what we call the Temperance House project. It may look like quite a straightforward building from the front elevation, but it goes around in a sort of L-shape and is quite a long, complicated layout of a building inside. It's a development of six flats. The commercial unit at the bottom will remain in place. Then we're going to be developing six flats above it and round the corner. It used to be an old solicitor's office. We bought the whole thing for £250,000. Ultimately the main value at the time that was attribute to the business on the ground floor because they had the lease on it, which gave a £200,000 valuation.

The commercial element to the property, including the basement, is worth about £200,000 or so. It meant that we got the development space for these six flats for around £50,000 and, despite that the building was built in the 1800s, it was in quite good condition. So, the development space costs £50,000 – for the purposes of the numbers assessment we will exclude the commercial unit, as that will remain untouched at its current value. It is going to be somewhere in the region of £610,000 for development costs. We have fees of somewhere in the region of £103,000, though that's all the stuff we were talking about for architects, engineers, principal designers, health and safety, finance costs, arrangement fees, legal fees etc. There is a lot that's involved in this type of development, and they're all sort of encompassed in these extra costs. So, our total costs are expected to be: £50,000 (Purchase) + £610,000 (Build cost) + £103,000 (Fees) = £763,000. The valuation, excluding the £200,000 commercial unit, is somewhere in the region of £1,000,000. That leaves £237,000 of profit.

This development at the time of writing is nearing completion and should be marketed for sale within the next month. You can see from the entranceway, which has a big oak staircase, it's quite an impressive building. It's going to be quite a high-end development.

Summary of the key numbers

Now you can consider the key numbers that we've covered. Here we have given you an understanding of how to calculate numbers, analyse deals, and get an overview of whether a deal stacks up in terms of its numbers. We've compared various strategies and looked at the returns that you could be making. We're using these key metrics. We've got gross yield, which is a high-level industry comparison that – as we said earlier – doesn't factor in things like direct costs of rent. It's high-level. You have no indication of how good a flat or a house investment in general is from that figure. Net yield is similar style calculation, but it's a better indicator on real returns. So, it's inclusive of the direct costs of rental, but the main drawback is that it's still based on the value of the property, not the amount of cash that you've invested in the deal, so it's still not quite a real return.

In this sense, they give you a high-level understanding and are quite easy to calculate, but they don't give you a comparable investment-to-investment type percentage – the kind of thing if you were trying to compare this investment type against the likes of a return from such-and-such, be it the return from shares, etc. Net cash flow is quite simply the cash that you get from the rental. So it's your rental income, less direct costs. It's the monthly cash in the bank and, as we said before, it doesn't include maintenance. The Returning on Cash Invested formula is the most comparative percentage, as it shows true returns on a cash for cash basis. So that one really is the focal point.

I think for many, when they're assessing return, we tend to look at annualised return, which is just trying to compare the time value of money. So, we can add 100% return on this investment and 50% return on another investment, and the first investment takes a year, the second investment take six months, then the annualised return is the same. We've been through the example of how to calculate profits for different types of strategies and outlined some of the costs that you must think about for the various strategies.

We've been through several examples now. Whilst we are covering the calculation of the numbers net before tax calculations, you do still have to think about tax when you when you're looking at any strategy. And that's something we've already covered in a lot more detail within the chapter dealing with an introduction to property taxes elsewhere in this *Fast-Track to Property Millions* book. It's the final piece of the puzzle when you analyse the numbers as to understand how much you made and how much tax you now must pay. What that does is help you see the benefits of your strategy, as well as recognising that are some significant implications from tax that you need to be aware about.

Examples of new-build properties being constructed and developed by the
REWD Group.

Chapter Eight

Multiple Streams of Income

Laurie Duncan

THIS chapter is about multiple streams of income, because although we are very biased about the success of buy-to-let, we do have various other income streams in the form of our various other businesses. As I'm sure you know, buy-to-let is awesome. It is very passive, and it brings in what is called investment income. We have to do very well for that cash and, month by month, our letting agent takes care of all that income for us. But the other businesses produce revenues in different ways as well. As I've mentioned, we've got buy-to-let, which provides a month-by-month cash flow; very passive. We then have REWD Training, which brings in cash depending on what events we have. At any one time we will have current developments, which are focused on larger lump sum returns; ultimately that's a longer-term play. We have to wait on the developments to be fully completed and sold off before any profits arise. However, when the profits do come, for developments then they are a bit more significant. We've had to wait a bit longer for them. So, if we're waiting a bit longer, the rewards should be greater.

So there are different schemes. The building company is quite gradual. We constantly have cash coming into the business to fund the various building company projects. So that's a bit more of a gradual profit-making scenario there. But really the point of this summary is to get you thinking about the various different ways that you can bring more income into your business and to your life. It doesn't have to be all that complex. It doesn't have to just be assisted sales. It doesn't just have to be traded deals. You can combine all these things, and the more you can invest the money and network with people, the more work you do and the more experience you will get. Ultimately, it becomes easier to bring these other income streams into play. So that's the purpose of having multiple streams of income.

Let's now go into some of the detail about some of the income streams you could employ. There are lots and lots of different methods of producing and bringing cash into your life. The most common initially is employment; everybody has their day jobs, and most of us do our bit. Employment income is where you are paid a salary or hourly rate for doing a job for your employer. It's most commonly how people start out, and most commonly people are trying to make a move away from this model because they are becoming increasingly frustrated by their jobs with big companies generally. They feel like they're overworked and underpaid – all the rest of it. They don't enjoy the feeling of entrapment. I myself was just forced to leave my day job recently. We planned for that. It was all good. We've been building things for a couple of years to allow us to make that move.

If you can build up your property business on the side while you still have employment income, that's awesome. Why would you not take advantage of that scenario if you can get it? So employment income is just normal income, if we can call it that. Keep that going for as long as you can, I would say. Some people 'burn the ships' and just dive right in; they just kind of go for it with no particular plan in place. Sometimes that's motivating for people. For me, it was too risky. I like to plan, and that's exactly what we've done. Keep your employment going as long as you can. In the background, though, your property business can be taking shape.

Property investment income and trading income

Now, the first type of income that I want to talk about is property investment income. We'll be talking about investing and we'll talk about trading, because these are different types of income. It's just the way that

HMRC looks at the different ways you make money, and you can be taxed very differently. For instance, buy-to-let and HMO are different things; there is no HMO that we would consider as part of the buy-to-let strategy. But as you'll have seen from earlier chapters, we've made a few moves ourselves and it's a very different animal from a buy-to-let. HMO, or a house of multiple occupancy, is where you rent out the individual rooms rather than the whole flat. In our case we've actually rented out the whole flat or facility occupied by people from the one tenancy company. But each room is occupied by an individual tenant, so there are a lot of complexities and legislation that are involved with this type of thing. It's very different from buy-to-let, but the returns can be much more significant. We've certainly done well with our HMOs but, regardless, the HMO is classed as residential premises, just like buy-to-let is classed as residential premises. So they are both investment income in the eyes of HMRC, and are taxed accordingly. Be aware that any time we're talking about tax, the legislation changes constantly. Do your best to seek advice from your accountant as to the best way that you should be set up.

We have already talked a little bit about corporate structuring and tax, so you'll have a basic understanding of these differences. But it's a very good idea to keep the day job going as long as you can, while in the background you can start building up your buy-to-let portfolio and your investment income.

The next type of income is what's classed as trading income. That's really for any developments that you do, and can be known as 'flipping' properties − or buy-to-sell. We are very focused on buy-to-let, as you know, and when we refinance, we can make more money than most people do on residential flips.

The difference is that if you do a refinance on a buy-to-let, the cash loaned from your bank is not taxable because it's not a profit; it's just an increased bank loan. If you sell something, or if you trade something, you (hopefully!) make a profit between the costs and the sale value, that's trading activity, and then you need to pay tax on these profits. So we go on and on about people who do up a flat for £5,000, or £10,000 or even £20,000 profit − something like that. By the time they've factored in all the costs and taxes, really there's not a lot of profit left in it. Again, it depends how you're structured, and in terms of your corporate structure it may vary if you're a sole trader, an LLP, a limited company... all these types of things apply. But it might make more sense, if you're looking at single units, to do them as a buy-to-flip on occasion; maybe you don't have enough cash flow coming in after the projected refinance, so maybe you get cash back from the deal or something like that. So you have to ask yourself – is the asset you're looking to purchase worth your while to do a flip? We did buy two flips on a commercial scale. They are classed as developments because they are on the larger scale of land developments and commercial residential developments.

Ultimately if you're buying something, you're adding value and you're selling it to make a profit. So it's the same thing. There's absolutely no reason why you can't have your income from employment, and alongside your day job income you are building up a buy portfolio on the side. Then you can be doing some flips. It makes sense for larger sums of cash to come into your business. Very cool stuff. As you start doing more and more business, you build your network, you build your power team, and you have a lot more stakeholders. You have a lot of people that are doing similar things as you are, and people are happy to pay for referral business. They're happy to pay for affiliations. They see it as a way everybody would understand that it is a way of generating more business for themselves through your efforts. We have affiliations with different people, and it makes sense. It's good to get your name out there to get people talking about you, and it opens up a lot of doors to your network. It's such an easy way to boost your business by paying someone for their affiliation.

Likewise, why would people not pay for you to refer them some business? Think about that, because this can be going on in the background. All of these things that we're talking about now can be happening at the same time. You don't have to just focus on one. You don't have to just do one buy-to-let deal. You might buy three buy-to-let units and do one flip in the one year, and have some referrals coming in as well. So all these things have to get you thinking about extra revenue coming into your business, coming in your life, trading and brokering – whatever you want to call it.

There is one very commonly talked-about type of strategy in the property market. Take it with a pinch of salt. It's not as easy as others make it out to be! It's known as 'sourcing', and it's basically just on and off-market trading or brokering of property sales, but there are very few people that are serious about it. There's definitely a lot of people who talk the talk when it comes to sourcing. Everybody agrees that the sourcing aspect of property acquisition is important, but how many people are actually spending money on the marketing and how many people are actually getting good-quality deals? Then…! How many people, when they do get good-quality deals, are going to sell them on to you rather than keep them themselves? You've really got to think about that.

When I first got started out, I began with a sourcing business, and it was my intention to be trading deals. But then every time I found an opportunity, I was negotiating with my best interests at heart. That is to say, any time I secured a really good deal, I bought it myself. Of course I did! Every other source is going to be the same, unless you find a source who's just brokering deals for themselves but not buying. That's not going to last for too long before they do start buying themselves, once they get educated and get all the financing in place. So when I started, ultimately the sourcing business didn't work out because I kept buying the deals myself. Therefore there were no sales coming into the business. Without sales coming into the business, you don't have a business. I had to knock this thing on the head. We are now getting back into it, so if you are looking for opportunities and you're already working with us and at a high level, reach out to us because we regularly have deals coming to us. Not even necessarily through our own marketing efforts, although that is something we're doing again too. But just because of who we are and what we're doing in the market. They know we've got solid financial backing, they know we can get deals over the line, they know we pay the fees upfront – all that type of thing.

Sourcing can be very good and, again, people are very happy to pay a certain fee if the deal stacks up. If you're going to get into sourcing, there's a lot of stuff that goes along with that. There's a lot of compliance and various other things you need to take into consideration. So make sure you're playing the game and adhering to all of the legislation. But it can be a very good way to make some extra coin. For whatever reason, you might not want to buy a property. Say you've got five deals in one month, and you're only buying four of them. It makes sense to capitalise on the other deal. So look for people to sell that opportunity to. I think the biggest fee we paid was about £20,000 on a portfolio, so you can make a lot of money. They start at anything from £1,000 up to whatever. It depends on the nature of the deal. These fees will get factored in to the brokering service provided by the sourcing agent.

Referrals and affiliations is quite an attractive strategy too, but you really need to know what you're doing. You need to get educated on that, and you need to be serious about it. Then you've got to think about your team. For a build, you're going to have a refurb team, and they need to be flexible. You're going to have a build team, you'll need a refurb team, and the refurb team may charge £10,000 to do a job. If you are the person who is managing that build team and you're pushing all the work their way, why don't you make arrangements to supply that build team to other people in your network? You don't even have to do any work. You literally just feed the team. They invoice you, you invoice them, and you can make an extra fee. It's another way to bring more income into your property business. Don't get caught up in just doing one thing. You can do them all.

Monetising business opportunities

Think about how you can monetise any situation at any time, and put this stuff into practice because all of these little fees coming into your business can make a big difference. And some of these things are really easy, so do them all if you can. If you're ever looking at punting stuff on for whatever reason – say it doesn't work for you – then run it by us, because we can usually find an exit to make sure you still get paid something rather than nothing. Everybody can win from that scenario. So why don't you do these ones too? You could loan out funds – maybe your own funds, maybe other people's funds (with their consent in place, it goes without saying) – but you can loan out funds and get paid an interest for those funds. There are various different ways that you can get access to finance and, again, while we've already gone into this in a lot of detail, we as a group are excellent at raising finance. We could not be doing everything that we are if it wasn't for our skills in raising finance. We teach about that in a lot of detail on our courses. If you're interested in that, then by all means reach out. But you can loan out your own funds, you can loan out other people's funds, you can make cuts for referrals as an incentive, or you can make money by interest.

Why aren't you taking consultancy fees, consulting with people on whatever it is that they want to know? You might think about doing property training in the future. Awesome. It's no walk in the park, I can tell you that. There's a lot of work that has to go into it, like it always is when you're starting up a new business. But when it comes to property, you've got to ask yourself: why are people going to come in and learn from you? And what will they learn? So whether you're consulting on a one-on-one basis or you're running events like property training events, ask yourself why are people going to come and learn from you or take consultation from you.

We always had ambition to start a training business – and not necessarily an events business, where you are just running events all the time. We wanted a training business where people can learn from us. We always had the ambition, but until probably the end of 2020 we never had a story to tell. We are passionate, driven, ambitious guys, but we felt as though we never had much of a story to tell. It was only after we concluded on the launch of the Lanarkshire portfolio, which was 82 properties was up to the end of 2020, that people actually started getting in touch with us and asking, 'Hey, how did you do that?' I guess it was that realisation that made us think about more seriously about property training.

Before that, we had our mastermind group, and it was a free thing. We just used to run these events once a month on a Zoom call. In fact, because this was all during the coronavirus lockdowns, we all had to communicate via Zoom. We would create different topics and different presentations, and people would come and join them and try and learn from us. We would be offering them free content all the time for nothing.

But nobody should be giving their time away for nothing. Time is precious. Life is precious, and if you've got good quality content, people are going to pay for that and you should monetise it.

REWD Group is all about generational wealth. This chapter is about creating and maximising multiple streams of income. And we want you to think about those multiple streams of income. There might be synergies between us as we move forward. You may want to come and do some of your own presentations at a training event. Who knows? Nothing's ever off the table. When you're consulting on your own area of expertise, you need to have some degree of credibility. That's the point. All the work that you do between now and that point – if you decide to become a consultant or do some training – all the work that you do until you reach that point, that is your story and that is your credibility. That is why people are going to pay you for your time: to consult with them, to train them, to mentor them, to push them forward, to help them achieve their goals. But they want to see that you have achieved your goals first. That's what we've done at REWD Group. We set ourselves some big crazy goals, big enough that everybody laughed at us. Then we achieved them. And that's what you should do, too. But then, once you've got that credibility and are taken seriously, this stuff is a great way to bring extra revenue into your business. You should think about it, absolutely. It is a great method of generating more income. Always keep thinking about multiple streams of income, and the better your portfolio the more you can offer people.

Portfolio building and project management

Portfolio building services are where you build other people's portfolios on their behalf, and there can be so many different ways of making money within that service. You can have a front end source fee, or you can have a back end source fee. You can have the build team's extra margin, which we talked about earlier. You can take a fee for managing the project as well. There are so many different ways and, by the time you add all these numbers up, that's a decent amount of income.

This was another thing that I did when I got started professionally, before I began my work with the group; it was something I was going to offer as a service, because you can see how lucrative it can be. Though as it happens, the group has diversified into various other businesses. Those various other businesses have their own income streams, and currently portfolio building isn't one of them. But it's never off the table, as it's something we've been talking about doing for people. The more we get back into sourcing and trading, the more we're going to have opportunities to sell on these leads to people. Building other people's portfolios is a great thing to have as an income stream as part of your business. So again, think about that: if the deal doesn't fit for you, you can sell it to someone else. It may meet someone else's criteria, they can start building their portfolio and they're going to pay for it.

The more opportunities you find, the more use you can be when it comes to the buying and selling of property. For instance, you have assisted sales. That's another thing we've talked about in terms of a number of strategies. It's actually quite a simplistic process, where you just assist the person selling the property. You agree whatever your commercial terms are with them, but you might arrange to manage it too. For instance, maybe our property needed some TLC. You can manage the refurbishment, and you get that all done. Well, the other person still owns the property, but then if you get an increased uplift because of the condition of the property, you might agree to split the profits 50-50 or maybe even 75-25. They might be happy with that. You're doing all the work you're managing, so anything that you make above that by doing whatever the seller wants, you can keep for yourself. It's a really great strategy to increase your returns rather than just taking a sourcing fee, because you can get in at the front end.

Doing an assisted sale, you may end up making a bit more profit but it can be more complex. You can organise all this through lawyers. It's just a legal agreement; very straightforward. The main thing is, don't worry if it seems scary right now. All this stuff might seem scary, because it's new. It's a natural human emotion. We may have a fear of the unknown, but it's definitely a great way to make some extra cash. So consider assisted selling. But there's so much more you might also do.

Take project management, for instance. We've talked about this a little bit already. You might have people who sponsored you and your

business, where they paid you funds and you have some kind of promo-
tion for them running in the background. It might be another business
owner, maybe even somebody in the same industrial park, city or offices.
In fact, it could be anyone. We recently sponsored a local festival; we
knew the organiser from school, and we paid for the sponsorship of the
VIP area of this festival. So we paid them for the pleasure of advertising
our brand at their festival, and I think there was anything from about
4,000 to 5,000 people at that festival. Something like that. If you plan to
bring sponsorship funds into your business, think creatively. There's absolutely no reason why you couldn't do that. Just think about the
different types of sponsorship available to you.

Commercial lettings and lettings agencies

Commercial lettings are something that we have become involved in by
accident, really. We had no real intention of starting a commercial lettings business, but because of our commercial to residential conversion
projects, we ended up buying whole buildings in order to have control
over the development. You really need to buy the whole building, because if you don't own this part of the building or that part of the
building, or you don't own this access route or whatever it might be, it
can quickly become very complex and it can cause you a lot of problems.
So if we are buying a whole building, it gives us control over the project.

However, within the whole building there's maybe only a certain
space that we can develop; perhaps there are other spaces on the ground
floor, for example, which already house retail units. Thus we've actually
ended up with something like 11 or 12 commercial units where we would
generate an income actually from these commercial lettings. Because
we've got so many of them now, just because of the efforts we've made in
the commercial residential conversion development business, we're now
looking at starting a lettings business or a commercial lettings business
and having the commercial lettings run through our pension fund.
There's a reason for that. We go into a lot more detail about those types
of investment strategies in our advanced level training courses, so consider those because there's definitely a lot to learn that can be very lucrative.

In fact, the rents on commercial lettings are significantly more than residential buy-to-let lettings and could be comparative to HMOs, because sometimes HMO income is substantial – like we've demonstrated on our own. But with commercial lettings, you might find the income to be the same as those. You may stumble across these opportunities and you may end up with commercial properties that you've paid for that produce income, and that can be a great way to bring other income into your business as well. Why not be thinking about it?

We've not really talked about commercial residential conversions on here. We did talk about developments earlier on in the presentation, but developments – business, commercial, residential conversions – are also great ways to produce a lot of extra cash. For lettings, you just admit the tenants and they have to pay the rent. More often than not, that's on the basis of filling a vacancy and ensuring a lease, which means that the tenants take care of absolutely everything; you have no maintenance to do and you've no other costs, like you would do in a residential buy-to-let scenario.

The best commercial lettings can be very attractive, and it's something that we are going to end up developing in time – just because of what we have ended up with in terms of these buildings that we've acquired. So we start thinking about that. Why not holiday lets and serviced accommodation, though? Those are different to the HMO strategy, right? If you are servicing something that attracts VAT, which can massively increase the cost of your rental to your tenant, you need to be aware of that fact. So keep that in mind if you're thinking about setting up a holiday let or some service accommodation.

Again, for holidays, think about the demand for Airbnb that's currently going on. You notice a massive boom in those short-term lets, where you can let a flat in a decent location even for one night in the big cities. It might be £200 for the night. So if you get even a 60% to 70% occupancy rate, which is what we understand to be typical in that market, that's a significant amount of money – much greater compared to normal buy-to-let. Granted, it's not as passive, because you have to have a bit more involvement than you would with the holiday service accommodation-style model, but really if you get a cleaner or have it managed

● ● ●

through an agent, you can still make a lot of money off that even by the time these other costs have been taken off.

You know the sort of thing we're talking about: beachside tourist destinations, city breaks... all of these opportunities. It's excellent to have a think about and, again, it's another strategy that we are looking at just now because currently we don't have any holiday lets or service accommodations. But I think we might have some in the pipeline, or are certainly looking at making some acquisitions. So it can be a great way to boost your monthly cash flow. Think about the particular areas of interest if you're going to get into that, because it has to be somewhere with a strong demand; ideally somewhere that has a known annual demand, regardless of the time of year. Perhaps it's in a particularly busy place. That's the type of demand that you want, because otherwise you have peaks and troughs all throughout the year. You have income and you don't have income, then you do and then you don't. You'd be best to keep that steady, if at all possible.

Then there is a letting agency. Another thing that is on the radar for REWD Group, perhaps obviously. What we are talking about here is a residential letting agency. There's no reason why an agency cannot also control the commercial properties currently, as it does for us. In fact, it can control the residential side and the commercial side, but once you get to a certain size it might make sense to bring a letting agency into your structure. Now, don't get confused here; don't get me wrong. I'm not saying I want to be our own letting agent. I'm not saying you want to be an agent, as being a letting agent is massively time consuming and it's not necessarily all that profitable. We don't want to be involved in the running of that company in terms of director-level management. But we are keen to have a stake in a letting agency, because we are growing at quite a significant rate. And we have ambition. We do work with a massive national letting agency, and that often forms part of our growth plans for future. So think about that. Don't get consumed by the time involved in being a letting agent. But as you grow, you might want to bring that letting agency's income stream into your structure.

Business synergies

Then there are auction houses, business synergies. I talked earlier about groups and business synergies. We've got the buy-to-let side, we've got the developments business, we've got the building company, and we've got the training business. There are other businesses we are looking at all the time to try and bring more synergy into what we do.

Now, auction houses are another thing. Ultimately auction houses are sourcing machines, and people who own auction houses are buying up many, many opportunities themselves before stuff even gets to auction. So it can be a way to bring in significant amount of acquisition leads for yourself or for training clients, for example. That can be a great way to bring that synergy into the group structure. So it's another thing we are looking at, and it's another thing you might be looking at.

Look, you don't need to do all of these things, but you should be aware of all of the different ideas out there that can bring money and income into your business. Certainly earlier in this chapter we talked about the day job and how we came to it through investment and trade, sales and developments, referral sales, trading sources and brokerage, build team referrals and margins. You should definitely be doing all of that. Some of those other strategies are maybe a little bit more advanced so, depending on the stage you're at, you might want to think about these down the line a bit. You might not, of course, but be aware that these are all things that you can bring into your own business. We would encourage you to go after massive growth and massive business. We want that for all our training clients, and we'd love to hear your stories once you've achieved some cool things. It can be really satisfying – but then, that's all part of the training business. When you see people that have achieved things that previously they thought weren't possible, it's always an exciting thing.

There are lots of different methods out there, so lots of different ways of producing income. That's what this chapter is all about. We've talked about lots of different methods of generating income, but I want to look at different types of income and – having touched on a little bit of that – I just want to go into greater detail on it. Let's think about income for a moment. Income is very different from passive income. If we look

● ● ●

back to the start of this chapter, we were talking about the day job and income from employment. That is, income that you work for. Then the next part of that section was about passive income, and specifically passive income from buy-to-let. You can combine the two when you're getting started, to milk the day job for as long as you can. But you need to put time into those efforts, and you need to put your time into doing your day job because then you'll be paid for that. But then you will also have buy-to-let income, where if we put 1% of our time in – and I think that's being overly generous – it's very passive. That's the point.

Every business should be an asset. So whatever asset we are creating when we're starting that asset, it can be very time-consuming. Right? But as we progress as we move things forward, we systemise that new asset, and then it becomes more and more passive in time. You working for money soon becomes money working for you; the process can become passive in commissions, referrals, affiliations... all that type of stuff. You can get paid commissions on the side. I know we talked about raising funds, so you can just raise different types of income and that can include passive income, commissions, interest, and then business income. How many businesses have you got on the go? Are you already thinking of a group structure? There are various benefits to that, actually.

You may already be thinking about a group structure. We always had a vision of having a group structure. We had a vision of all these different businesses working together as part of the group, and we had that vision of these businesses bringing in an income and all the different ways businesses can generate funds from passive income. Business income is my favourite type of income. It can be a challenge to start getting things up and running, but then – as and when things get going – business income just flows. You can create a great team of staff that brings income into the business. But systemise those strategies. If you have good people, you have a good business.

So what other types of business do you have going on? What other businesses can you start? What other business income can you generate? Are you a good receiver? How many times is somebody giving you a compliment? How many times does somebody give you a compliment, and your natural reaction is to shy away? Well, if you don't know how you receive then you're not a good receiver. When someone gives you a compliment or when someone gives you a gift, try to overcome this natural resistance that exists. Many of us – probably most of us, including myself – have to confront this. I'm getting better at it. When you receive a gift of some sort – and that can be a financial gift, it might be a bottle of whisky, it might be an invitation to dinner, it could be a corporate hospitality invitation – then welcome it with open arms.

It's important to be a good receiver, and gifts are just another way of generating more income into your life. It doesn't have to be financial. There are lots of benefits through corporate gigs, and the massively beneficial thing is that you don't need to spend a penny the a whole day. If you want to come and hang out with us at some of our own corporate hospitality gigs, we've got a few different ideas coming up. In the coming years we may offer you a gift. If so, receive it with open arms.

Considering the future

Have you considered the consequences for the future? It's a really interesting thing, because a lot of people haven't. What I mean by this is that a lot of people talk about this job security thing, and I just wonder how secure jobs really are. Look, I get this. Being an entrepreneur now, there are people who care about us, love us, and are just looking out for us. Mainly they are our parents, aunts and uncles, friends and all the rest of it. And they'll say things like: 'Just get a normal job. Why aren't you interested in job security? That all sounds too risky.' All of that sort of thing. The old chestnut of 'just get a normal job' versus being an entrepreneur. It's interesting to think of it, because if you are an employee – and there's nothing wrong with being an employee – not everybody wants to run a multi-group business, but people also like having job security. However, if you are an employee then how secure is your job?

That question of security can be relevant whether you are the employee or you are the entrepreneur. If you're the entrepreneur, you're responsible for the security of your employees. And at any point, various different things could happen in business that could impact on that security. That normal job could be affected by any number of factors. So although people talk about that security, I would ask, have you considered the consequences? Have you really thought that through? Whilst there is definitely a place for employees, staff, jobs and all that, we have a great team here and we're constantly expanding it. We're always looking for good people. That might even be you. But have you considered the consequences of not having some passive income? Not having some other trade, and not having multiple streams of income in your life? I love that we try to create an awesome working environment here so that our staff can love what they're doing, and they love being part of everything we set out to achieve. But we would encourage all of them – absolutely all of them – to consider their income streams. Of course, working here, they're going to get great opportunities anyway, just through the nature of what we do here over time. But we would encourage them to think about multiple income streams as well. Because there's more to life than what you know, and our future is based on our opportunities.

I would be baffled if everybody didn't start their own portfolios and stuff like that. I will be hammering that point home, because there can be various external factors that impact on business. So how secure is that job? What other income do you have coming in? Really, think about that. I need that to hit home for you. Do your job, love your job, be paid well for your job. But think about other income streams coming into your life as well, because it's important to build up these income streams. Think about them, and think about them a lot. Maybe this is very different than what you previously expected. Can you do both? Can you do all of them? Absolutely you can. You can do them all. All of these different things we've talked about throughout this chapter. You can do them. So do. Or at least do some. Give a few of them a try. That's the point. Just have some extra cash coming in. Whether you get that cash from other businesses, synergistic businesses, property-related businesses... all these different methods that I've been talking about earlier. There can be big consequences if you don't have these. What happens if you're made redundant tomorrow? You should have some other income.

That's our business strategy, absolutely. Honestly, this is how we are operating: group-level management, thinking about other assets and other businesses to bring on-stream as part of the group. There is no limit to the size; absolutely no limit. Letting agency, auction house, the commercial route... all these different things. There are new businesses, and we may start within the next six months. You should start thinking about that, definitely, as part of your own property business. Now, initially you just might want to get started. That's cool. But don't let anyone tell you that you can't go after these things. You can go after more business, and with them comes more synergy.

The beautiful thing as well is that all these synergistic businesses I'm talking about, they just work so well together with the ultimate goal of all property: they support one another. Property-related support businesses are awesome. And it doesn't just have to be property-related. You might want to be hired as a virtual assistant – a VA, if you've not heard the term before – which can provide good support. If you are a freelancer, you might do a bit of web design or graphics on the side. You might be a drop-shipper, which is basically like where you go to those big warehouses that have massive amounts of stock, you do all the marketing in the middle, then you sell the stuff to a customer from the warehouse and you get paid at the checkout. That's drop-shipping. But don't let it distract you from your property venture. Just check it out, even if just out of curiosity.

I would hate to distract you from your property venture just because I've mentioned drop-shipping and these multiple streams of income, but it might be a way for you to produce some extra income if you don't normally do that kind of thing. You might be a high-flying marketing executive for all I know. I looked into this kind of thing at one point. If all of that fails, you could do some mystery shopping where you go and you pretend to buy a pair of trainers or some clothes, and you provide feedback to the company about how good the service was that you received from the customer service agent. I think you get paid a couple of hundred quid. So there are different methods, different consequences to think about, and don't limit yourself by income streams. Consumers are endless, and you should have lots of opportunities.

Realisations

Just to tie things up on the subject of multiple streams of income, I have purposely finished with the topic of realisations. Why? Because there are certain things that you, and everyone else, must realise. For one, that unlimited money is everywhere. Many people have resistance to that fact. But whatever you do, don't limit yourself on your current reality. I spoke about this before. Whose reality do you want to be in? Don't limit yourself by the confines of your current reality now, because our reality two years ago looked very different to our current reality. What is real right now seemed unrealistic to us two years ago. You must go and develop loads and loads of strategies. Don't just use one. Don't just use private investors, don't just use SSAS, don't just use credit cards, don't just use bank loans, don't just use overdrafts.

There are so many different financial strategies that we have covered. Use them all. Why would you limit yourself by not using them all? You just need to just get started. Whatever you do, however you do it, it's always going to require great effort. You will need to put the work in. You need to take action. I cannot emphasise this point enough. We meet so many people who go on other training courses and then get in touch with us. They talk the talk but they take no action. They make no effort whatsoever. And it baffles me, because back when we started the group, we were hungry. We were going out, doing all sorts of different things, and just going after that because we were driven. We were hungry, driven characters, we put in a lot of effort, and we didn't even know what we were doing most of the time. But we put in the effort, and we pushed through the fear. We moved forward. But realise that this new life you're after is not just going to come and fall on your lap. Nothing's going to come and fall in your lap in this life. Nobody's just going to bring your new life to you on a silver plate. You've done a training course, and congratulations – here's a new life. Come on. Whatever you do, it will require effort. Realise that and get ready for it.

Put in the effort and soon you'll be sitting on a particular amount of cash in your bank. You're earning a particular amount of cash right now. Your income will be of a particular level right now. What you spend your money on and what you spend your time on, it's completely up to you. It's your life. I assume that everybody reading this book will also have read *Rich Dad, Poor Dad* by Robert Kiyosaki. As I mentioned earlier, if you've not read that book yet, make sure that you do. It's all about creating assets and putting money in your pocket.

Liabilities, on the other hand, take money out of your pocket. Now, we all want the finer things in life. I certainly do. I want super-cars, super-yachts, multiple international homes. There's no limitation on what I want. I want to live my life to the fullest, and I want to spend money on liabilities. I want to, but I want my infinite returning assets to pay for those liabilities. The assets should pay for the liabilities that I choose to purchase. Create infinite returning assets to pay for your liabilities, create the assets, and then buy what you want.

But don't spend your money, or others' money, or money from a bank or a credit card provider, on liabilities. Spend that money on creating infinite returning assets, and use the income from the asset to pay for the liabilities that you want in your life. Please do this, because that's what separates the rich from the poor. Create assets to pay for the liabilities. The poor use things like credit cards and bank loans to pay for the liabilities. Because of that, they never get out of the rat race. So realise that if you continually create more and more assets – infinite returning assets – the more assets you create, the more income you create, and the more liabilities you can buy. It's not your money; it's the money generated from your assets. Essentially the asset is putting money in your pocket for you so that you can pay for your liabilities.

Look, don't let yourself get distracted. I've just been talking about different ideas that will make you think about other types of income. You might bring in an asset, or you might think about virtual assistance, free-lancers, drop-shipping or even mystery shopping. I don't know what you want to do with your life; it's up to you. It's your life. But definitely get good at one thing before you move on to the next. Before we got into developments, before we got into commercial residential conversions, we got good at buy-to-let. And we *are* good at buy-to-let. We knew what we were doing, let it take care of itself, and that allowed us more time to focus on our business as we got more and more into buy-to-let. Then it was more about commercial conversions, and then more about the developments generally, and we realised that we had massive value to bring to the masses. So we started REWD Training, but we didn't just start all of these on day one.

The number one thing we did start on day one with our group was our holding company. We started the holding company because we wanted to plant that seed and were conscious about group structure, massive growth, synergistic businesses and all of that. Then over time, as we got better and better at everything we were doing with all these different businesses, one by one we started to grow. Only now, like I mentioned earlier, since we've got these other things up and running are we able to think about bringing more businesses into our structure. But each time we don't start a new business until we've got the previous one set up, running systems and producing an income. So be very aware about that and don't let yourself get distracted. Don't go off trying to do lots of different things at once. Focus on one thing. Get good at it. And then move on to the next one.

Get good at one thing first. And look, I've mentioned this a few times throughout the course of this chapter: your life is your life. 'Multiple streams of income' is your choice: do it or don't do it. But why else would you be reading my advice to you about all these different ways that you can generate more income? Why would you not do it? Otherwise what was the point in you buying this book in the first place? Just be inspired to go after your ambitions. This book will be much more valuable than that to you if you choose to make it sooner. You're either going to produce multiple income streams or you're not. Perhaps it'll be just one extra income stream or maybe 10 or 20... whatever it might be. You are either going to produce multiple income streams or not.

I want you to find your own interest in real estate, in wealth development, in real wealth. Be purposeful and bold. It's about *real wealth*. And you can achieve that. Absolutely. There's no limit to the number of income streams that you can have. But recognise that it's your choice. Your decision is not up to anyone else but you. So do or don't.

Mentorship is something that you might consider. We often offer mentorship, and we only deal with mentorship clients after they've studied with us on REWD PRO. Likewise, we don't necessarily deal with every client that we once mentored. You have to be willing to put the work in. You have to be willing to make the moves. You have to be willing to step through the fear. You have to be willing to be uncomfortable. And all of that goes along with being an entrepreneur. However, it can definitely help you stay on track if that's something that you're looking for.

We were really excited to announce our property mentorship program. This is a very specific one-on-one training program for a limited number of people, to help support them in building a massive buy-to-let portfolio. This isn't the next cattle market property training course to teach generic strategies. Instead, it's a specific one-on-one tailored mentorship program for people with high ambitions. We will be teaching specifically how to build a large buy-to-let portfolio with none of your own money, using detailed techniques and strategies that we employ ourselves. Our objective for our clients is to achieve generational wealth. We will only be opening this up to a small group of people. The best thing about mentorship is that it can help you stay on track and move you forward towards your goals, whatever those goals might be. If you're thinking about property mentorship and you're interested in working with us, then get in touch. We will be happy to discuss it with you.

Do you want to produce some steady income? Do you want enough multiple income streams coming into your business to allow you to leave your day job? Maybe not. Perhaps you might love your day job, and that's cool. You don't have to leave your day job if you love what you're doing. That's awesome. If you work for awesome people, it's sensational if you have a great working environment because that's what life is all about. Everyone should have a great place to work. I came from a toxic employment environment previously, and one of the things I'm very passionate about doing here at REWD Group is ensuring that we do not have a toxic work environment. We have a welcoming, enjoyable, exciting environment, and I think we do a good job with that.

You need to have some kind of income, and you will always be thinking about generating bigger income in the future. What else can you do? What other income can you bring in? What other businesses can you start? What other passive income can you generate? What can you do that is really simple which could bring you in an extra £100, £500, £1,000 or £5,000 a month? Whatever it might be for you, depending on what stage you are at, you should always be thinking back to income and the future, and whatever else you can do to move yourself further forward towards that goal.

REWD Group management overseeing property development in the Falkirk area. (Images Copyright © Sara Amelia Photography, all rights reserved.)

Chapter Nine

Buy to Let at Massive Scale

Conar Tracey

THE final section we have for you is all about buy-to-let at massive scale. Throughout this book you've probably picked up on the fact that we are heavily biased towards the buy-to-let strategy. The reason we are biased on this approach is purely down to the fact that our focus is on creating infinite returning assets. Consistent cashflow and passive income – that's what it's all about, and it is something that is achievable for everyone by following the correct strategies and implementing the right systems. You can achieve incredible things by investing in property and leveraging the power that buy-to-let has to offer on a significant scale. You can replace your full-time income in a very short period of time, and go on to create significant wealth that your friends and family will all benefit from.

You may have started this book purely to get an understanding of how all of this property investment stuff works. You may only have aspirations to purchase one property – perhaps you're saying to yourself, 'I just want a little nest egg that will give me a bit of extra income and I can have it as part of my pension for when I retire.' Now, don't get me wrong: owning more than one property, more than just your principal residence, is significantly more than most people will ever achieve – especially in the UK. But once you know how easy it is to do these things at an incredible scale, do you really want to set your aspirations to just one property to make an extra couple of hundred pounds per month? Is this genuinely all you want?

I guess I'm just trying to get your mind accustomed to the fact that there's so much more out there. Simply by understanding these things and knowing how to do this stuff, why the hell would you stop at just doing one? Why would you not want to continuously repeat the same step-by-step model that can provide infinite returning assets and support you in whatever it is you want to do in life? Whether you want to focus on having more time at home, spend more time with the family, or maybe if you want to travel more – you can do whatever you want.

Everybody needs income, but it doesn't mean you have to be exchanging every available hour to get paid. There are ways that you can be clever about how you invest your time. Finding ways that will pay you while you sleep! Getting paid while you're doing whatever the hell you want to be doing day in, day out! Also, by creating something that allows the future members of your family to benefit; there really is no limit to this. The same strategies can be used many, many times. Once you get your head around the concept of following the correct instructions and you put things into practice, simply by implementing this advice, you can literally achieve whatever you want and continue to grow your income. You can continue to grow your personal wealth and ultimately create generational wealth.

As individuals we all have a specific purpose that we want to be doing all of this for. We are investors and developers first and foremost – that is our primary focus. The building company, the training company... they are subsidiary businesses that support what we are all about. We are out there playing this game exactly the same way that you should be. We have simply found a process that works, and now all we're trying to do is replicate that process to get bigger and bigger, producing more income and adding more assets. It's really straightforward once you know what it's all about. Once you've identified how to do things, you just follow the same plan for every transaction; one by one, portfolio by portfolio. This is an unbelievable thing that is available to everybody that is willing to learn and put a bit of work in.

Fundamentally, you need to realise that there is another world out there. You may be living in this one version of reality right now, simply because you're not aware of how to do these things. You might see other people or you may even have looked at ourselves, and asked yourself, 'How the f*** are those guys doing that?' Maybe that's what's drawing you to actually read this book. Just to gain an insight into how we do things. We are scrutinised all the time, challenged by other professionals in the industry and other outside sources that believe what we are doing must be dodgy, or there must be something to it that we're not being transparent or honest about. Ultimately, the answer is f*** them, because the truth is that we are transparent. We are fully open and honest about how we do things, and we want to teach others how to do it and support their growth.

That's why we created the training business, because there is a significant undersupply of homes within the UK and that has created serious issues that need to be addressed. The government isn't going to do it. If you can benefit personally and your family can benefit financially as you continue to grow by solving a core problem in the UK property market, what is the harm in that? If you're following legal strategies and are being clever in how you spend your time and effort, simply by having the knowledge as to how to do all of this, you're only going to improve your life and the lives of those around you. We want to show you how to do exactly that.

Landlords and property investors

We want to support you as you continue to grow through this process. Like I said, we are playing this game to the end, and we love it. It just comes down to whether you want to learn about how you can play as well. If you want to go and achieve buy-to-let at significant scale and you want to benefit from all that extra passive income and all those infinite returning assets, you have to accept your responsibility as to what you are, which is a professional landlord and professional property investor.

There are clear responsibilities that come with being a landlord which you have to appreciate. First of all, you are solving a problem. You are providing a product to the market that there is significant demand for. You are supplying homes to people. These include people who are looking to rent accommodation, because they need shelter. They need a home to bring up their families. They need a home for themselves, to feel safe. You have to do that by being professional at providing that service. Therefore, you must be a registered landlord in every local authority where you own a property – you must be registered so that everyone can identify who owns the property and who is responsible. You, as a professional, must be willing to put your hand up and say, 'Yeah, that's me. I own that property and they are my tenants. Here are my registration details if you need to contact me.' You must also ensure that all of your properties, whether you only own one or thousands, are fully compliant and meet current legislation.

Make sure that tenants' concerns are addressed every single time they are raised. If you can keep on top of that, you're never going to have any comebacks to say that you did something wrong. It's not even worth thinking about. So just make sure that you're doing your part, but your letting agent should take care of managing all of this for you.

Tenancy agreements are another important element to protect yourself as a landlord. You must have the right letting agent who can fully support you in taking care of your tenants and your assets, and this starts with having a detailed understanding of the current legislation when it comes to tenancy agreements and ensuring that right agreements are put in place before allowing someone to occupy your property. In any business, you want to treat your customers well – and as we've already discussed, in your role as a professional landlord, your customers are your tenants. It's important you have a good relationship with the tenant and that your letting agent is dealing with any issues as efficiently as possible, as you want the tenants to treat you asset with respect and take care of it which will hopefully reduce your costs on maintenance and refurbishment.

If you want to build a successful buy-to-let business, you have to address some important questions to find out if you have what it takes to be able to take good care of your investment portfolio. Do you have the right systems in place? Are you able to manage this business with minimal time by yourself? Because ultimately, you're creating this opportunity so that you can live your life on your own terms. You're not trying to just replace your current job with another one. You're not going from a job you dislike where you're working solidly all the time only to suddenly realise that you've just replaced that with another headache because you're now trying to manage all of your rental properties yourself. All of the systems have to be in place, and it's important to recognise what part you play. As a professional property investor, it certainly isn't going out to a property to have a look at a problem at four o'clock in the morning. All of those things should be delegated to the appropriate member of your power team.

It's important to ensure that you have the correct team in place, because you need to make good use of everyone you have instructed to support you. You may feel like a bit of a puppet master pulling the strings, with everyone else on the ground doing various tasks for you all the time, but you have to ensure that you can trust them and that they're efficient and effective at the job. You're not going to ask your lawyer to go and manage your properties. Rather, your lawyer is going to ensure that the conveyancing process for your acquisitions goes through smoothly and that it goes through as fast as possible, and you don't get stung with any extra caveats. It's not their job to be going out to a property to give it a lick of paint! Everybody has to identify what role they play and you must ensure you have selected the best team that is aligned with your ambitions and plans for growth.

Power Team

- Solicitor
- Letting Agent/Estate Agent
- Mortgage Broker/Finance Specialist
- Refurb Team/Contractor
- Insurance Broker
- Mentor/Coach

If you want to achieve anything – if you want to start and be serious about achieving significant results – then you have to consider creating something with a bigger purpose than just yourself. You might be an individual with very clever ideas and be very specific about how you're going to do things, but there are so many other competitors out there, so many other people trying to do this, that you have to stand out and you do that by creating a brand and a brand vision.

We wanted our stakeholders and investors to be able to buy into something more than just the three of us. This is why, beyond the core business that provides multiple services to multiple different industries, people recognise the REWD Group brand on its own, without necessarily thinking of us as individuals. Yes, people will link the brand and us – absolutely they will, and we want them to because we're constantly working on growing our personal and group brands. But we want people to identify the REWD Group brand as a serious force in the property investment space. The group, as the brand, attracts investment and attracts deals which – when combined – accelerates our growth massively. What a powerful statement, to be an organisation that people know. We can deliver, and people know what we do. Therefore, when someone has a property or a complex portfolio that they're looking to sell, they will bring it to us because they know it's something we're interested in and they know that we can complete very quickly. They'll know that we are constantly raising capital and that we're constantly doing deals. When opportunities arise, we get them! Why? Because of our brand and the position we have actively put ourselves in to be recognised at the dominant force in our space.

Finding the right strategy

Start thinking about how you're going to make a plan of action and ask yourself, 'What is going to help me get where I want to be?'

As well as all of our efforts to actively find investment opportunities for ourselves, one of the core benefits to working with us is that we supply heavily-discounted property deals to our training clients – EXCLUSIVELY!

Do you want to learn exactly how you can scale a life changing property portfolio and have direct access to the right deals that will accelerate your wealth position? To piggyback and benefit from our reputation, and to be fed heavily discounted property deals by people you can trust?

The route through our mentorship is to get you from starting with zero properties to a £1 million property portfolio within 12 months. Think about that... if you can go from now to a year later, having a £1 million buy-to-let portfolio, producing an average of £3,000 per month in net cashflow – how would that impact your life? That level of passive income is a game changer to so many people, and it's achievable just by by working with us to understand how to do all of this. To be fed opportunities and learn how to attract your own deals, whilst ensuring you put yourself in the best position possible to be ready to buy portfolios that generate cashflow from day one. If that's something that you want to achieve, you seriously need to consider learning how you can do this with the support of people who are already doing this at an advanced level like ourselves.

If you are serious about becoming a professional property investor and want to change your life, you absolutely must understand the following four key elements.

Foundations

You will not succeed if you do not build a solid foundation from which you can scale your property business on. This starts with your mindset. If you do not believe this is possible and you're not willing to put the effort in to create it, you will fail. You must answer these questions with absolute clarity:

- Why are you doing this?
- Who do you want to be?

Everything you do in life and business all depends on how honestly you can answer those questions. If you don't have a clear answer to those questions right now, you must identify what matters to you the most and put a strategy together that fits your level of commitment and vision.

Have a clear definition of your goals and ensure you have the most efficient corporate structure to maximise the benefits of building a successful buy-to-let portfolio. Don't let the tax man take more than they're due!

Systems

You must find the most efficient way to manage your property business so that you can focus on growth.

The *Pareto Principle – the '80/20 rule'* – states that in many cases roughly 80% of consequences come from 20% of causes. Simply put, this basically means that 20% of what you do will produce 80% of the results, and if you break this principle down further it equates to 4% of your input producing 64% of your results. As a property investor, your only focus – and therefore your 4% – is to FIND DEALS and FIND MONEY. Nothing else.

Leverage the team around you. Identify the role that everyone plays and delegate to the appropriate person. Focus on the value-added activities.

Deals

This is where your wealth is created. The assets you buy and the kind of deals you do will define the success you achieve. You must understand what a good deal looks like – especially when you're working on multiple units. You have to be aware of all the complexities involved in order to make sure that you have a positive outcome. If you don't have an exit, you don't have a deal!

Implement the Buy-Refurbish-Rent-Refinance strategy to maximise the rate you can grow and constantly recycle the capital invested to keep buying more. Ensure you have a constant flow of investment opportunities by building relationships and credibility with property sourcers, auction houses, estate agents and letting agents, etc. Create your own direct-to-vendor marketing strategies – use every resource possible to keep your deal flow coming.

Finance

The world offers UNLIMITED MONEY. Accept that statement. Believe it. Think about it relentlessly. Visualise it.

There are endless opportunities to raise finance and use other people's money to grow your investment portfolio. You are not asking for a favour; you can bring serious value to your investors and provide them with a return for capital that is likely depreciating in value sitting in the bank or underperforming elsewhere.

There are so many ways to raise finance to fund your dreams... GO AFTER THEM ALL!

The route of least resistance is available to you: real data to guide you through the whole process. Until you get these four fundamental areas locked down and understood in detail, you will not be successful in buy-to-let at massive scale. By understanding the foundations, the systems, the deals and the finance, you're going to be able to operate on a level above those who already call themselves professional property investors, because they will not know the level of detail that we show you when you work with us.

Finding success

Success is very, very easy. It's creating a plan and turning up every day to implement it. Day by day, one bit at a time, let the efforts lead you to success. Once you've got that mindset, you can start to look at the technical areas of the business that will drive growth.

If you want all of this, if you want to live a life on your own terms and have a significant income – are you ready to get to work?

The number one thing that keeps people from succeeding, that keeps people where they are, that keeps people poor, they end up going through their life accepting what they're dealt, doing what they're told and they end up at 50 or 60 years old wondering what the f*** happened. Well, we're going to tell you what happened...

You talked yourself out of going after what you were supposed to go after. You talked yourself out of your purpose. You talked yourself into the idea that success is magic, luck or fairy dust, and not cause and effect. That's what happened. And that's the number one thing that keeps people from succeeding.

It's the 'What if?' story that they tell themselves over and over and over again as to why they can't move forward and other people can. Why, even if they do the work, it still isn't going to work out.

Success is easy; it's really f***ing easy. It's making a plan and executing the plan every day. It's that simple.

Conclusion

That brings us to the end of this chapter, and it also brings us to the end of *Fast-Track To Property Millions*. I want to summarise with six absolutely necessary realisations:

- You MUST have the right mindset.
- You MUST use other people's money.
- You MUST buy at a discount.
- You MUST have the right team in place.
- You MUST put the effort it.

...and YOU MUST BE EDUCATED!

You wouldn't be reading this if you didn't already understand that you must take the time to get educated before making any moves in property. If you don't fully understand all the things we've discussed in this book, you're going to set yourself up for failure. The purpose of getting educated and learning from those who have achieved the things you want to go after, is to minimise the risk of failure and increase the potential for a successful outcome dramatically. You want to fast-track the entire process. Step one, The reason that we provide training and mentorship is to stop people making the kind of mistakes that we have made in the past and to share our knowledge and experience so that you can replicate it.

If you don't want to have a large property investment business with over 200 units in your portfolio, that's fine. If you just want to create something on a smaller scale, that's up to you, but try and get to ten properties as quickly as possible so that you can enjoy it. By the time you get to that point, and you do so in the first year, maybe you will do it again. Why wouldn't you do it again and again if you know how?

We're here to support you and bring you into the game that we're playing. We are creating a life on our own terms and we want the same for you.

If you're ready for the next level... TAKE ACTION.

To start your *Fast-Track to Property Millions* journey now, scan the QR code below:

About the Authors

LAURIE DUNCAN

Laurie began investing in buy-to-let property back in 2010, acquiring his first investment simply because it was across the road from where he bought his first home (it had been on the market a while, and he got a good deal on it, of course!). Since then he's been building his own portfolio, as well as REWD Group's together with Alex.

He has over 20 years' experience in international sales and business development, with a track record of building both top and bottom lines, to enable business expansion into new markets and product ranges.

Laurie is constantly seeking out new potential to push the company on to new areas and opportunities.

Laurie, if not at his desk, can most often be found snuggled up on the couch with his totally awesome wife Emma, his baby boy Daniel, and their German Shepherd Dog, Kobi! Alternatively, he may be running around Grangemouth, doing a bodyweight workout in the garage, or in the sauna or steam room!

ALEX ROBERTSON

Alex is a self-made property investor and businessman. He comes from a financial background, gaining a degree in Accounting and Finance and then going on to Qualify as Chartered Management Accountant (CIMA).

Alex gained a huge wealth of experience in business within the oil and gas industry, working to build businesses and aid geographical expansion throughout Europe and the Middle East, in roles from Finance to Project Management and General Management.

In 2010 Alex began to invest in property and apply his business skills to this new field. He combines strong financial analytical skills, project management (APM qualified), a passion for property and experience in building businesses, all towards the goal of growing REWD Group.

Alex often works behind the scenes of the business, guiding strategy and driving investments. The two co-founders are very different in personality; however, their skills complement each other perfectly to create a very well-balanced business.

CONAR TRACEY

Conar entered the world of property as a 'Trainee Estate Agent' when he was 18 years old, and quickly progressed to becoming the youngest Property Valuer in Scotland at only 19. Since then, Conar has become an industry expert and has brokered over 1,000 property transactions across the whole of the UK and gained further qualification in commercial property and building surveying.

He has almost 10 years' experience in the property industry and has been responsible for running

operations for some of the largest quick sale estate agents and property auctions in the country. With a reputation as one of the best in the industry, Conar can find investment opportunities in any market and present deals to investors that most would never even think possible.

Conar first met Laurie and Alex in 2018 before REWD Group had even been formed. They began their working relationship straight away, getting their first deal done together only a week after meeting. Since then, Conar has sourced over 25% of REWD Group's massive buy-to-let portfolio and continues to lead the way in maximising profitability across all companies within the group as Head of Business Development.

To find out more about REWD Group and the work that they do, please visit their company website at: *www.rewdgroup.co.uk*

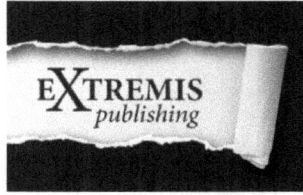

For details of new and forthcoming books from
Extremis Publishing, including our monthly podcast,
please visit our official website at:

www.extremispublishing.com

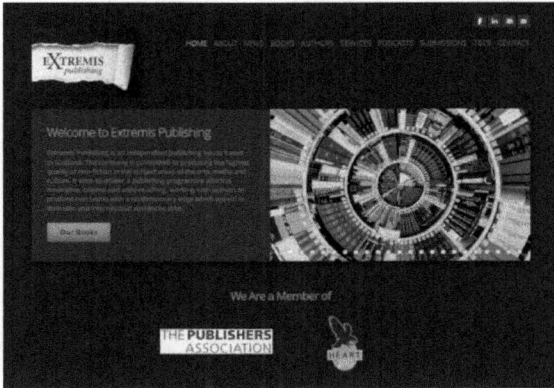

or follow us on social media at:

www.facebook.com/extremispublishing

www.linkedin.com/company/extremis-publishing-ltd-/

CPSIA information can be obtained
at www.ICGtesting.com
Printed in the USA
BVHW052053261222
654951BV00011B/405

9 781739 854379